EXECUTIVE ACTION
634 WAYS TO KILL FIDEL CASTRO

About the Author

FABIÁN ESCALANTE FONT was born in Havana, Cuba, in 1940. As a young political activist he suffered persecution and was imprisoned for his activities against the dictatorship of Fulgencio Batista. Following the 1959 Cuban revolution, he joined the newly created Department of State Security, where he carried out varied activities against counterrevolutionary organizations and the Central Intelligence Agency of the United States, including the latter's Operation AM/LASH — a plan to assassinate Fidel Castro.

He directed the investigations that the Cuban government carried out at the request of the US Select Committee of the House of Representatives, when the investigation into the assassination of US President John F. Kennedy was reopened in 1978.

Fabián Escalante was a Division General of the Ministry of the Interior and between 1976 and 1982 was head of the State Security Department (G-2).

He is internationally recognized as an authority on the CIA and its operations in Cuba and Latin America.

EXECUTIVE ACTION
634 WAYS TO KILL FIDEL CASTRO

Fabián Escalante

Ocean Press

Melbourne ▪ New York ▪ London
www.oceanbooks.com.au

ISBN 10: 1-920888-72-1
ISBN 13: 978-1-920888-72-5
Library of Congress Catalog Card No: 2006934546

First Printed 2006

Available from Ocean Sur in Spanish as
Accion Ejecutiva, ISBN 13: 978-1-920888-55-8

PUBLISHED BY OCEAN PRESS

Australia: GPO Box 3279, Melbourne, Victoria 3001, Australia
           Fax: (61-3) 9329 5040 Tel: (61-3) 9326 4280
           E-mail: info@oceanbooks.com.au
USA: PO Box 1186, Old Chelsea Stn., New York,
           NY 10113-1186, USA
           Tel / Fax: (1-212) 260 3690

OCEAN PRESS TRADE DISTRIBUTORS

United States and Canada: **Consortium Book Sales and Distribution**
           Tel: 1-800-283-3572 www.cbsd.com
Australia and New Zealand: **Palgrave Macmillan**
           E-mail: customer.service@macmillan.com.au
UK and Europe: **Turnaround Publisher Services**
           E-mail: orders@turnaround-uk.com
Cuba and Latin America: **Ocean Press**
           E-mail: oceanhav@enet.cu

www.oceanbooks.com.au
info@oceanbooks.com.au

Contents

Glossary

AM/LASH Refers to both the CIA covert operation to assassinate Fidel Castro and agent Rolando Cubela

Assault Brigade 2506 Bay of Pigs invasion force

CANF Cuban American National Foundation

CDRs Committees for the Defense of the Revolution

CIA Central Intelligence Agency

CRC Cuban Revolutionary Council

DD/P Deputy Director of Plans (CIA)

DIER Rebel Army Investigations Department

DSE State Security Department

ELN National Liberation Army

FBI Federal Bureau of Investigation

FRD Revolutionary Democratic Front

G-2 Cuban State Security Department

JGCE Junta of the Cuban Government in Exile

MDC Christian Democrat Movement

MID Democratic Insurrectional Movement

MRP Revolutionary Movement of the People

MRR Movement for the Recovery of the Revolution

OAS Organization of American States

Operation ZR/Rifle CIA program to assassinate foreign leaders

OSS Office of Strategic Services

RCA Anticommunist Civic Resistance

SAS Special Affairs Section

SIM Military Intelligence Service

TSD Technical Services Division (of the CIA)

Introduction

On July 20, 1961, I was assigned to the Attacks Bureau, the Cuban Security Department unit responsible for investigating plots and conspiracies against revolutionary leaders. It was a memorable day, not only because it marked my debut as an operative officer, but also because I had the pleasure and honor of meeting the people who, from that moment, would be my *compañeros*.

The first was Mario Morales Mesa, known as Miguel — our chief, who had been an internationalist combatant in the Spanish Civil War and was a communist and a born investigator. A small, slim man with a fine mustache like those worn in the 1940s, he possessed an ironclad will and personal courage in the face of every test. Dozens of anecdotes were related about him, some from his time fighting in the International Brigades in Spain. In one story, he was made responsible for a light submachine gun of Soviet manufacture known as a Maxim, and was thereafter known himself by that nickname, as he had a particular way of firing the gun so that, his *compañeros* claimed, it imitated the sounds of a Cuban rumba.

Later, as some of his *compañeros* related, he was taken prisoner and placed in a concentration camp in fascist-occupied France, where he managed, in conjunction with the Senegalese guards who looked after the prisoners, to open a little store which sold milk to the capos of the place and gave it away free to the most needy.

Mario was a real character who lived for 80-plus years. When I met him, I had returned to Cuba after training in the Soviet Union, with lots of theory but little practical knowledge of the realities that I would have to confront. Mario taught me skills in daily combat and investigative skills that cannot be acquired in any school, however good it might be.

He was an unpredictable person. On one occasion when, tired and hungry, we went to eat hot dogs from a van parked behind the famous Hotel Nacional in Havana, he recognized one of the owners of the place as a former officer in the army of the Batista dictatorship.[1] After identifying him as a sympathizer of the general [Batista], he set about conspiring with him, while indicating to me that I should eat as quickly as I could. When we had finished eating, the subject took us to a corner of the van, and with some pride, showed us a crate of incendiary devices, explosives manufactured with a "live phosphorus" base, at that time one of the CIA's most sophisticated inventions for acts of sabotage. Quick as a flash and without giving me time to react, Mario pulled out his revolver and arrested them all, seizing those mechanisms of destruction.

Perhaps because of that rapidity with which he always acted, he utilized a particular expression when he was talking: "You understand," which he insistently repeated every time he was referring to something.

I also remember Carlos Enrique Díaz Camacho, whose nickname was Trillo, one of the *compañeros* who most deeply impressed me and with whom I was friends until his death in 1964 at enemy hands. He was a man in his 30s, an old man to those of us who had just passed 20. One day I found him in Mario's house, where our office was located, with a cache of valuable jewels in his hands, wrapped in a woman's handkerchief. The jewels came from the Cuban bourgeoisie who were frantically trying to get them out of the country. Trillo was an agent who, by right, belonged to the small world of the Havana bourgeoisie, and who hung out with people of

---

1.   Fulgencio Batista: Cuban dictator who came to power through a coup d'état and ruled from 1952 to 1958.

his own social milieu aware of his solid links with various European ambassadors, through whom they hoped to get documents, valuable jewelry and assets — not always legitimately obtained — out of the country. On many occasions — and justly so — those riches were returned to the people at a time when they were most needed.

Once, we were with Trillo in the anteroom of the office of Captain Elíseo Reyes, known as San Luis,[2] then chief of the G-2 revolutionary police. Two other police officers were also waiting there, one of them known to Trillo. In a low voice, he exchanged words with the individual, making him believe that I had brought him in as a prisoner, and in a few minutes he had exposed him as an active conspirator within the police ranks.

I recall Trillo always wearing a light suit, with a mischievous look in his eyes and an expression on his lips: "Tell you later," which of course he never did.

Another of my *compañeros*, José Veiga, better known as Morán, who had worked undercover in the United States and who spoke English perfectly and enjoyed opera, had an inexhaustible imagination. He always had an idea at the ready, even if it was impossible to realize.

Carlos Valdés, Pedro Piñiero, Mayiyo and others completed that group of no more than a dozen men who played an outstanding role in the fight against the assassination plots of the CIA and its Cuban associates against revolutionary leaders, particularly *compañero* Fidel.

Many recollections come to mind of those years, when sometimes we didn't have a working budget or a cent to buy something to eat, while in the desk drawer there were thousands of pesos, dollars or valuable jewelry, and it never occurred to us to take something to satisfy any need, including that of our work.

---

2.   Elíseo Reyes: a captain of the Rebel Army who fought with Che Guevara in his Bolivian campaign and was killed in the struggle for Latin American independence.

All of my *compañeros* are present in this story, not just those that are mentioned, but also many more who gave the best of themselves in this silent war against terrorism. In addition to performing these heroic deeds, in many cases they have been witness to the incidents related. This story is a tribute to that group of anonymous combatants, dedicated to them with all the love and affection that emerged from the heat of the years and adventures we experienced.

Perhaps readers will find it strange that I have used the word love in introducing the theme expounded in the following chapters. I can explain by affirming that love of the homeland and our people has been, is, and will be the motivation for our undertakings and struggles, as well as the basis of this great adventure that is the Cuban revolution. To it and to my *compañeros*, present and fallen, my eternal gratitude and remembrance.

Preamble to an Obsession

He consulted his watch again. For several minutes he had been concealed in the dark doorway of an empty house facing the little airport of Fort Lauderdale. His gaze was fixed on some lights in the airport administration area. At his feet was a can of gasoline, waiting to be put to use. Suddenly, the lights went out and the guard left in the direction of a nearby café.

The watcher picked up the can of fuel, crossed the street and entered the airport with swift and sure steps. Once there, he headed for an area where three P-51 Mustang aircraft were parked. He opened the container and diligently spilled its contents around the planes until it was empty. He then retreated to a prudent distance and threw a lit match in the direction of the three aircraft, which were rapidly engulfed in flames. A voracious fire illuminated the night, while the man made his getaway in a car waiting for him nearby with its engine running. As the car pulled away, the sirens of a nearby fire fighting unit began to wail.

Alan Robert Nye had been recruited a few months earlier by the Federal Bureau of Investigation (FBI) to penetrate groups of Cuban émigrés who were conspiring against the Fulgencio Batista dictatorship. He was a pilot and had apparently been expelled from the air force after his base chief received an anonymous note accusing him of conspiring with the Cubans to launch air attacks on military targets in Cuba.

In fact, the "expulsion" was a plan carefully laid by the FBI to give him a solid introduction to the Cuban émigrés fighting the Batista dictatorship. However, the plan spiralled out of control when the Cubans, enthusiastic over the project to "bomb military targets on the island," acquired various aircraft to undertake the mission. Nye found himself in a blind alley, because if he didn't attack the proposed objectives, the émigrés would become suspicious. As a way out, the FBI ordered him to destroy the planes and to blame supposed Batista agents for the sabotage.

After that action, the FBI introduced him to Efraín Hernández — the Cuban consul in Miami and an agent of the dictatorship responsible for keeping the émigré community in Florida under observation — in relation to a new project that was underway. Hernández briefly explained that the FBI had entrusted him with an important mission in Cuba. The details would be provided later but he assured Nye that a large sum of money would be paid for his services, and that top members of the US administration were aware of the plans.

Nye didn't know much about Cuba, only that it was a paradise for tourism, gambling and prostitution, so he approached the task as a Caribbean vacation. On November 12, 1958, he arrived at Havana airport, where a black automobile was waiting for him at the bottom of the aircraft steps. The vehicle drove him at speed to the Comodoro Hotel, located across from the beach in a tranquil Havana neighborhood.

Impatiently waiting for him there were colonels Carlos Tabernilla and Orlando Piedra — the former, chief of the air force, and the latter, head of the secret police. After the usual introductions they moved to the hotel bar, where they began to talk at a table set at a distance from the others. Tabernilla briefly explained to Nye the details of the plan in which he was to be involved. It was to assassinate Fidel Castro, the rebel leader who was challenging the Batista dictatorship from the country's eastern mountains.

The idea seemed simple enough. Nye was to infiltrate the rebel ranks in the area where Castro was operating. Once with him, he would outline his "revolutionary" credentials and the project to bomb military airports from Florida. The colonels were convinced that Castro would be seduced by Nye's personality. They had two reasons for this belief: one, Nye was a US citizen, a Yankee representing the most powerful nation on earth; and two, the rebels needed planes to respond to Batista's air force, which was constantly bombing the civilian population in the rebel zones and causing significant destruction. Nye was a pilot and had an impressive letter of introduction from the émigrés in Florida, and thus would be an ideal pilot for any small aircraft in the possession of the rebels, which could also be used to strike at Batista's military positions.

Tabernilla and Piedra explained to Nye that he would be protected by an army command, and most importantly, that $50,000 would be placed in his bank account once Fidel Castro was eliminated.

That same afternoon, the three men headed for the Columbia military camp, the headquarters of the national army, to coordinate the project there with Colonel Manuel García Cáceres, chief of the fortress in Holguín, capital of the northern region of Oriente province. Nye and García Cáceres quickly agreed that the former would travel to the colonel's command post within a few days and initiate the operation from there.

Despite the brevity of his stay in Havana, Nye found the time to visit the capital's main nightclubs and was able to understand why his fellow countrymen were interested in maintaining the government of Batista, who was guaranteeing them a paradise of gambling, safe investment and entertainment.

On December 20, Alan Robert Nye was in Holguín going over the main aspects of the homicide plot with Colonel García Cáceres. Four days later, in the company of a squadron of soldiers in the vicinity of the town of Santa Rita, he was infiltrated into the operational zone of Fidel Castro's rebels. That night, they stashed a .38-caliber revolver and a Remington .30-06 rifle with a telescopic sight in a previously selected site, and Nye bade farewell to the troops.

The following day he went on alone. Within a few hours he was captured by a rebel patrol and he informed them of his desire to join the revolutionary combatants and to meet Fidel Castro. But things did not go according to plan from the outset. The young officer commanding the patrol did not appear very interested in him, and confined him to a camp where wounded soldiers were recovering, explaining that, in due course, his case would be considered.

That didn't bother Nye very much. On the contrary, it provided a way for him to familiarize himself with the territory. He imagined that as soon as Castro, who was operating in that area, knew of his presence, he would send for him and the opportunity would come. He would just have to wait until nightfall to get to his cache, retrieve the weapons, and ambush him in a convenient location.

On January 1, 1959, he was stunned by the news: Batista had fled and the rebels were preparing to deal the final blow to the battered and demoralized government forces. His shock was total, because nobody had warned him of the possibility of such an event. In his conversations with the Batista officers he hadn't picked up on the weakness of their government, and far less that the troop of "bearded ones" were on the point of defeating it. In any case, he thought to himself, there was no evidence against him, and as soon as the situation normalized, the rebels would set him free, and if they didn't, he would turn to his embassy for help. At the end of the day, he concluded, he was a US citizen and his rights were guaranteed.

On January 16, he was transferred to Havana — for a routine investigation, he was told. An amiable rebel captain took a statement from him and then explained that he would have to wait for a few hours while his story was being verified. Nye committed a major error by mentioning the Comodoro Hotel as the place where he had stayed on entering Cuba. In a matter of hours the investigators had discovered two elements that convicted him beyond any doubt: one, the name he gave in the hotel — G. Collins — was not his real name; and two, his expenses there had been covered by Colonel Carlos Tabernilla.

The rebel officer interviewed him again and asked him to clarify the situation. Nye was unable to conceal the truth for very long: he confessed to the plot and named its instigators. In April of that year Alan Robert Nye was sanctioned by the courts and expelled from the country through the US embassy. That was the end of the first criminal attempt on the life of Fidel Castro undertaken with the participation of a US government agency — the FBI — in complicity with Batista's police force.

The assassination plans devised against Fidel Castro involved weapons such as lethal poisons, powerful plastic explosives, cigars containing dangerous substances, grenades to be launched in public areas, guns with sophisticated telescopic sights, poison-filled syringes so fine that contact with the skin would be unnoticed, rocket launchers and bazookas, and powerful explosive charges concealed in underground drains with a stopwatch ticking down the minutes and seconds.

A few months after the triumph of the revolution, the United States posed the need to eliminate the Cuban leader as the most expeditious way to overthrow his government — not an innovation in US politics, as various presidents, politicians and human rights activists have been assassinated to prevent their ideas changing that powerful nation's social base.

Leaders from other parts of the world have also been eliminated on the advice or encouragement of US ambassadors and consuls who perceived them as potential enemies of the political and economic strategies they were advocating, to the point that this method became an instrument of policy, the end justifying the means. All that was required was constant adherence to the practice of plausible denial.

The assassination of President John F. Kennedy in 1963 was doubtless one of the most traumatic episodes in US history. Over the years, various commissions were created in order to determine who was behind the crime and who executed it. Nevertheless, those investigations, supported by million-dollar budgets, have only produced various hypotheses and lists of groups possibly interested in the president's elimination.

Prompted by the Watergate scandal, which confirmed that CIA agents actively participated in clandestine activities against foreign politicians and US citizens, and under public pressure, in 1975 the US Senate created a commission headed by Senator Frank Church to investigate intelligence activity related to the assassination of leaders hostile to Washington's policies.

For the first time the existence of an institutional mechanism directed at political killings was exposed. Special weapons, poison and other sophisticated means were created in CIA laboratories to this end.

However, that commission only uncovered a minor part of the CIA's criminal plans. A complicit silence sealed the lips of the organization's agents and chiefs who, headed by Richard Helms, CIA director at the time, refuted and withheld information that would have unmasked the shady assassination mechanism concealed in the Agency's depths.

In the case of Cuba, the commission concluded that there were merely eight conspiracies hatched against Fidel Castro, some of which, according to the investigators, never materialized. This is far from the truth.

From 1959, the youthful revolutionary government had to confront acts of terrorism from Batista supporters, war criminals who had fled from justice, and organized crime elements who perceived the new regime as prejudicial to their economic interests. Later, with the official approval of President Dwight Eisenhower's administration, the CIA instigated the task of eliminating Fidel Castro and defeating the Cuban revolution.

The most powerful CIA base within US territory was established in Florida with more than 400 case officers and 4,000 Cuban agents who, backed up by maritime and aerial fleets, launched an unprecedented offensive against revolutionary Cuba. Some 300 clandestine organizations were formed, armed and directed from the

United States with the same purpose. An army — Assault Brigade 2506[1] — was organized, trained and landed in Cuba to defeat the revolutionary government. Given the extent of those forces, it is not hard to imagine the extraordinary dimensions of the US aggression, which even came to include bacteriological warfare.

Understanding how hundreds of conspiracies against the life of the Cuban leader have been frustrated and neutralized is not easy without comprehending the extraordinary work of the people involved in this undertaking. At the heart of this success are the men and women who made it possible to expose enemy plots, not only in Cuba but in the United States itself. The five patriots currently imprisoned in the US are an example of this.[2] The most important weapon in this clandestine warfare has always been the justice of the cause and the solidarity that this has engendered. The hundreds of men and women who infiltrated the ranks of the CIA and the counterrevolutionary groups, often without the most elemental training for the work involved, have been the real heroes of this feat.

In recent years CIA responsibility for the conspiracies against Fidel Castro has been questioned in the United States. Certain journalists and scholars have been seduced by the idea that a few bad apples within the Agency were responsible for such conspiracies behind the backs of their unwitting chiefs. The actions of William Harvey, Ted Shackley, Howard Hunt, David Phillips, David Sánchez Morales and others are presented as aberrations. This is completely untrue. If the Church Commission made one thing totally clear, it is that in early 1961 the two principal CIA chiefs, Richard Bissell and

---

1.   Assault Brigade 2506: the Bay of Pigs invasion force.
2.   In 1998 five Cubans living in Miami were arrested and charged with espionage offences. They had been monitoring terrorist groups operating out of Florida with the aim of preventing attacks on Cuba, but were convicted and are currently serving long sentences in separate US jails. Their story is told in *Letters of Love and Hope: The Story of the Cuban Five* (Melbourne & New York: Ocean Press, 2005).

Allen Dulles, ordered the creation of Operation ZR/Rifle, with the mission, according to declassified documents studied by members of Congress on the commission, of setting up the physical elimination of foreign political leaders.

That operation was directly or indirectly responsible for the hundreds of homicidal plots against Fidel Castro. In some cases the CIA both directed and funded them; it was also aware of others which it encouraged via the control it exercised over the counterrevolutionary organizations. It has utilized the extremely powerful weapon of psychological warfare, with thousands of radio broadcast hours transmitted from the United States inciting and exhorting the revolutionary leader's assassination.

The "Cuban American Mechanism" of the CIA and the Mafia, described in the following chapters, was activated in 1962 after the Bay of Pigs defeat, when President John F. Kennedy's government used it to unleash a civil war within Cuba — at a cost of millions of dollars. It took on a life of its own the following year, when it emerged as an independent force in the US political context. It is possible, as certain investigators maintain — including the author of this work — that this mechanism, having grown out of control due to political and economic conflicts with US ruling circles, played a significant part in Kennedy's assassination.

The incidents narrated in this book, extending up to 1979, are based on multiple investigations: the experiences of the author, who participated in some of them; dozens of interviews with participants; documentary evidence; and the generous collaboration of *compañeros*, officials and underground agents who dismantled the plots. Thus we can reveal the dimensions of this incredible conspiracy: the history of US plots to bring down the Cuban government over more than 40 years.

A select number of cases — the most significant, some of them unknown, whose connections with the CIA and the US Mafia are irrefutable — have been selected for this book.

While based in fact, certain fictional devices have been employed to make for easier reading, and to present the events and characters involved in higher relief, without affecting historical accuracy.

The book is therefore the history of how successive US governments tried to assassinate one man, Fidel Castro, who, like the mythological David, has defied Goliath in committing himself to the defense of his people's sovereignty and independence.

1 With the Tigers

The alarm clock awoke Colonel J.C. King, who mechanically switched it off, throwing it a glance to confirm the time. Still half asleep, he gazed up at the ceiling and tried to put his thoughts in order.

With the exception of Sundays, King got up at four in the morning. At that early hour, he devoted himself to studying the most important news that had come in the day before and meditating on the steps to be taken in his current projects. Afterwards he read an excerpt from the Bible, as, contrary to comments made by his detractors, he was deeply religious. He liked to compare certain passages of the Bible to actions he had taken, which gave him profound satisfaction.

This day marked an important moment in his career. He had been invited by his bosses, Allen Dulles and Richard Bissell, to give a special report on the situation in Latin America. For the first time during his years as CIA chief for the Western Hemisphere he felt intensely concerned. More and more organized political movements opposed to the policies of the United States were appearing on the continent, disturbing the peace and threatening the prospects of US investors. There had been earlier conflicts in what the United States considered as its backyard, but the triumph of Fidel Castro's revolution in Cuba had convulsed the usually passive Latin Americans like never before.

Cuba was once again the issue for discussion, as it had been in recent months since the United States had become aware of the need to remove Fulgencio Batista. It had become evident that political maneuvers to replace him "democratically" could not prevent the triumph of Fidel Castro and his rebels in the Sierra Maestra.

The political situation on the island had been worrying King for some years. The growing anti-US demonstrations, the strong communist movement built during the 1930s and 1940s, and finally, the assault on the Moncada Garrison[1] in 1953, indicated that communist subversion had reached the US border, and they could no longer sit back with their arms folded.

At the end of 1958, one of his closest friends, William D. Pawley, President Eisenhower's former ambassador and the owner of various businesses in Havana, had warned of the danger threatening the United States if Fidel Castro succeeded in Cuba, but his words went unheeded. It was assumed that Castro's rebels were just another group in search of power, but events had unfolded rapidly, threatening US interests.

King recalled that Robert Weicha, the CIA agent who operated as US consul in Santiago de Cuba, was convinced Castro's group was not communist. Another informant who had reported on the group was Frank Sturgis,[2] a mercenary who had joined an expedition led by Pedro Luis Díaz Lanz, then chief of the rebel air force.

Nevertheless, King still believed they could control the Havana government's future actions. Not only did they have Díaz Lanz in the Rebel Army, there were other "sympathizers" like Huber Matos and various government ministers, all of whom discussed

---

1. On July 26, 1953, Fidel Castro led a failed assault on the Moncada Garrison in Santiago de Cuba, the second-largest military fortress in Cuba, with the aim of arming the people and defeating the Batista dictatorship.

2. Frank Sturgis (Frank Angelo Fiorini): US armed forces veteran and member of the Rebel Army air force under Pedro Luis Díaz Lanz. Under CIA orders, Sturgis participated in attempts on the life of Fidel Castro and the training of the Cuban exile brigades that took action against Cuba. He was linked to the conspiracy to assassinate President Kennedy and was involved in the Watergate incident.

everything with the embassy. Still, Castro was unpredictable. His speeches on agrarian and urban reform in which he announced his intentions to lower rents and redistribute the land among the campesinos, and particularly the trials of notorious Batista followers, were a cause for concern. Therefore, independent action had to be prepared so that events didn't take them by surprise.

King rose from his bed, and as was his custom, shaved and dressed with care. A final glance in the mirror revealed the image of a man of military bearing, 50-something, white-haired and with a penetrating gaze. He felt satisfied at confirming once more that, although the years were passing, he retained his distinguished appearance.

He descended the stairs of his house with an agile step, headed for the kitchen, and prepared a cup of coffee. His long years of military service had taught him that it was better not to have a full stomach before battles or important meetings. With his cup in hand, he moved to a comfortable armchair in the large sitting room of his mansion. At that early hour the servants had not arrived for their domestic labors and he could allow himself the luxury of working there, where sunlight was beginning to filter through the large windows. He picked up his files, extracted various documents, and commenced reading attentively. One of them caught his attention; he reread it several times and then underlined two paragraphs in red pencil:

Castro has been in contact with communists — vanguard groups from his university days — and there have been constant reports of possible communist affiliations on the part of some of the top leaders. However, there is no certainty at the present time that Castro is a communist...

Castro would appear to be a nationalist and something of a socialist and although he has criticized and alleged US support of Batista, it cannot be said that he is personally hostile to the United States.[3]

---

3. "Special National Intelligence Estimate: The Situation in Cuba." *Foreign Relations of the United States, 1958–60: Cuba* (Washington: US Government Printing Office, 1991), 356.

He took the pencil and distractedly placed it between his lips. It was a personal habit that he adopted when he was absorbed in thought. He had before him the evaluation of the CIA station in Havana and had to consider it as the most authoritative; those opinions, however, did not concur with Washington's actual perception of what was happening in Cuba.

The diplomats were confused in their analysis of events. They thought that what was happening was merely the result of premature enthusiasm after the revolutionary triumph and that things would subsequently follow the usual pattern. Was there anyone who had defied the United States who could live to boast about it? Fidel Castro was not, as they saw it, an exception to the rule.

The clock marked 8:30 a.m. on January 13, 1959. His closest colleagues were expecting him in an hour to discuss the issue. There was an established procedure: everyone who worked under his command had to be heard before making any decision on a specific subject.

When he was ready to leave, the telephone rang. It was the operations officer who, as always, was responsible for ascertaining whether the colonel was ready to commence his daily agenda.

He went out into the garden and made himself comfortable in his automobile, a black, four-door Oldsmobile that gleamed immaculately. Willy, his driver, an elderly sergeant who had been in his service for years, switched on the ignition and moved off in the direction of the Agency's central offices, installed in an old army building known as Quarters Eye while its ultimate headquarters in the discreet district of Langley, on the outskirts of Washington, were under construction.

He walked to his office with a confident step, and to his satisfaction, found the people he wanted there ready for the briefing. Tracy Barnes, Richard Bissell's aide; Frank Bender, a veteran agent of German origin who had fought behind Nazi lines during World War II; Robert Amory, deputy director of intelligence; and various other officers. After the customary greetings, King asked Bender to relate the content of his talks with Augusto Ferrando, the Dominican consul in Miami, believing them vital for a multilateral evaluation of the situation in Cuba. In his particular Germanic style, Bender explained:

"Ferrando represents Colonel John Abbes García, head of Trujillo's[4] intelligence, and they want to know our official position on Cuba. They believe that Castro is a dangerous communist, who will take revolution to all the countries of the continent. He confirmed that President Trujillo is planning to form an army with exiles from General Batista's forces located in his country in order to block Castro's plans, but needs Washington's blessing. He proposed that we should send someone there to gain additional details."

When the report was over, King observed the rest of the officials and fixed his gaze on Amory. King didn't like him. He was a dapper, Harvard-educated liberal with a penchant for adopting a contrary position, particularly when it came to analyzing proposals from his division. King motioned him to give his opinion.

At one point in his career, Amory, a slim man with a long face, refined manners, and a solid background in matters of hemispheric politics, had aspired to a State Department post, but he'd lacked the necessary sponsors to secure one. He knew that King didn't like him and took advantage of any opportunity to irritate the colonel with his sharp political reflections.

"To me it seems premature to draw conclusions as to Fidel Castro's intentions. Trujillo sees phantoms everywhere and fears that his dictatorship could be attacked by thousands of Dominican exiles in Cuba and other parts of Latin America. As you know, Colonel, I have expressed reserve over the support we are still lending that government, as in my understanding it is compromising us with other nations on the continent. What we are doing in this

---

4.   Rafael Leónidas Trujillo: ruthless Dominican dictator also known as the Sultan of America; he earned himself the nickname of Metal Man due to his fondness for braid and medals. He died in May 1961, victim of a CIA conspiracy.

case is very similar to the experience with Batista, and look what has happened there."

Amory's words were followed by a silence. King's face was slowly changing color. He was aware that the "analyst" was attacking him for his public sympathies with the Batista government. Barnes, who knew what the colonel was thinking, intervened to avoid a sudden explosion from King, and explained that the Agency heads had not defined their position in relation to Castro and that therefore all options should be kept open, including that suggested by Trujillo.

Everyone meeting there knew that Barnes spoke for Richard Bissell and as long as the "great strategist" (as the deputy director of plans was called behind his back) kept an open mind, Allen Dulles, CIA director, would be receptive to any proposal.

The meeting concluded, King collected his reports and meticulously put them away in his briefcase as he always did, according to habits acquired in the army. On returning to his office he recalled, for a few seconds, his years as an officer, his ascent through the ranks and his service as a military attaché in various Latin American countries. That was his great school, where he had learned that one had to treat Latin Americans with a heavy hand so that their fragile democracies didn't collapse. That was why he had sympathized with Fulgencio Batista when he led the coup d'état in Cuba in the early 1950s. But Batista could no longer be kept in power, because of weak Washington politicians who refused to commit themselves to overt US involvement in the Cuban conflict. Bureaucrats like Richard Amory thought that communism could be contained with liberal theories, not realizing that in fact they were aiding it. King consulted his watch once more, and left his office to head for the meeting with his chiefs.

Allen Dulles, the much-admired director, received him with his customary pipe between his lips and the pleasant manner of a venerable, elderly man. He was the indisputable and undisputed chief of the CIA. Founder of the Office of Strategic Services (OSS), the CIA's predecessor, he played a dominant role in US covert actions in Europe during the war. There he undertook operations that were still legendary among young officers. His brother, John Foster Dulles, was secretary of state, and both had an established legal practice in New York that, among other clients, represented the powerful United Fruit Company.

Richard Bissell, a brilliant Harvard graduate in economics, was seated in a comfortable armchair, his long legs crossed. He saluted King with his characteristic professorial gesture.

After a brief exchange, King slowly read out the report and then gave a brief account of the conversation between Bender and the Dominican consul, deliberately omitting Amory's views. When he concluded his report, King waited expectantly. He knew Dulles perfectly well. He had the habit of asking his subordinates to express their opinions so as to attack them with sharp questions in order to discover the weak aspects of their proposals. On this occasion, however, he remained silent, a strange experience for the others in the room. After a few seconds that seemed interminable to King, he made a movement with his head in Bissell's direction. The latter, as if on cue, stepped in, interpreting the thoughts of the "great chief":

"We have nothing to lose in finding out what Trujillo has up his sleeve. I propose sending Bender himself so that he can report back, avoiding any commitment. Then we can make the pertinent decisions. In addition, it would be interesting to seek out one of the men we have in Havana for firsthand information on what is going on there. I fear," he concluded, "that our people are very polarized in one way or another and are not being objective."

Dulles, comfortable in his armchair, had his eyes half closed. He looked at King in a questioning manner.

"What is your opinion?" he asked.

King straightened in his chair, and with a rapid movement of his head indicated his agreement.

"Clearly, as Mr. Bissell says, we have nothing to lose by sending Bender."

The Tigers
Santo Domingo, Dominican Republic. January 1959

The day had been too hot in that Caribbean "winter." In the Presidential Palace two men were engaged in animated conversation. They were Rafael Leónidas Trujillo, president for life and "Supreme Father of the Homeland," and Fulgencio Batista Zaldívar, who, up until a few weeks earlier, had been the "strongman of Cuba." Long gone were the days when they contested the title of bloodiest and most reviled dictator on the continent, as well as the crumbs thrown them now and again by Uncle Sam. In his still-recent period of "democratic" urges, Batista had adopted a threatening attitude toward the Trujillo regime on more than one occasion. But Batista's time was now over, and apparently all disagreements had been overcome.

Both were impeccably dressed: Trujillo, spruced up for an imminent press interview, was decked out in a military suit covered in medals and braid; for his part, Batista was wearing an elegant white drill suit. Each of them held a glass of whiskey in their hands, from which they sipped from time to time.

The former Cuban dictator was starring in his new role as deposed president exiled in the Dominican Republic, after a hazardous journey in the small hours of January 1, 1959, when he had to flee Cuba, besieged by the triumphant revolution.

He couldn't complain at the treatment he had received. He was accommodated in one of the capital's finest hotels and even given a bodyguard. It was true that he had to pay for everything in hard cash, but between old foxes like these two men such trivialities did not cause offense. As the old saying goes: "You today and me tomorrow."

Trujillo was relaxed. He was satisfied, as he had demonstrated to the illiterate general that his regime was the stronger, and he was not going to miss any opportunity to show it. He took the floor, and after a "historical-political" preamble, explained his fears of the repercussions that Fidel Castro's victory might have for all of Latin America and particularly his country. In the final months of the previous year he had anticipated — in a meeting with his closest allies — the probable political outcome in neighboring Cuba and had devised a strategy in response. He would form a new army of anticommunist soldiers that would attack the neighboring island without delay, before the new Cuban government could fortify itself and before the thousands of exiled Dominicans resident in Cuba could organize themselves to counter the invading army.

Thus, during the initial weeks of January 1959, hundreds of men arriving from Cuba — many of them from the ranks of the dissolved regular army — joined the army that was being trained in Trujillo's camps, which were further swelled by mercenaries recruited from throughout the Americas.

In pursuit of that strategy, Trujillo had directed Colonel Ferrando, his consul in Miami, to evaluate the attitude of the CIA and the US State Department toward the new regime in power in Havana. The response could not have been more encouraging. In essence, it consisted of US approval for his plans, to be made concrete with the visit of a top-ranking Agency official. He could move ahead with the project and invade Cuba within six months, he figured.

Nevertheless, something was bothering Trujillo. Much of the daily news arriving from Cuba acknowledged Fidel Castro's enormous popularity and charismatic appeal. He would have to find a way to eliminate him. Without a leader, the people would be defenseless against external aggression and everything would be easier. That was precisely the subject of his conversation with Batista.

"Fidel has found a way to deceive my people," the defeated Cuban dictator explained. "His speeches, full of promises to improve the standard of living of the poorest sectors, are pure demagogy. That has been his principal error because it will lead to a direct confrontation with US interests. He is standing up to the Americans and those people won't forgive him for that. Perhaps the easiest thing would be to wait until they defeat him."

"I don't think things will be that simple," responded Trujillo. "Moreover, why wait? We have the necessary men and US backing in the OAS [Organization of American States] and the UN [United Nations] if necessary. I believe that now is the appropriate moment to resolve this conflict, and that in addition, the Americans would be appreciative…" Trujillo thought to himself, "this tight-fisted guy obviously doesn't want to invest and is thinking only of taking refuge on the beaches of Miami, but he's not going anywhere with his wealth. He'll have to get his money out and if he tries, I'll take it off him."

Batista appraised the situation and grasped Trujillo's strategy. The Dominican was not only after his collaboration but also his money. He got up and took a few paces around the room, an office decorated with antique furniture and heavy drapes. He reasoned: "He thinks that I'm going to return to Cuba in the eventuality of Fidel being overthrown, and in that he's totally wrong. I have been through many dangers in recent years and what I most want to do is rest. I'll have to find a way so that this little general doesn't suspect my intentions, and escape at the first opportunity to enjoy my fortune."

Batista halted in the middle of the room and, forcing a smile, nodded:

"General, I am in agreement with your plan. I understand that you are suggesting we find a way to liquidate our young enemy before your Caribbean army reaches Havana. With him dead everything would be much easier. I have attempted it before, and things did not work out as I had hoped, but I think I can take care of the matter. Obviously the costs will be down to me."

Trujillo assented: here was the cooperation he was looking for. Now he could fully dedicate himself to the invasion plans, while his colleague busied himself with liquidating the man who was giving them so many headaches.

After a cordial handshake, the two dictators separated. Batista hurried to his luxury hotel in the Dominican capital.

Once there, he got rid of his wife Marta and some of the hangers-on awaiting him, and asked for a phone link to Miami. A few minutes later he was talking to one of his henchmen, Rolando Masferrer Rojas, known as the Tiger.[5]

Masferrer was living comfortably in Miami, where the authorities had confined him not so much for his political record, but for his illicit activities and businesses. He was a personal friend of Santos Trafficante[6] and was in ready contact with Colonel J.C. King.

Batista confided in his man:

"Rolando, I need you to send me someone you trust completely for a matter requiring an urgent solution. It has to do with our own future..." He left the rest in suspense.

Realizing that something big was cooking, from the other end of the line, Rolando responded: "I don't think there will be any difficulties, General. You remember El Morito? Yes... the one who was chief of the Tigers in the Manzanillo area. Well, I'll give him instructions to travel there immediately."

Washington, March 1959. CIA Headquarters

Colonel King was standing in front of the large window of his Quarters Eye office, meditating on political events in Cuba. Despite his recommendations, the administration was going in the wrong direction. With every passing day the communists were gaining a more significant quota of power in the Havana regime. Fidel Castro already had several of his loyal men in key government positions. Raúl, his younger brother, was virtual chief of the

---

5. Rolando Masferrer Rojas: politician in the pre-revolutionary period who organized the so-called Tiger death squads under General Fulgencio Batista and was responsible for hundreds of killings among the civilian population, principally in the eastern Cuban provinces.

6. Santos Trafficante: capo of the Florida Mafia and its representative in Havana prior to 1959.

army; Camilo Cienfuegos was chief of his general staff; and the dangerous Argentine Ernesto Guevara was behind all the populist and communist initiatives being announced in Havana. According to King's agents in the embassy, with every passing day the communists were gaining control over key positions, even though these agents were constantly meeting with people from the new government allied to their ideas to give them fresh instructions. Events were proceeding in the most disagreeable direction for the United States.

King was so absorbed in his thoughts that he failed to notice the presence of his secretary, who was patiently waiting with a cup of steaming coffee.

"Here is your coffee, Colonel. If you have no other orders, I'll be going, as it's already past 9:00 p.m."

King took the cup. With a gesture he indicated that she could go and he once more buried himself in his thoughts. He had to convince his chiefs to do something to reverse the course of events on the island. He knew of Trujillo's plans, but mistrusted the old dictator, whose alliance with Batista was very frail; besides, Trujillo was placing a lot of confidence in the internal forces that he claimed could be mobilized within Cuba to support his invasion. Moreover, King was concerned at Trujillo's lack of prestige with other Latin American governments. In the case of the invasion materializing, that factor could prompt significant political and moral support for Cuba.

King sat down at his desk and flipped through various reports until he found the one he wanted. It was an interview by case officer Bill Alexander of Rolando Masferrer, an exile who was forming an organization with branches in Cuba to fight against the revolutionary government.

Masferrer proposed to the CIA agent his anti-Castro plan, explaining that it included the assassination of Castro and that he could count on various men prepared for every contingency. His only condition was that he be given the post of government minister in the cabinet to be formed after the collapse of the revolutionary government.

The report concluded by affirming that Masferrer had become one of the most influential figures within the exile community in Miami, controlling the group of ex-Batista soldiers there, and that he was privately opposed to the Trujillo plan, given his understanding that the Dominican dictator wanted to sideline them from his project.

King tapped the intercom and asked for Bill Alexander. He wanted to know the operative's opinions at first hand.

"Colonel," Alexander stated, "I believe that Masferrer is our man. He has very powerful allies within the exile movement, including Eladio del Valle,[7] a former member of Congress in the Batista government who is closely linked to Santos Trafficante. It would seem that these people are offering him solid economic backing and want Castro out of power as quickly as possible."

"And how are they thinking of executing the plan?" asked King.

"The idea is to infiltrate a command of men to prepare an ambush for Castro in the vicinity of the Presidential Palace. They have people ready and trained for this task and it will not be difficult to shoot him. Without their leader, the revolutionaries will get involved in power struggles and that will create an opportunity for the United States to bring order to the island."

---

7. Eladio del Valle Gutiérrez: known as Yito. A captain in the merchant marines who devoted himself to trade in contraband merchandise from 1941 onwards in complicity with the Cuban government of the time. He was given a position in Batista's government and in 1952 held the post of deputy inspector of the National Secret Police. One year later he entered the Military Intelligence Service (SIM). In 1959 he left Cuba for the United States and became linked to the Junta of the Cuban Government in Exile (JGCE) headed by Carlos Prío Socarrás. He was an active participant in the CIA's acts of subversion against the Cuban revolution and was suspected of participating in the assassination of President Kennedy. He was brutally murdered himself in 1967.

Miami, March 1959

Hundreds of kilometers from Washington in his Miami residence, Rolando Masferrer was giving his plan its final touches. He deeply loathed Fidel Castro and anything that sniffed of communism, perhaps because of his past. In the 1930s he had fought in the International Brigades on the side of the Spanish Republic during the Spanish Civil War. In that period, he was a passionate defender of anarchist ideas. However, after the conflict ended in victory for the fascists, he perceived that he had been profoundly mistaken and speedily changed his allegiances. Initially, he made contact with various gangster groups acting in Cuba under the protection of President Ramón Grau. Later, he realized that he didn't have to depend on anyone else and that he could be a family head himself, and thus he created his own gang. After Fulgencio Batista's coup d'état of March 10, 1952, he joined that gravy train and soon obtained control of a newspaper, a position in Congress, and a paramilitary army called the Tigers that acted as an executive arm of the dictator. The mere mention of his name terrified people. His gangs acted with particular remorselessness in the eastern part of the island. There they executed, tortured and imparted their "justice."

On January 1, 1959, he was forced to flee in haste to avoid being tried for the crimes he had committed, and his new lair was Miami. There he had influential friends, particularly in the organized gambling sector. Being an enterprising man, he set to work immediately and soon his friend Santos Trafficante, chief of the local Cosa Nostra, made him responsible for extracting the money from the Havana casinos, which remained concealed in the homes of loyal friends. In the depths of his obscure consciousness he wanted to do something for his country, and when Batista required him to "eliminate" the revolutionary leader, he dedicated himself to the task with renewed energy. In Havana he could count on certain safe houses belonging to former associates where he could hide his point men. There were no problems concerning clandestine entry into Havana: some of the residences of his collaborators adjoined the banks of the Almendares River a few meters from its estuary, where he could land in a small vessel on a dark night.

The two men selected for the assassination were Obdulio Piedra, nephew of Orlando Piedra, infamous former chief of Batista's Police Investigations Bureau, and Navi Ferrás, alias El Morito, a notorious Tiger from the death squads. Both had a reputation as hard and unscrupulous guys. Their faces were disguised with thick mustaches, perhaps to disguise them for their flight from Cuba.

The conversation was brief. Everything had already been said.

"I have confidence in you," affirmed Masferrer. "You are well prepared and I can also inform you that the Americans are supporting us, it's just that they don't want to appear to be involved. This support will be very useful when the time comes because the FBI will take the pressure off us and it will be easier for us to operate our businesses. Plus, Trafficante's people are prepared to pay good money, so we win on both sides."

He continued: "Over there you have to move carefully. You are known and I have news that Castro is developing an efficient police force. You should get in contact with the group that Ernesto de la Fé[8] directs from prison and conclude the task as quickly as possible."

The two assassins asked for certain details. They were particularly interested in the pay and how they would return to Miami. After their doubts were allayed they went to arrange the preparations for the journey.

Colonel King received the news at the precise moment that the two killers left for Cuba. His officer, ensconced in Miami, kept him abreast of all events.

---

8. Ernesto de la Fé: minister of propaganda during the Batista regime who was detained in 1959 and sentenced by the revolutionary courts for his activities in support of the Batista dictatorship.

He replaced the receiver and informed Bissell that the operation had begun. "Everything is going according to plan. With luck, we'll have finished with Castro in a few days," affirmed the CIA division chief.

Havana, March 1959. DIER[9] Headquarters

...After illegally entering the country at the end of March, Obdulio Piedra and Navi Ferrás — two notorious Masferrer men — were discovered with various collaborators of Ernesto de la Fé, a former Batista minister currently serving time in prison for his past crimes. The two were hiding in one of the safe houses owned by the group in the Vedado district of Havana. In initial meetings between the new arrivals and various counterrevolutionaries, our agent was unable to discover the objective of their infiltration, and so did not detain them at that point.

A few days later, the two men asked for a car and began to reconnoiter the vicinity of the Presidential Palace. Alerted by our agent, we directed a National Revolutionary Police patrol to stake out the location and, as soon as they appeared, apprehend them and take them to the closest police station.

On the third day after the aforementioned orders were dispatched, the patrol located the suspect vehicle, and when the agents moved in to identify the two men, Navi Ferrás opened fire with a submachine gun. The police returned fire, leading to an exchange of shots in which nobody on our side was wounded.

The counterrevolutionaries managed to evade the police pursuit and left the country that night in a vessel awaiting them at a wharf in the Almendares River estuary.

---

9.   DIER: Rebel Army Investigations Department.

The house serving as the command hideout of Masferrer's men was searched, resulting in the seizure of valuable information on counterrevolutionary plots and the planned assassination of Fidel Castro.

A few days later, on March 27, *Revolución*, the newspaper of the July 26 Movement, reported the abortive attempt:

> The police authorities discovered a plot to assassinate *Comandante* Fidel Castro led by Rolando Masferrer and Ernesto de la Fé, two notorious Batista supporters linked to elements of the US Mafia located in Cuba prior to the revolutionary triumph...

2 A Tough Guy in Havana

Havana, April 1959. US Embassy

David Sánchez Morales was a Chicano. With his dark hair, almond eyes and round face he could not conceal his Mexican origin, and this had presented him with numerous difficulties in his career within the CIA. He had a strong, brutal character and an uncontrollable taste for liquor.

He was accepted into the CIA for his willingness to take on dirty jobs. However, when it came to giving him better paid and more comfortable positions, everyone vacillated, giving him a pat on the shoulder and promising him better luck next time.

He was part of the task force in the US intervention in Guatemala to liquidate Jacobo Árbenz's "communists," responsible for training the forces of rebel colonel Carlos Castillo Armas, a former collaborator of the US embassy in that country. The native Guatemalans that he trained in the "arts of subversion" mockingly called him "El Indio" (The Indian), and the nickname stuck. Everyone in the Agency called him that behind his back.

When he was appointed as a "diplomat" in Havana in 1958, he perceived that his great opportunity had finally arrived. Cuba was a sought-after placement for young officers, not only on account of the agreeable climate and high salary, but for the contacts that could be made with US entrepreneurs based there, particularly those related to organized gambling and drug trafficking, who could guarantee any young diplomat a promising future in return for their cooperation. The triumph of the revolution and the subsequent economic measures taken by Fidel Castro cast shadows on Morales's horizon. Several of his agents had warned him that the democratic discourse of the new regime concealed a skillful international communist maneuver to seize Cuba, and he had expressed this belief in various reports sent to Quarters Eye. There was nobody better authorized than him for such analyses: he had agents infiltrated into the Rebel Army, the National Revolutionary Police and other government agencies.

In April, Morales received an urgent call from one of his principal agents, Frank Sturgis, a US mercenary who had joined the revolutionaries in the final months of their struggle against Batista and had occupied an important position within the Rebel Army.

After talking for a number of hours with his agent, Morales was left feeling totally convinced that the United States could not allow the Cuban regime to advance in its political project. Through *Comandante* Pedro Luis Díaz Lanz, chief of the air force, Sturgis had discovered that one month later Fidel Castro was to decree a radical agrarian reform act that would affect the large proprietors of land and US sugar mills.

Sturgis insisted that the only way to solve the Cuban situation was through Castro's elimination. Díaz Lanz had confided to him that various reformists in the cabinet headed by Manuel Urrutia could channel the process in another direction and eliminate the communists led by Raúl Castro and Ernesto Che Guevara who, in his assessment, were promoting the revolution's radicalization.

With another US collaborator, Gerry Patrick Hemming,[1] a parachute instructor and explosives expert, Sturgis had a plan to effect Fidel Castro's assassination.

---

1.   Gerry Patrick Hemming: US citizen who was in Cuba in 1959 with a group allegedly training to fight in Nicaragua. He was named as an instructor of the Green Berets in the Panama Canal Zone and is linked to Cuban exile groups operating against Cuba from US territory.

That same afternoon, Morales met with Jim Noel,[2] head of the Havana station, and put to him the plan suggested by Sturgis. The plan, he explained, consisted of attracting Fidel Castro to the air force headquarters for a meeting and then detonating a powerful explosive previously concealed in the meeting room.

Noel, following his custom of not taking responsibility for any operative who did not provide 100 percent security, posed some of the dangers he could foresee and finally decided that he did not have the power to approve the proposal. To Morales's total dissatisfaction, Noel decided to consult with the new ambassador to Cuba, Philip Bonsal,[3] a pragmatic diplomat and a specialist on Latin America who was opposed to CIA incursions into foreign policy. Observing Morales's face, Noel ended the interview:

"In any case, I authorize you to travel to Washington to go over the plan with Colonel King; he will know what is most in keeping with the winds blowing over there."

Morales met once again with Sturgis and Hemming to go over the details of the planned operation. Afterwards, through Marjorie Lennox,[4] one of the secretaries at the station, he reserved a seat on the first available Pan American flight from Havana to Miami. Once in that city, he phoned Washington to inform them that he would be there in a few hours, and requested an interview with King.

---

2.   James A. Noel: head of the CIA station in the US embassy in Havana from 1958 to 1960, and head of the Madrid CIA station from 1961 to 1964.

3.   Philip W. Bonsal: US career diplomat, a liberal with knowledge of Latin American affairs; appointed ambassador to Cuba in 1959 after previously serving there as a junior diplomat.

4.   Marjorie Lennox: secretary at the CIA station in the US embassy in Havana. She was detained in 1963 along with several CIA officials while attempting to place concealed microphones in the Chinese Xinhua press agency.

Washington, April 1959. CIA Headquarters

As soon as Colonel King knew of David Morales's presence he called him to an urgent meeting. He was not accustomed to receiving colleagues at night but the wire from Havana intrigued him. In the wire, Noel informed him of the need to discuss an emerging plan that could change the course of events in Cuba. This was what he had been waiting for, King reflected. He knew the men in the Cuban capital very well and their numerous contacts within the government and opposition ranks. Through certain reports that had reached headquarters, he had picked up that a bloc against Castro within the regime was beginning to appear and organize itself. Maybe the moment to act had arrived.

It was the first time that Morales had met with such a high-ranking chief. Walking through the corridors of CIA headquarters he could sense a growing emotion. He had in his hands a vital plan, and if it met with success, his future would be assured.

Once in King's office, he explained in a wealth of detail the plot to assassinate Fidel Castro and the collaborators who would accompany him in setting the trap, concluding with a confident statement:

"Sturgis is a proven man. He fought in the Pacific during World War II and was wounded on three occasions. Later he worked with the Army Security Agency. In the mid-1950s he joined the Carlos Prío group exiled in Florida and established good contacts with the Cuban revolutionary movement. He travelled to Cuba with arms for Castro's rebels and recruited various officers, including Díaz Lanz, chief of the armed forces. He enjoyed much respect within that group and Gerry Patrick Hemming, a contract agent and demolitions expert, worked with him…"

Morales continued expounding on the conspirators' credentials and the project's possibility of success.

King reflected while he was listening. He would lose nothing by authorizing the plan because its principal executors were from the

Cuban regime itself. Although two US citizens were to be involved, the United States had nothing to do with them... apparently. He was aware that the Agrarian Reform Act would divide the Cuban government and that he had elements who could neutralize the communists and who — in the absence of Fidel Castro — would take over control.

"Very well Morales, I approve the plan with two conditions: one, that our embassy is not seen to be involved in the action; and two, that this project stays between us: you, Noel and myself."

David Morales knew precisely how to interpret what the colonel was saying. Accordingly, he asked his chief for justification for an irregular visit, and once the details were agreed, took the first plane to Miami to continue his journey to Havana from there.

Miami, July 1977. Testimony of Frank Sturgis[5]

In April 1959, as captain of the air force in Castro's army, I proposed to David, my case officer and an embassy official, that the solution to the problem in Cuba was the elimination of Castro. By that date it was clear to all of us that the communists controlled the main government positions and that after the drafting of the Agrarian Reform Act, land and sugar refineries owned by US citizens would be confiscated. There was also the issue of tourism. We already knew, through Díaz Lanz, that the casinos were going to be closed definitively, which would ruin many friends in the gambling syndicate.

Many people were looking to us, Americans in the Rebel Army, hoping that we would give them a signal to act, and we couldn't lose any more time. Raúl Castro and Che Guevara were placing

---

5.   Interview with Frank Sturgis by a collaborator with Cuban intelligence, conducted under the cover of an article for the national press.

their cadres everywhere and would soon control the main posts within the armed forces.

This was what we proposed to case officer David Sánchez Morales for Castro's execution.

A few days later, Morales returned from a trip to Washington and gave us the green light. I remember that at the beginning of May, we met in Díaz Lanz's office and made the decision. Hemming would plant the device that we had prepared, and we would then wait for Fidel to visit the selected location.

One afternoon, in the middle of that month, we placed the explosive device in the meeting room of the air force command. We took advantage of two large marble ashtrays there and placed the charge inside them. Then, with some fine cables concealed under the carpet of the room, we took the connection out to the park. There, conveniently hidden among some bushes, we left everything ready to install the electrical connection that would explode the device at the desired moment.

We waited for Castro's visit with much tension during those days. Díaz Lanz had invited him to a meeting with the central command, but as always, he (Castro) never said when he would come, in order to appear unexpectedly as was his habit.

In the meantime, we established contact with other army commands, with, among others, *Comandante* Huber Matos, head of the Camagüey military fort, whom we knew was against Castro's socialist direction. The idea was that after he (Castro) was eliminated, they would join with us to form a provisional government which would select a civilian figure to head the country.

Sergio Sanjenís, chief of the Aviation Military Police, came to see me one day highly concerned. He had received information that G-2 [the Cuban State Security Department] was investigating Díaz Lanz and myself, and explained:

"Frank, these people have got you under observation. I think that Fidel wants to send out a warning by detaining some of his detractors, and many people know that you are virtually part of the opposition. I'm leaving the country at the earliest opportunity and I would advise you to do the same."

When I spoke to Díaz Lanz he got very nervous. He told me:

"Frank, it's over. Castro suspects us and that's why he hasn't come to the air force command."

Hemming retrieved the explosive device at the request of Díaz Lanz, who, without saying anything to us, took a launch and headed for Florida. When I consulted with David, he ordered me to leave Cuba as quickly as possible, to avoid G-2 discovering the embassy connection. I was left with no alternative but to steal a plane and leave with Gerry... That was how this conspiracy on the life of Fidel Castro failed, due to the cowardice of certain people who these days, in exile, want to boast about actions that they never had the valor to carry out...

A Faustian Opera
Washington, December 1959. CIA Headquarters

Colonel King found himself extremely busy that afternoon in the final days of the year. He was examining various cables from the CIA station in Havana, and one of them had really caught his attention. It noted the contacts made by Major Robert Van Horne, military attaché at the embassy and a CIA official, with various counterrevolutionary groups active in the Cuban capital.

The month had been decisive in terms of the creation and organization of the counterrevolutionary movement in Cuba. The dismantling of the conspiracy organized by Huber Matos and his associates had forced many people to choose which road to take. Manuel Artime[6] founded the Movement for the Recovery of the

---

6.   Manuel Artime Buesa: participated in the armed struggle against Batista on December 28, 1958, but quickly turned against the revolution. He was a leader of the Assault Brigade 2506.

Revolution (MRR), and the Christian Socialists went underground, renaming their party — which had previously played an active role in national politics — the Christian Democrat Movement (MDC). After leaving the government, Manuel Ray founded the Revolutionary Movement of the People (MRP), and thus commenced a lengthy list of counterrevolutionary groups, almost all of which, at that point, originated in the lay structures of the Catholic Church.

Nevertheless, King's attention was focused on another organization that had already been operating for a few months. It was the Anticommunist Workers Movement (MOA), composed of bourgeois elements, landowners and businesspeople who, fearful of the measures taken by the revolutionary government, had decided to join together in a counterrevolutionary coup.

One of the principal leaders was US citizen Geraldine Shamman, who was married to a Cuban businessman with a large personal fortune. Shamman — a covert CIA agent — was the MOA's link with the US embassy and affirmed that the group had organized units in all the island's provinces.

Colonel King noticed that events had moved forward rapidly on the island. The cable listed some of the group's proposed activities and one proposition had caught his attention: an attempt on the life of Fidel Castro during one of his visits to the residence of *Comandante* Ramiro Valdés,[7] head of G-2.

"Perhaps," mused King, "this is the opportunity that I was waiting for. Only in this case," he concluded, "they will have to act directly so as to ensure success. We mustn't repeat the errors of the past."

Nevertheless, they needed to cover their backs; to find a way to eliminate the leader without appearing to be involved. King knew

---

7. Ramiro Valdés Menéndez: Moncada Garrison assailant, expeditionary from the *Granma* cabin cruiser and one of the combatants who was very close to Fidel Castro. He was chief of G-2 and subsequently minister of the interior.

that Dulles and Bissell would support him, but Harvard liberals and academics in all the government structures would protest at or even oppose such an extreme measure.

With those thoughts running through his head he took up his pen and began to write a long report. When it was finished, he read it through again and decided to stress one paragraph:

> A far left dictatorship now exists in Cuba which, if permitted to stand, will encourage similar actions against US holdings in other Latin American countries... Thorough consideration [must] be given to the elimination of Fidel Castro. None of those close to Fidel, such as his brother Raúl or his companion Che Guevara, have the same mesmeric appeal to the masses. Many informed people believe that the disappearance of Fidel Castro would greatly accelerate the fall of the present government.[8]

A few hours later Allen Dulles received the report and, after consulting with Richard Bissell, who had already been informed, noted in a corner of the document:

> APPROVED. HANDLE THE MATTER WITH MUCH DELICACY. DO NOT INFORM THE AMBASSADOR AND TAKE THE NECESSARY MEASURES TO AVOID THE UNITED STATES BEING SEEN TO BE OFFICIALLY INVOLVED IN THE OPERATION.

Miami, January 1960. Testimony of Luis Tacornal, "Fausto"[9]

I was sitting in the lobby of the America Hotel in downtown Miami when I overheard a conversation on the situation in our country. I immediately caught on that the people meeting there were against

---

8. Senate Select Committee (Church Commission), *Alleged Assassination Plots Involving Foreign Leaders* (Washington: US Government Printing Office, 1975), 92.
9. Luis Tacornal: Cuban security agent infiltrated into Rolando Masferrer's counterrevolutionary group.

us, so, perceiving the opportunity to establish a friendship with them, I followed the current...

Two days later, Masferrer himself appeared at 9:30 a.m. accompanied by four friends: one called Antonio, who is lame; El Morito; and two others, one of them a relative of Orlando Piedra. In that first meeting they told me that they had planned a joint action with the people of Huber Matos and Tony Varona[10] in Camagüey, that the plot had failed because events had moved faster than expected, and that he wanted me to get in contact with his man in Havana. That was what we talked about in the first meeting.

A second meeting was agreed for 3:00 p.m. that same day.

At the agreed time Masferrer reappeared, accompanied by the lame one, Antonio. El Morito didn't leave me alone for a second. I think they maybe checked me out in Havana, or something like that, because they arrived more ready to talk. On that occasion they asked me to learn by heart a note with the addresses of certain people in Havana, and they explained what code to use with each one of them in order to make contact.

Some weeks later, Masferrer phoned me again at my house in Miami to explain the plans they were preparing, which were related to an invasion of Cuba...

They believe that with State Department support they can obtain the moral and material aid necessary for going ahead with their invasion plan. At the point when they land and initiate the battle, the State Department will ask the OAS to intervene in Cuba, backed up by six to eight Latin American countries. In the case

---

10. Manuel Antonio de Varona Loredo: prime minister during the Carlos Prío Socarrás government (1948–52). He was president of Congress and headed the Cuban Revolutionary Party (*Autenticos*) during the 1948 presidential campaign. He led the Revolutionary Democratic Front (FRD), a front organization organized by the CIA that brought together Cuban exile counterrevolutionary organizations in the United States. Later, he joined the Cuban Revolutionary Council (CRC), a similar organization, whose objective was to form a provisional government in Cuba after the Bay of Pigs invasion.

of the OAS deciding to intervene in the Cuba issue... President Eisenhower will designate Admiral Burke[11] to command troop-landing operations...

Colonel King from the CIA, in charge of the Latin American division, is the man in charge of reviewing and presenting the plans of the different groups, which in their turn are called to Washington to discuss them. The day before I left Miami, Colonel King called Rolando Masferrer and told him that he was thinking of approving his plan and, as it was impossible for him to go to Washington, some CIA agents would visit him in his house in Miami to discuss the plans more thoroughly.

Masferrer thinks that at "Zero Hour" the men can leave Miami for the intermediate base in the direction of Guatemala, as if they were going on a work contract... with another group leaving from Tampa supposedly en route for Panama... that they would meet up on a little island they had in the Bahamas and subsequently land in Cuba. Once they had taken power, they would convene elections as soon as possible and impose a "democratic regime."

During this meeting in Masferrer's house, Yito [Eladio] del Valle came to visit him. Masferrer explained that he was going to Washington to meet with Carlos Márquez Sterling and also with CIA agents. He asked me to accompany him to Washington...

As soon as I have fresh information I will send it via the same channel.

Luis Tacornal Saíz (Fausto), was educated in New Orleans. The triumph of the revolution surprised him there while he was involved in establishing the July 26 Movement in that city, but he soon realized

---

11. Arleigh Burke: chief of the US Army, a friend of Dwight Eisenhower; he had amicable relations with the government of Fulgencio Batista, from whom he received various decorations. He belonged to a group of Pentagon officers proposing the defeat of the Cuban revolution by means of direct US military action.

that his duty was elsewhere, within the ranks of the enemy which was already organizing to attack the revolution.

He became an infiltration agent for the [Cuban] Security Services, which selected José Veiga Peña, a young officer whom he had known when they were both students in New Orleans, to work with him.

Fausto and Veiga were an inseparable pair. They moved to Havana, and from Geraldine Shamman's residence, infiltrated the conspiratorial network, whose Cuban State Security code name was Caso Ópera (the Opera Case), until it was dismantled in November 1960 with the arrest of most of the conspirators.

Both of them exposed themselves to innumerable dangers, but as Lieutenant Colonel José Veiga recalled, the most difficult experience was when the counterrevolutionaries received a CIA directive to assassinate Fidel Castro.

Havana, November 1994. Testimony of José Veiga Peña

At the end of 1959 and beginning of 1960 I made contact with Geraldine Shamman, who lived on First Street in Miramar and operated as the link with the CIA station in Havana located in the US embassy, and who was also Manuel Artime's representative in Cuba. Up until that point Shamman had dedicated herself to hiding war criminals and refugees from the Batista regime.

We were aware from the first meeting that she reported directly to Major Robert Van Horne, military attaché at the embassy and one of the CIA chiefs on the fifth floor of the building. His secretary was called Deborah and his typist Mildred Perkins.

Van Horne was almost always accompanied by Lieutenant Colonel Nichols, who, according to her, was in charge of military intelligence.

We met both of them in the Methodist church on 110th Street, Miramar. One Sunday Fausto and I received instructions to organize Masferrer groups nationwide and have them ready to effect an uprising in the Escambray, to engage in sabotage and to execute an attempt on the life of Fidel Castro, for which Geraldine would act as our support.

On a number of occasions we observed Geraldine filming and taking photos of the house adjacent to hers, the home of *Comandante* Ramiro Valdés, head of G-2. She said that that material was for Van Horne and that was correct, as I accompanied her to his office on various occasions to hand over the film. In fact, they were studying the possibilities of assassinating Fidel on a visit to Ramiro's house.

On inquiring what ideas they had to execute the attempt, she explained that three groups would take part in the action: two would seal off the streets and the third would fire on the *comandante* from the attic opposite. I discovered that she already had M3 submachine guns and grenades and only needed telescopic rifles that the Agency was going to provide.

Bearing in mind the group's dangerousness, we decided to focus on delaying the operation, which resulted in the visit to Havana in January 1960 of a high-level CIA figure to put pressure on Fausto to speed up the assassination attempt on the commander-in-chief.

Given the CIA pressure, we proposed to simulate an attack on *Comandante* Abelardo Colomé Ibarra,[12] likewise an enemy objective, and when that failed, to go underground and divert the main project.

The supposed attack on *Comandante* Colomé was organized on the corner of 20th and Third Street in Miramar, with a shootout that allowed Fausto and me to flee with the arms, which, as we explained afterwards, we threw into the sea, thus neutralizing the operation.

---

12. Abelardo Colomé Ibarra: operations chief of G-2, 1959–61. An outstanding combatant in the revolutionary war who rose to the rank of *comandante* and was a founding member of the Cuban State Security Department.

Geraldine hid Fausto in her house for a few weeks, having advised the US embassy, which confirmed the attack on *Comandante* Colomé but added that the US government was not planning to give it publicity… I was hidden on 21st Street in Vedado in the house of counterrevolutionary Isabel del Busto, until headquarters decided to activate the case…

On December 28, 1960, the Havana *El Mundo* newspaper published the following news on its front page:

27 DETAINEES SENTENCED IN LA CABAÑA…[13]

Report from the public prosecutor… that the individuals tried some months ago were conspiring against the stability of the state, in conjunction with the enemies of the revolution who are attacking the Cuban government from abroad… Those sentenced had conspired to assassinate senior government figures and to plant bombs… according to the testimony of José Veiga Peña, Manuel Franco, Antonio Cervantes, Luis Tacornal Saíz and the investigation of the armed forces.

----

13. La Cabaña is an 18th century fortress complex located on the eastern side of Havana Bay.

3 La Cosa Nostra

A cold front had swept over Washington, obliging its residents to swathe themselves in heavy overcoats and walk rapidly along the almost deserted streets and sidewalks. An important meeting was underway at CIA headquarters, which had brought together a large number of chiefs and officials of the Western Hemisphere Division. Under discussion, and not for the first time, were contingency plans to combat and defeat the regime of Fidel Castro in Havana.

In one of the air-conditioned rooms set aside for special meetings, with white walls and no windows, soundproofed and with rigorous protection measures against bugs, a group of men who had recently arrived in Washington from various countries were talking animatedly around a large oak table.

They were all high-profile specialists in various espionage sectors and veterans of PBSUCCESS, the secret war plan that had defeated the "communist" government of Jacobo Árbenz in Guatemala in 1954.

Moving from left to right, the first was Jack Esterline, who had been chief of the CIA station in Venezuela until news had arrived that something "important" was being prepared against Cuba. He had been in Caracas when Fidel Castro visited there in early 1959, and had realized then that the man was a very dangerous leader for the United States. That was why, as soon as he heard that a task force against the Cuban revolution was being organized, he offered his services. Bissell immediately accepted him and placed him at the head of the task force.

Then came Howard Hunt, back from Uruguay after an incident with the US ambassador assigned there, who accused him of refusing to accept orders in front of President Eisenhower during the president's visit. The ambassador was inflexible with his staff and immediately demanded that Hunt be replaced as head of station there.

The next person was veteran OSS spy Frank Bender, of German origin, who had been personally recruited by Dulles during World War II and was the CIA's link to the dictator Trujillo. He was handling the mercenary action through which the Dominican dictator was unsuccessfully trying to defeat the Havana government. He already had solid experience and knowledge of the Cuban exile groups, with which he had established close connections.

David Atlee Phillips,[1] a specialist in psychological warfare who had recently operated underground in Cuba and had an excellent base of agents, came next. His credentials also included participation in the conspiracy that brought down the Árbenz government in 1954.

The cowboy of the group was William "Rip" Robertson, who belonged to the legendary paramilitaries, always ready for action. It was true that he had blundered on certain occasions and was still recovering from the huge error committed in Guatemala when CIA aircraft, acting on his instructions, mistakenly sank a British cargo boat in the belief that it was a Czechoslovakian vessel. The United States had to pay substantial compensation to Britain, and since then he had been somewhat left out in the cold.

---

1.   David Atlee Phillips: recruited by the CIA in the early 1950s in Chile, where he published a national newspaper. In 1954 he was part of a CIA task force to overthrow Jacobo Árbenz's government in Guatemala. At the end of the 1950s he established himself in Havana under the cover of a publicity agency. He later became chief of the CIA's Western Hemisphere division.

Finally came Tracy Barnes, with his slicked-down hair, dark tailored suit, the Agency's rising star, an advisor to Bissell and his logical successor in the event of the latter's promotion to CIA chief.

The conversation was animated and Barnes read out President Eisenhower's recent instructions to move ahead on a covert operation to overthrow the Cuban government. The language employed was sinuous but clear enough for everyone to get an exact grasp of the strategy they were to execute. Stripped of verbiage, the essential aspects of the strategy were the setting up of a responsible and unified opposition to the Castro regime outside of Cuba; the development of mass media for the Cuban people as part of a strong propaganda offensive; the creation of a secret intelligence and action organization in Cuba to follow the orders and instructions of the opposition-in-exile; and the development of a paramilitary force outside of Cuba for future guerrilla actions.

Once Barnes had finished, Colonel King, who suspected that the decision to establish an independent task force would once again keep his command sidelined from any action, asked to speak:

"In general, I think Barnes's notes summarize the mission to be executed. However, I insist that if Castro is not removed from the field, our plans could fail…"

A silence followed the colonel's words. The rivalry and differences between the head of the Western Hemisphere Division and Bissell's principal advisor were no secret to anyone. The same thing had occurred with the intervention in Guatemala. Everyone thought that King was too slow for such complicated tasks. Without any doubt, it was for that reason that Dulles had directly subordinated Esterline and his group to the leadership. Richard Bissell, sitting in the corner of the room, looked at him intently and his myopic eyes, hidden behind heavy-lens glasses, reflected an explosion of anger.

"Colonel, as you will understand, such recommendations cannot be written in an official memorandum that has to be signed by the US president. You have the approval of Dulles and myself for that task, which — I repeat again — is highly compartmentalized. What more do you want?"

With a brusque gesture, he moved on, setting March 1 as the date for each person to submit plans in their area of expertise for Dulles's consideration. These plans would then go to the president for inclusion in a National Security Action Memorandum that would require the president's signature.

Give Me a Death
Washington, January 1960. CIA Headquarters

At the end of the task force meeting, Colonel King, still annoyed at the treatment he had received, headed for his offices. He was approached in the passage by David Phillips, who asked him for an urgent meeting.

Once seated inside the office, Phillips said:

"Colonel, as you know, I participated in the recruitment of Cuban exile Manuel Artime. He is a very useful man who heads the MRR with the support of the Catholic Church and influential sectors within the national business community. We are training some of his men and he thinks he can be ready to liquidate Castro within a couple of months."

King settled himself in his chair. His bad mood had begun to dissipate. This was an attractive proposal that he couldn't ignore. If everything worked out well, his position within the CIA would be strengthened and maybe he could even get the chief off his back.

"Very good," he said, softening his expression, "explain the matter to me in detail."

Phillips embarked on a long explanation. The project was essentially based on the access of certain members of Manuel Artime's group to the University of Havana, a location frequently visited by Fidel Castro. It would be easy to fire at him there and then melt back into the crowd.

After listening to Phillips, King felt more relaxed. He shook Phillips's hand when he was leaving and affirmed:

"I have confidence in you, keep me up to date with the plan. I would only ask that, for now, it stays between the two of us."

He accompanied Phillips to the door and patted him on the back with an affectionate gesture, unusual for him.

"And who do you suggest should coordinate the plan?" asked King.

"I think Howard Hunt is our man. He has been in Havana and is an experienced agent."

"Very well, take care of the details. Of course, if everything goes according to plan, I would like to have you on my team, and who knows, maybe in post-Castro Havana!"

Havana, Early March 1960. Testimony of Howard Hunt[2]

...Our cover personnel gave me the documents in support of the operational alias under which I would live while the project lasted; I got a travel advance and flew to Tampa where I boarded a National Airlines flight to Havana.

I installed myself in the Vedado Hotel and changed my dollars for Cuban pesos, checked out my small and miserable room and set off to reconnoiter the Cuban capital.

The atmosphere of repression hit me almost straight off. Uniformed bearded men brandishing Czech submachine guns guarded the hotels and other confiscated assets. Women and girls in military attire marched through the main streets in a one, two, three, four cadence. "Long live Fidel Castro!" Obviously, the cult of personality had been appropriated by Cuba.

---

2.   Excerpt from the book *Give Us This Day* (New York: Arlington House, 1973), where Hunt relates his experiences in Cuba and comments on the failure of the Bay of Pigs invasion. (Editor's note: re-translated from Spanish.)

Newspaper stands that once exhibited *Life, Look, Time* and *Vision,* offered strident imports from Peking, the Soviet Union and the National Institute of Agrarian Reform. I walked to the Malecón and saw long lines of Cubans queuing for visas outside our consulate. From there I returned to Sloppy Joe's, where I lunched on a light beer and a miserable sandwich, alone in the large bar where previously you had to fight for service...

I slept until I was awoken at midnight by the squeal of brakes in the street...

I looked out of the window and saw the flashing lights of police cars escorted by two jeeps. Uniformed bearded men jumped out and headed for some neighboring apartments, where lights began to come on. A few minutes later two men and one woman were brought out and pushed into a Black Maria.[3] Submachine guns threatened the crowd. The three cars sped away... I had witnessed revolutionary justice in action...

The next morning I flew back to Tampa and took a connecting flight to Washington, where I drafted a report of my impressions. When they asked for my recommendations in terms of the project, I listed four: to assassinate Fidel Castro prior to or during the invasion; to destroy radio stations; to destroy shortwave transmission systems just before the start of the invasion; to discount any idea of a popular uprising against Castro until the matter is militarily decided.

Havana, April 1960, DIER Headquarters.
Testimony of Carlos Arocha Pérez, "Eduardo"

...According to our sources, on April 9 this year elements infiltrated from the United States under the orders of Manuel Artime Buesa and the CIA planned to unleash a series of terrorist attacks, including the dynamiting of various electricity stations and oil refineries in

---

3.   Black Maria: English term for police van.

the country. At the same time, armed gangs would take charge of assassinating national leaders and army and militia officers.

A commando force comprising counterrevolutionaries Rogelio González Corzo, Juan Manuel Guillot Castellanos and Roberto Quintairos Santiso, previously trained in Miami, were to attend a commemorative event at the University of Havana for those who died there on April 9, 1958. There, dispersed among the public, they would attack *Comandante* Fidel Castro and assassinate him.

Our man, responsible for facilitating the two cars to be used in the action, was detained by the police who, under instructions, held him all day with the explanation that the vehicles had incurred outstanding traffic fines, which was a fact.

Meanwhile counterrevolutionaries José Quintana García, Joaquín Benítez Pérez and Martina Otero Salabarría, coordinators of the attempt, were arrested. This led to the dispersal of the group and allowed us to continue its penetration for higher objectives.

A Present for Castro
Washington, July 1960. CIA Headquarters

Sheffield Edwards was a career officer who served for many years in the Defense Intelligence Department, where he rose to the rank of colonel. There he received merits not in the combat trenches, but within the institution's bureaucracy. He was a sharp person who knew how to perform in the presence of senior chiefs at the right moment. Some time back, his friend J.C. King had proposed him to head the CIA Office of Security, a unit set up to oversee the protection of secrets within the Agency, and he had accepted. The CIA would certainly offer new horizons very different from military life, he thought.

Six foot tall, with whitish hair, blue eyes and a military bearing, Edwards enjoyed a reputation among his colleagues as a reserved, loyal and disciplined man.

One day in mid-July 1960, Richard Bissell and J.C. King called him to an important meeting. After the habitual greetings, they discussed events in Cuba and the state of the project to defeat the regime. While Bissell was explaining details, Edwards wondered why he was being informed of such compartmentalized plans, which had nothing to do with his usual work. He didn't have to wonder for long. When the Harvard professor had finished, King took the floor to give him a mission, just as he had done previously when both of them were in the army.

"We think that you could play an important role in helping us get rid of Castro. Some of your personnel have relations with the Las Vegas gambling syndicate. They are as interested as we are in solving this problem. Using a solid front, perhaps posing as the representative of businessmen who have lost a lot of money in Cuba, select the most appropriate individuals and offer them a contract on Castro's life."

The request did not take him by surprise. Under the cover of protecting CIA secrets, Edwards was developing a secret program, one of whose objectives was to maintain relations with individuals involved in organized crime who would occasionally take on dirty operations in which the Agency didn't want to or couldn't be involved. They were the experts in assassination and extortion, which were prohibited to the elegant, clean and delicate men of the CIA.

The conversation continued for several hours, with the participants all proposing different solutions, from a shootout in the streets of Havana to the use of poison.

It was not the first time that US intelligence had used the services of the Mafia to promote US foreign policy interests. At the end of World War II, the OSS proposed and achieved the release from prison of Lucky Luciano, one of the principal Mafia capos, to serve as ambassador to La Cosa Nostra in Sicily, where the US troop landing in southern Italy had been planned.

At the end of the meeting, Bissell suggested that Edwards should meet with Joseph Scheider, head of the Agency laboratories, who had been successfully experimenting with synthetic botulin — a powerful poison more effective than cyanide that left no traces — with the objective of confirming the state of his research and assessing his usefulness in the plot.

Some hours later, alone in his office, Edwards analyzed the various proposals discussed for effecting the crime and decided not to reject any of them: poisoning, a surprise shootout, or the use of a lone assassin.

He picked up the phone and dialled the number of one of his men, Jim O'Connell, operational support chief, under whose mantle the Mafia contacts were concealed. That night, O'Connell and Edwards met in a dark Washington parking lot, since matters of that nature were not discussed in the offices.

O'Connell was very pale, blond and over six foot tall, weighing 200 pounds and with the look of a killer. He always carried a revolver hidden under his arm. He was notorious for his crude habits and was an appropriate person for the task recommended to him.

After Edwards's detailed explanation, the agent understood what was required and assured his chief that he had the means and the appropriate people for the mission.

The following day, O'Connell met with Scheider who, like a traveling salesman, offered him a variety of products: a lethal poison and chemical agents capable of inflicting temporary disorientation, uncontrollable euphoria and hair or facial hair loss.

When O'Connell left the meeting, he was elated. He hadn't imagined that the Agency would have such a variety of means for undertaking that type of order. The era of waiting with submachine guns at the exit of some public place was ending. Now, one could not only kill, but also leave the victim crazy, beardless or subject to constant and uncontrollable fits of laughter. Marvellous, he thought.

As soon as he got back to his apartment he took a hot shower and made coffee. He dialled a New York phone number and waited a moment until someone picked up at the other end of the line.

"Mr. Maheu, please."

He waited a moment while the servant advised her boss. Seconds later, a familiar voice answered.

"How are you, my friend? I imagine you must be surprised by this unexpected call, but I need to see you urgently."

"Yes, yes, I could get there…"

"OK. I'll be on the first plane and I'll call you."

Robert Maheu was a veteran CIA agent who had started his career in the FBI. Afterwards, he became a private investigator and lent the Agency valuable services. At that time he was working as head of public relations for Texan multimillionaire Howard Hughes. Short, brown-eyed with a doglike face, he could rub shoulders — without calling attention to himself — with the regents of the gambling city of Las Vegas, where Hughes had important businesses.

As soon as he reached New York, O'Connell took a taxi to the luxury apartment of his old collaborator. There, sipping a glass of bourbon, he brought Maheu up to speed with the reason for his visit: a contract on the life of Fidel Castro.

It wasn't the first time that Maheu had received a task of that nature. He had solid links with the right people for such jobs. The little guy moved about the room. "Perhaps," he thought, "John Roselli, one of the right-hand men of Giancana, the capo of La Cosa Nostra in Chicago, could be the man." He knew that Roselli had sufficient friends in Florida, which was the location of the largest number of Cuban exiles. Santos Trafficante, the czar of gaming in Havana before Castro took power, was also there in Florida. "Yes, Roselli's the man," he concluded.

Roselli and Trafficante would be the individuals given the task. They would surely find appropriate individuals for the job among their contacts in Havana.

For his part, O'Connell would seek out other ways of executing the plan. He knew that in the near future — in September — Fidel

Castro would be attending a UN meeting in New York and maybe the opportunity they sought would present itself there. "Perhaps a public activity at which to place an explosive device," he mused.

Washington, November 1975, US Senate.
Report of the Church Commission[4]

From March through August 1960, during the last year of the Eisenhower administration, the CIA considered plans to undermine Castro's charismatic appeal by sabotaging his speeches. According to the 1967 report of the CIA's inspector general,[5] an officer in the Technical Services Division (TSD) recalled discussing a scheme to spray Castro's broadcasting studio with a chemical which produced effects similar to LSD, but the scheme was rejected because the chemical was not reliable. During this period, the TSD impregnated a box of cigars with a chemical which produced temporary disorientation, hoping to induce Castro to smoke one of the cigars before delivering a speech. The inspector general also reported on a plan to destroy Castro's image as "The Beard" by dusting his shoes with thallium salts, a strong depilatory that would cause his beard to fall out...

A notation in the records of the Operations Division, CIA's Office of Medical Services, indicates that on August 16, 1960, an official was given a box of Castro's favorite cigars with instructions to treat them with lethal poison. The cigars were contaminated with a botulin toxin so potent that a person would die after putting one in his mouth. The official reported that the cigars were ready on October 7, 1960...

---

4. Church Commission: Senate Committee created under the presidency of Senator Frank Church in 1975 to investigate CIA assassination attempts on foreign political leaders.
5. Report on assassination plans against Fidel Castro, published with an introduction by Fabián Escalante as *CIA Targets Fidel* (Melbourne & New York: Ocean Press, 1996).

In August 1960, the CIA took steps to enlist members of the criminal underworld with gambling syndicate contacts to aid in assassinating Castro... According to the 1967 inspector general's report, "Bissell recalls that the idea originated with J.C. King, then chief of the Western Hemisphere Division."

The earliest concrete evidence of the operation is a conversation between DD/P [deputy director of plans] Bissell and Colonel Sheffield Edwards, director of the Office of Security. Edwards recalled that Bissell asked him to locate someone who could assassinate Castro...

Edwards assigned the mission to the chief of the Operational Support Division of the Office of Security. The support chief recalled that Edwards had said that he and Bissell were looking for someone to "eliminate" or "assassinate" Castro.

Edwards and the support chief decided to rely on Robert A. Maheu to recruit someone "tough enough" to handle the job... The operational support chief had served as Maheu's case officer since the Agency first began using Maheu's services, and by 1960 they had become close personal friends.

Sometime in late August or early September 1960, the support chief approached Maheu about the proposed operation. As Maheu recalls the conversation, the support chief asked him to contact John Roselli, an underworld figure with possible gambling contacts in Las Vegas, to determine if he would participate in a plan to "dispose" of Castro...

The support chief had previously met Roselli at Maheu's home...

The inspector general's report states that "Edwards and Maheu agreed that Maheu would approach Roselli as the representative of businessmen with interests in Cuba who saw the elimination of Castro as the first essential step to the recovery of their investments."

According to Roselli, he and Maheu met at the Brown Derby restaurant in Beverly Hills in early September 1960. Roselli testified that Maheu told him that "high government officials" needed his cooperation in getting rid of Castro, and that he asked him to help recruit Cubans to do the job…

A meeting was arranged for Maheu and Roselli with the support chief at the Plaza Hotel in New York. The inspector general's report placed the meeting on September 14, 1960.

…Michael J. Murphy, chief inspector of the New York police, entered the suite of the Waldorf Astoria, a luxury hotel that served as headquarters for his men in charge of protecting Castro, and met there with a CIA agent waiting for him with a hair-raising story.

The Agency had a plan to place a box of cigars in a location where they could be smoked by Castro. If and when he lit one, the agent said, the cigar would explode and blow his head off…

Murphy, who could hardly believe his ears, was dismayed, as it was his responsibility to protect Castro rather than to bury him. If the CIA agent was pulling his leg, it was a joke on too crude a subject. But the worst thing was that it seemed the agent was talking in all seriousness…

The Dynamiter
New York, September 1960. Central Park

John Martino was one of the top Mafia strongmen in the casino of Havana's Hotel Nacional. His chief, Mike McLaney, afforded him privileges over and above those enjoyed by the rest of the gangsters operating in organized gambling. Within a few years he had bought a house in the Cuban capital, while also occupying a suite at the neighboring Capri Hotel, where he was constantly visited by the most beautiful chorus girls from Havana's cabarets. The revolution complicated his life. He soon realized that the Cuban government was going to eradicate gambling and prostitution and would do away with the lucrative businesses they had set up.

One afternoon, at the beginning of August 1959, McLaney instructed him to begin to smuggle the Mafia's money out of Cuba via the maritime link between Havana and Key West in Florida. However, a tip-off to the Cuban police resulted in his detention on October 5 with a suitcase full of dollars.

Cuban police were waging a full-scale battle against organized crime figures, who, through the use of couriers, were attempting to save their fortunes. One such courier was Jack Ruby, who some years later would be Lee Harvey Oswald's assassin.

Martino was detained in the Havana jail in the lower part of El Príncipe Castle, an old fortress dating back to the colonial era. Only the payment of a large bond made his release possible, whereupon he fled the country aboard a yacht bound for Miami.

In September 1960 the opportunity arrived for taking his revenge on Fidel Castro, the man who had taken away his decadent lifestyle and then put him in prison. Through the New York press, which gave front-page coverage to the activities of Fidel Castro on his second visit to the United States, Martino learned of a public event organized by Cuban émigrés in Central Park in honor of their leader. A telephone call from the "godfather" Sam Giancana was the catalyst for his decision that the park was the appropriate place to assassinate the revolutionary leader.

He called his brother Walter, a gunman under his orders, and told him to place a powerful dynamite charge under the platform to be used by Castro and his followers.

He couldn't have known that US police agents would surprise Walter in that operation, arrest him, and inform the press, thus unmasking the homicidal plot.

That same month, *Bohemia* magazine in Havana circulated information collected from the US news agencies:

> During the visit by Prime Minister Fidel Castro to New York, police agents in that city surprised US citizen Walter Martino attempting to place a potent 200-pound TNT explosive device in Central Park, where the Cuban leader was to attend a public meeting.

A Contract to Kill
New York and Havana, October 1960

At the end of the 1950s Sam Giancana, also known as Momo, was chief of one of the most important Mafia "families" in Chicago and possibly the country. His relations with various trade union groups assured him control of legitimate businesses in the ports and road transportation, which were highly lucrative. He was a descendant of Italian émigrés who had fought hard to give him his position. More than one of his colleagues had to pay very dearly for trying to muscle in on one or another of his businesses. His "family" had commercial interests in many countries, including Cuba and its leisure industry.

Informed by Roselli of the CIA proposal to take out Fidel Castro, he understood that in providing his services, not only would he be doing the Agency a favor which he could call in when necessary, but he would also be solving a problem that was affecting everyone. Since the revolutionaries had taken power on the island, everything was going backwards and businesses were collapsing; for that reason he decided to accept the contract and designate one of his most outstanding captains for the operation.

Giancana's choice was Richard Cain. He had a background in the police force, as did many members of the "family," through which he had acquired experience and useful contacts for his current work as a private detective, which provided a cover for his activities as a link between CIA agents and the Mafia.

Two telephone calls to Santos Trafficante produced what Giancana needed: a backup in Havana who could help Cain set up and execute the mission. The choice of the thug was ideal: he was a former associate of Trafficante's from his time as director of the casino in the Sans Souci cabaret, Eufemio Fernández.[6]

---

6. Eufemio Fernández: a notorious gangster from the 1940s who was arrested in 1961 when he was coordinator of the Triple A organization.

It was early October 1960 when Richard Cain arrived at Havana airport. From there he went to the Hotel Riviera, and after changing into lighter clothes, phoned Fernández to arrange a meeting in L'Elegant, the hotel's discreet bar.

Tortoiseshell spectacles framed the cold eyes of the US killer while he assessed his new Cuban acquaintance. Both sat down at the bar and ordered rums, one in an expectant pose and the other mentally weighing up his words. Finally, Cain spoke:

"Mr. Trafficante told me that you were a man he could trust, prepared to do anything to serve him. Is that still true?"

"My friend," Fernández replied, "All I can say is that I have only one word and that is pledged to *Señor* Trafficante. Tell me how I can help you."

Considering every word, Cain explained what was required of them. At the end, as if in passing, he assured Fernández that he was a good shot and would have no objection to directly participating in the action.

"These people are crazy," thought the Cuban gangster. "They don't realize how much Havana has changed." He had to find some way of making the American understand so that he wouldn't think he was scared of the mission. Trafficante might still return to Cuba one day, which would give him a chance of recouping his job as front man in the capo's casino.

Choosing his words carefully, Fernández explained why what Cain proposed would not be at all easy. Fidel Castro moved about at high speed and had no fixed habits. Moreover, he had loyal men who could not be bribed. "However," he stated, "I would like to consult with some friends…" Noting the look of displeasure reflected on Cain's face, Fernández went on:

"Don't worry; they are proven people whom Trafficante knows very well. I'll vouch for them."

And after a courteous farewell, he left the hotel with a smile on his thin lips.

The next day they met up again. This time Fernández came with a tall, light-skinned black man with gleaming white teeth, whom he introduced as Herminio Díaz.[7]

"This is Santos's latest bodyguard in Havana."

The three of them made themselves comfortable at the bar of the 21 Club — an elegant establishment opposite the Capri Hotel — and began to talk. The Cubans tried to explain to him that the proposed operation would not be easy. It could take months, given that it involved stalking the victim. But there was another factor that could not be overcome: Castro's personal guard was too tight and well trained.

Cain realized that his collaborators were right. "In any case," he thought, "I could make various sorties around Havana and study the matter more closely."

He thanked his new friends and told them that he would let them know when he left the island, which, naturally, he did not do.

Washington, November 1975, US Senate.
Report of the Church Commission

It was arranged that Roselli would go to Florida and recruit Cubans for the operation. Edwards informed Bissell that contact had been made with the gambling syndicate.

---

7.   Sandalio Herminio Díaz García: a gangster and extortionist since the 1940s who had been arrested on several occasions and served prison terms for various crimes. At the end of the 1950s he was closely linked to Santos Trafficante and through his influence and that of Major Robert Van Horne at the US embassy in Havana, was named chief of police at the Hotel Riviera, owned by the Mafia. In 1962 he left Cuba for the United States, where he was linked to Santos Trafficante and Carlos Prío Socarrás, former president of Cuba. A member of the Commandos L terrorist organization, he took part in various actions against Cuba. He is suspected of having participated in the conspiracy to assassinate President Kennedy. He died on March 26, 1966, attempting to infiltrate Cuban territory via the northern coast of Havana province with other counterrevolutionaries.

During the week of September 24, 1960, the support chief, Maheu and Roselli met in Miami to work out the details of the operation...

After Roselli and Maheu had been in Miami for a short time, and certainly prior to October 18, Roselli introduced Maheu to two individuals on whom Roselli intended to rely: "Sam Gold," who would serve as a "back-up man," or "key" man, and "Joe," whom "Gold" said would serve as a courier to Cuba and make arrangements there...

The support chief testified that he learned the true identities of his associates one morning when Maheu called and asked him to examine the "Parade" supplement to the *Miami Times*. An article on the attorney general's 10-most-wanted criminals list revealed that "Sam Gold" was Momo Salvatore [Sam] Giancana, a Chicago-based gangster, and "Joe" was Santos Trafficante, the Cosa Nostra chieftain in Cuba...

The CIA inspector general's report quoted the support chief stating that "the Agency had first thought in terms of a typical, gangland-style killing in which Castro would be gunned down. Giancana was flatly opposed to the use of firearms. He said that no one could be recruited to do the job, because the chance of survival and escape would be negligible. Giancana stated a preference for a lethal pill."[8]

---

8. Senate Select Committee (Church Commission), *Alleged Assassination Plots Involving Foreign Leaders* (Washington: US Government Printing Office, 1975), 76–77.

4 The Sacred Monsters

Wherever the Agency needed experienced men, William Harvey was to be found in the front line. He was one of the CIA's "sacred cows," belonging to the group of officers trained in the heat of the Cold War. Six foot tall, 200 pounds in weight, fair-skinned and with a habit of making crude gestures that had earned him the reputation of a man of action and few scruples, he enjoyed wandering around the Agency, toying around with the .45-caliber pistol that always accompanied him.

For a number of years he led the task force spying on the Soviets in West Berlin. He was responsible for the construction of the much-publicized tunnel that crossed the border to the eastern part of the city, through which communications from Soviet troops stationed there were intercepted.

Nevertheless, he was unlucky. Soviet counterintelligence had discovered the tunnel project from the outset and initiated a disinformation campaign that confused US spies for quite some time.

Of course, that fact was not widely publicized. Supported by his Langley protector Richard Helms, then second to Bissell, Harvey made out that the Soviets had discovered the tunnel after it had been functional for some time, and that the information acquired in the first few months was authentic. Thus an aura of success surrounded Harvey, granting him inclusion in the highest-level CIA operations.

Nonetheless, Richard Helms had pulled him out of Berlin to

prevent Harvey's constant bragging from revealing the truth about the tunnel and damaging the CIA's prestige, assigning him to a bureaucratic post, albeit an important one: Chief of CIA foreign intelligence, with responsibility for agents and collaborators involved in essential Agency operations all over the world.

Harvey was working in that role when, one January afternoon in 1961, he received an invitation to meet with deputy director Richard Bissell.

"I've sent for you because we have an urgent and delicate mission for you. Given certain failures and disagreeable experiences, we have decided to organize a secret operation within our organization to create the capacity to overthrow and eliminate political leaders hostile to the United States in any part of the world. As you will understand, this is a very delicate matter, above all because our country cannot be seen to be openly committed to this program. Moreover, the incoming Kennedy administration doesn't know anything about it, and we think that the less they know the better. Your job is to select the appropriate people, train them, and when the need arises, we will give you the relevant orders."

Harvey swallowed. He was no novice and he knew that this kind of thing went on, but he never imagined that it would be elevated to the point that it was structured. Regardless, he was not a man to wilt in the face of difficult tasks, and thus he agreed, asking about the modus operandi and the objectives to be prioritized.

Bissell explained: "We want to give you a cover for the operation, so we'll appoint you chief of Division D, in charge of deciphering the codes utilized by our allies. Under that cover, you will organize the ZR/Rifle program. Your job is to find people with the capacity for this kind of work from among our agents, and to contact the lab chief and also Colonel Edwards, who is working along similar lines. Our priorities are Fidel Castro and Rafael Trujillo. As you know, Trujillo was our ally, but he is becoming a nuisance. Castro is a dangerous communist. A plot against Castro is already underway and you need to check it out and give it the OK. We need to eliminate him before the exile brigade training in Guatemala lands in Cuba. That is our chief priority."

Harvey experienced a feeling of satisfaction. Once again he was in the field of action and with a project in his hands worthy of a significant rise through the ranks. With a "Thank you very much, sir" and a smile on his lips, he took his leave of Bissell and rapidly immersed himself in Agency files, searching for his criminal candidates.

Washington, November 1975, US Senate.
Report of the Church Commission

Sometime in early 1961, Bissell instructed Harvey — who was then chief of a CIA foreign intelligence staff, to establish an "executive action capability," which would include research into a capability to assassinate foreign leaders...

"Executive Action" was a CIA euphemism, defined as a project for research into developing means for overthrowing foreign political leaders, including a "capability to perform assassinations." Bissell indicated that Executive Action covered a "wide spectrum of actions" to "eliminate the effectiveness" of foreign leaders, with assassination as the "most extreme" action in the spectrum.

The inspector general's report described Executive Action as a "general standby capability" to carry out assassination when required. The project was given the codename ZR/Rifle by the CIA.

William Harvey testified that he was "almost certain" that on January 25 and 26, 1961, he met with two CIA officials: Joseph Scheider, who by then had become chief of the Technical Services Division, and a CIA recruiting officer, to discuss the feasibility of creating a capability within the Agency for "Executive Action." After reviewing his notes of those meetings, Harvey testified that the meetings occurred after his initial discussion of Executive

Action with Bissell, which, he said, might have transpired in "early January"...

Harvey testified that the Executive Action capability was intended to include assassination. His cryptic handwritten notes of the January 25/26 meetings, preserved at the CIA, contain phrases which suggest a discussion of assassination: "last resort beyond last resort and a confession of weakness," "the magic button," and "never mention word assassination." Harvey confirmed this interpretation...

Bissell ultimately testified that the development of an Executive Action capability was "undoubtedly," or "very much more likely" initiated within the Agency. He had acknowledged on his first day of testimony that this would not have been unusual: "It was the normal practice in the Agency and an important part of its mission to create various kinds of capability long before there was any reason to be certain whether those would be used or where or how or for what purpose. The whole ongoing job of... a secret intelligence service of recruiting agents is of that character... So it would not be particularly surprising to me if the decision to create... this capability had been taken without an outside request."

Washington, January 1961. CIA Headquarters

Harvey picked up the intercom linking the Agency's principal chiefs and dialed Colonel Edwards's number. After greeting each other briefly they agreed on a meeting for the next day in a well-known but discreet Washington restaurant.

At the appointed hour, Harvey and Edwards installed themselves at a secluded table, and while savoring spaghetti a la Milanese accompanied by an excellent rosé wine, discussed pending issues. The colonel explained that the failure of attempts to eliminate Fidel Castro up to then was the result of poor professional planning on the part of the executors.

"It is essential to liquidate Castro before the invasion takes place," Edwards insisted. "We have various plans underway. The first consists of infiltrating a team of Cuban agents trained in Panama who, in collaboration with the internal resistance, will gun Fidel down outside his secretary Celia Sánchez's house, which he frequents regularly. The second, consisting of two alternatives, is to give poison capsules filled with botulin, an invention of our laboratories, to two groups associated with Santos Trafficante operating on the island. We plan to execute the third option through a young agent who is one of the leaders of the Cuban underground movement and should be infiltrating Cuba in the next few weeks to lead the internal front. This option consists of blowing up the meeting room of a minister who Castro regularly visits. What's your opinion?" he asked.

"It's foolproof," Harvey replied. "Thanks for the information, and if there's no problem I'll meet with O'Connell and Scheider to go over some of the details."

The Covert Agent

Félix Rodríguez Mendigutía was a CIA man. He came from a wealthy family in the Sancti Spíritus region of central Cuba. Like many of his friends, after the triumph of the revolution he escaped to the United States and there immediately placed himself at the command of anyone who talked of attacking Fidel Castro. Thus he came to the CIA. In January 1961 he was in an Agency safe house in Miami. Some months previously he had been recruited by the special missions groups organized in Panama to develop subversive action within Cuba in order to pave the way militarily and psychologically for the brigade of mercenaries which was to invade the island via the Bay of Pigs.

He had proposed Fidel Castro's elimination to his chiefs as the most expeditious means of defeating the Cuban government. His plan had the backing of an underground group on the island, which would give them the necessary support. He thought about the plan a lot before disclosing it, but everything seemed relatively easy to him. It was true that he didn't have up-to-date information on the internal political situation, but he knew the locations selected to commit the crime, and his training was excellent.

Years later, Mendigutía would go on to participate in the murder of Che Guevara in Bolivia, the US adventure in Vietnam, and finally, the war against the Sandinistas in Nicaragua.

Miami, January 1961.
Testimony of Félix Rodríguez Mendigutía[1]

One day I was talking to a friend of mine who had served in Díaz Lanz's group. We talked about our infiltration teams' chances of success and I put it to him that assassinating Castro could save many lives. He agreed with me and I drew up a plan for the interim camp commandant, an American we knew as Larry, to whom we had offered our services.

Afterwards, Larry told me that my idea had been accepted by the people in charge of the matter. In early January we flew to Miami, where a third Cuban, who would be our radio operator, was assigned to us. He gave me a special weapon, a long-range automatic rifle with a telescopic sight. For its part, the resistance had acquired a location in Havana facing a place that Castro visited frequently in that period, and they were setting up the assassination attempt.

The Americans transferred the complete infiltration unit to a location in Homestead while we waited for our boat. You could see an old motel and a field of tomatoes. The place was organized for us to practice with rubber dinghies that we were to use as trans-

---

1.   Taken from Félix Rodríguez's autobiography *Shadow Warrior*. (Editor's note: translated from Spanish.)

portation from our boat to the shore. From our "headquarters" we went by car to the cays where we flicked the headlights at a prearranged spot and a small boat came to the shore to pick us up, taking us out to the yacht we would use to reach Cuba.

We tried to infiltrate into Cuba three times with that damned rifle and we failed three times. The yacht we used had the power of a cruiser and was around 40 feet in length, with air conditioning, luxurious fittings and wonderful cabins. The captain was American, but the entire crew were Ukrainian. They didn't speak Spanish — at least with us — and regarded the sons-of-bitches carrying Soviet automatic weapons with distrust.

Our problem was that we never worked out a way to reach the shore. We were supposed to land close to Varadero beach, a place that I knew really well from my childhood. From there we would make contact with the anti-Castro resistance and then head for Havana. We would be supplied with a safe house from which we would leave for the location where we were to gun down Fidel, and we would try to escape in any way possible.

We were all ready for our third trip to Cuba. The American captain cancelled the mission. He reasons he gave were a hydraulic failure in one of the yacht's engines. When we returned to Florida, they collected the rifle and munitions and told us that they had changed their minds about the operation…

Lethal Aspirins
Miami, January–March 1961

Santos Trafficante was 41 when he arrived in Cuba on December 26, 1955. He was "a prosperous US businessman interested in developing tourism" who had been in Havana on a number of occasions and had decided to install himself there permanently. He promptly opened the Sans Souci casino; a few months later he bought shares in the Comodoro and Deauville hotels and extended his activities to other commercial spheres, particularly trade in contraband items from the United States.

A Cuban police report of that same year noted:

> Having expanded the investigation you ordered with the purpose of identifying "the high-level government official," it has been discovered that it is *Señor* Amleto Barletta, the owner of the hotel where the objective Santos Trafficante is staying… He is currently representative of one of the parties supporting the government. In relation to the paragraph: "with the gaming business in Havana," in my assessment, it lacks specific importance, bearing in mind that the informants used a generic term, which is used to refer to those who live off and exploit gambling in any country, using the word business because — licit or illicit — it is without doubt a business, just like the word traffic is used meaning trade… Attached is a press cutting from the March 26 edition of the *Miami Herald*, which reveals that the objective and his brother Henry violated the gambling laws, were detained and charged on those grounds, and also have a record of being imprisoned for the crime of bribery and for infringing the Lottery Law, having been given five years on each count…

Slowly but surely, Trafficante became the owner of, or principal shareholder in, Havana's most important casinos. According to the ruling to request his expulsion from the country, drawn up by the director of public order in the Cuban government:

> Trafficante was arrested in November 16, 1953, in Tampa, Florida; on May 29, 1954, also in Tampa… on June 15, 1956… by the Cuban police. He made more than 30 telephone calls to racketeers in the United States during the final months of 1957, as reported by Lieutenant Pena of the Cuban police. The accused attended a grand Mafia council at the house of Joseph Barbara in Apalachin, New York, in November 1957, in which gambling and other illicit operations in Havana were considered an important agenda item, and geographical divisions were designated to each gambler. The territory of the Republic of Cuba was included in the eastern zone of the United States…

Trafficante was detained on those grounds by the Cuban police on June 11, 1959, and interned in a camp for undesirable foreigners until August 18 of that year, when he had to be released given the absence of any extradition claim on the part of the US authorities.

A DIER report dated November 11, 1959, lists the main members of Trafficante's band as Eufemio Fernández Ortega, Néstor Barbolla, John T. Rivera, Sam Mondell, Joseph Bedami, Ciro Beluccia, Joe Cacciatore, John Martino and Mike McLaney.

In January 1960, Trafficante was arrested again by Cuban authorities in the Hotel Riviera along with his bodyguard Herminio Díaz García on account of their criminal and counterrevolutionary activities, and was finally expelled from the country.

Once back in Miami, profoundly resentful of the revolutionary process, he called together various Cuban émigrés he knew from his commercial dealings on the island, including Manuel Antonio (Tony) de Varona, a veteran politico and former collaborator in major illegal operations.

Varona headed Rescate, one of the largest underground groups acting against the Cuban government, composed mainly of characters from his political party at the end of the 1940s.

The strategy elaborated by Trafficante was clear. He was backing one of the most important exile groups, sponsored by the CIA and the State Department. Its members would be part of the new Cuban government once Castro was defeated, and all their goods and privileges would be restored to them, which would considerably increase Trafficante's influence.

Towards the end of that year the news he received of the US government's decision to overthrow Castro proved him correct in his decision. He had made a sound medium-term investment.

As soon as Roselli was contracted by the CIA to assassinate Fidel Castro, Trafficante knew about it. It was he who facilitated the contact with his friend Eufemio Fernández in Havana when Richard Cain traveled to that city to fine-tune the details of the crime. However, Trafficante kept his distance. He wanted government officials to come to him, asking for "favors." Finally, Roselli called him, informing him that "somebody" from the CIA wanted to meet with him, to which he agreed with pleasure. The opportunity to offer a noteworthy service to the US national security interests had arrived.

Trafficante had various additional options for the contract. One of them was an old friend of his, Juan Orta Córdova, an individual linked to the organized gambling syndicate who at that time was acting as office chief for the Cuban prime minister. Orta owed him a lot of favors and couldn't refuse a request from him. The other alternative was Tony Varona's group in Havana. He would dispatch the poison capsules to both of them, so that one of them could take out Castro.

"It can't go wrong," the gangster thought. Orta could mix the poison in one of the many coffees that Fidel Castro consumed in his office, and if that didn't bring about the desired result, Tony's people could use one of their men who worked in the Pekín Chinese restaurant, patronized on a regular basis by the Cuban leader.

Washington, November 1975, US Senate. Report of the Church Commission

Edwards rejected the first batch of pills prepared by TSD because they would not dissolve in water. A second batch, containing botulin toxin, "did the job expected of them" when tested on monkeys. The support chief received the pills from TSD, probably in February 1961, with assurances that they were lethal, and then gave them to Roselli.

The record clearly establishes that the pills were given to a Cuban for delivery to the island some time prior to the Bay of Pigs invasion in mid-April 1961...

The inspector general's report states that in late February or March 1961, Roselli reported to the support chief that the pills had been delivered to an official close to Castro who may have received kickbacks from gambling interests. The report states that the official returned the pills after a few weeks, perhaps because he had lost his position in the Cuban government, and thus access to Castro, before he received the pills...

Roselli told the support chief that Trafficante believed a certain leading figure in the Cuban exile movement might be able to accomplish the assassination. The inspector general's report suggests that this Cuban may have been receiving funds from Trafficante and other racketeers interested in securing "gambling, prostitution and dope monopolies" in Cuba after the overthrow of Castro...

The Cuban claimed to have contact inside a restaurant frequented by Castro. As a prerequisite to the deal, he demanded cash and $1,000 worth of communications equipment. The support chief recalled that Colonel J.C King, head of the Western Hemisphere Division, gave him $50,000 in Bissell's office to pay the Cuban if he successfully assassinated Castro...

The money and pills were delivered at a meeting between Maheu, Roselli, Trafficante and the Cuban at the Fontainebleau Hotel in Miami. As Roselli recalled, Maheu "opened his briefcase and dumped a whole lot of money on his lap... and also came up with the capsules and he explained how they were going to be used. As far as I remember, they couldn't be used in boiling soups and things like that, but they could be used in water or otherwise, but they couldn't last forever... It had to be done as quickly as possible.

The attempt met with failure. According to the inspector general's report, Edwards believed the scheme failed because Castro stopped visiting the restaurant where the "asset" was employed. Maheu suggested another reason. He recalled being informed that after the pills had been delivered to Cuba, "the go signal still had to be received before in fact they were administered..."

What really happened was that Orta took fright at measures being adopted against people conspiring in one way or another against the revolution, and sought asylum in the Venezuelan embassy. And when the Pekín restaurant employee realized the enormous risk he was running if something should go wrong, he took refuge in another embassy to wait for the mercenary invasion that everyone knew was on the point of landing in Cuba.

Operation Generosa
Miami, February 1961. JM/WAVE Base

Miami was a hotbed of Cuban exiles. They all knew of the brigade that was receiving military training in Guatemala and the special missions groups training in Panama whose objective was to spearhead the internal counterrevolution when the mercenaries invaded the island. Of course, what they were trying to do wasn't at all easy: to organize an army while developing leaders for an internal resistance movement that, like the exiles outside Cuba, was profoundly divided by competing ambitions. In their political training, all of them were demanding a specific quota of power when the revolutionaries were expelled from Cuba.

Well aware of these problems, the CIA had designated one of its most outstanding negotiators to unite these groups into one sole internal front. This was Howard Hunt, who rose to fame some years later as one of the Watergate "plumbers."

Nevertheless, Hunt had a clear preference for one particular group, the MRR, having reached certain agreements with Manuel Artime, its leader, on some of the latter's personal interests after the defeat of the revolution.

The Cuban Revolutionary Council (CRC) was invented to group together the exile movement. Dr. José Miró Cardona, a former dean at the University of Havana, who was prime minister in the initial revolutionary government, was selected to head it. The other appointees were Manuel Artime, as the Assault Brigade 2506 political delegate; Tony Varona; Manuel Ray; and other leaders from the Cuban community in Miami. But the most delicate issue was the question of who should be in charge of directing the underground groups?

Various meetings were needed to reach agreement among the exile leaders. They all proposed their own delegates, because they realized that it would be those in Cuba who would take the posts in the provisional government they envisaged.

Finally, they came to an agreement. Rafael Díaz Hanscom, an engineer allied to Varona's group who had left the island illegally, would be general coordinator; Humberto Sorí Marín, an ex-commander of the Rebel Army who had also been minister of agriculture in the first revolutionary cabinet, would be military chief; and Rogelio González Corzo, Artime's delegate within Cuba, would act as the link with the CIA and thus be in charge of supplies.

The decision in favor of Díaz Hanscom was not accidental. He had recently arrived from Cuba, where he worked in the National Savings and Housing Institute, bearing a plot to assassinate the leader of the revolution in the days leading up to the planned invasion.

Havana, November 1994.
Testimony of Mario Morales Mesa

Around the time of Girón [the Bay of Pigs], I was designated to organize a counterintelligence unit in charge of investigating plots and conspiracies to assassinate revolutionary leaders, particularly Fidel, who was the focus of all the hatred of the counterrevolution and the CIA.

We had received various reports on planned assassination attempts on Fidel in the run-up to the Bay of Pigs attack. These were clearly intended to decapitate the revolution — which those responsible believed would make the invaders' task easier.

At that time we had coordinated with Federico Mora, the captain of G-2 who, on Fidel's instructions, was handling the case of Humberto Sorí Marín, who had fled to the United States in early 1961 after being involved with the US embassy in Havana in various conspiracies.

Mora had infiltrated an agent into the group: Alcibiades Bermúdez, also a captain in the Rebel Army, who had been instructed by Sorí to create an uprising in the Pinar del Río mountains and to prepare the ground for a landing of men in support of the Bay of Pigs invasion.

In that way we knew about the landing of Sorí, Díaz Hanscom and a group of CIA agents on March 13, 1961, who entered the country at a point on the border of Havana and Matanzas provinces.

In their initial conversation, Sorí informed Alcibiades of their plans, including the unification and arming of all the counter-revolutionary groups, the unleashing of an internal war in support of the invaders, and the assassination of the *comandante-en-jefe* [Fidel]. The codename the Americans used for the assassination plot was Operation Generosa.

Informed of the plans and their imminent execution, Captain Mora passed on the details to our chief, *Comandante* Ramiro Valdés, who authorized an operation against the infiltrators after the necessary consultations.

Through our intensive investigation we discovered that the internal front unification meeting was scheduled for March 18 in a house in Reparto Flores, Marianao. Headquarters designated *compañero* José Luis Domínguez head of the operation and at 1800 on the day indicated, our *compañeros* surrounded the house and raided it before the counterrevolutionaries had time to react. There we seized a large number of weapons, plans and sketches, and, most important of all, details of a plan to assassinate Fidel on March 26 during a meeting scheduled to take place in the Housing Institute to discuss a construction project to house poor families. That particular project involved Rafael Díaz Hanscom, who had absented himself for a few days in order to travel clandestinely to Miami, and he was one of the people invited to the meeting. The plan consisted of placing an explosive device in the meeting room to be detonated by remote control.

That day dealt the first blow to the invasion plans, given that the counterrevolutionary general staff and various CIA agents specifically trained to sabotage the country's industries were captured. But, above all, one of the most dangerous conspiracies to assassinate *Comandante* Fidel Castro prior to the attack at the Bay of Pigs was dismantled.

Havana, March 28, 1961. DIER Headquarters

In accordance with instructions received, the house at 110 106th Street, Reparto Flores, Marianao, was searched and its occupants arrested. They were:

- Rafael Díaz Hanscom, in charge of the internal front, who, according to documents seized, was to assassinate Dr. Fidel Castro, prime minister of the revolutionary government, at the Savings and Housing Institute.

- Rogelio González Corzo, with false documents from the CIA in the name of Harold Boves Castillo. González was the MRR representative, a CIA agent and the coordinator of a plan to create a provocation at the US Guantánamo naval base to coincide with the invasion of our country currently being prepared by the United States.

- Humberto Sorí Marín, a former commander of the Rebel Army, a traitor to the revolution, involved in conspiratorial efforts with individuals from the US embassy in Havana dating back to the previous year, and associated with notorious counter-revolutionaries Manuel Artime and Huber Matos. In early 1961 he fled the country for Florida. There he received instructions from the CIA to join an internal front on the island, intended to unite all the counterrevolutionary groups, which would act as a fifth column as soon as the Yankees attacked us. One of his basic tasks was to try to recruit as many officers as possible from our armed forces for this purpose.

- Manuel Lorenzo Puig Miyar, CIA agent.

- Nemesio Rodríguez Navarrete, CIA agent, former leader of the MDM [Martí Democratic Movement], who traveled to Miami in January 1961 to receive instructions.

- Gaspar Domingo Trueba Varona, CIA agent, responsible for training military chiefs of the counterrevolutionary movements affiliated to the new united internal front.

- Eufemio Fernández Ortega, ex-collaborator of mafioso Santos Trafficante when he managed Trafficante's gambling room in the Sans Souci casino in Havana. Chief of the Triple A counter-revolutionary group and one of the leaders convened for the internal unity drive. A large quantity of arms and military equipment were found in his residence.

Also detained were counterrevolutionaries Dionisio Acosta Hernández, Pedro Céspedes Compay, Felipe Dopaso Abreu, Orestes Frías Roque, Eduardo Lemus Pérez, Narciso Peralta Soto, Gabriel Riaño Zequeira, Yolanda Álvarez Balzaga and Berta Echegaray Garriga.

In various searches undertaken and in the Reparto Flores house itself the following weapons were seized: 11 Colt .45 pistols, six M1 rifles, eight M3 submachine guns, six boxes of ammunition containing more than 5,000 bullets for different weapons, 11 cans of security flares, 16 rolls of time fuses, 13 rolls of detonator fuses, 15 boxes of M2 fuses, 12 boxes containing 120 incendiaries, a box of 21 fragmentation grenades, 24 packets of nitro-starch (11 in jute sacks and 13 in backpacks). Additionally, one radio and a transmission plant, maps, minutes, orders, six manuscript pages of plans to be executed and a document signed by a group of counterrevolutionary organizations constituting a so-called United Revolutionary Front...

5 Alternatives to the Crisis

The heat in Colonel King's office was intolerable. The air conditioning had broken down and the rigid security measures in place for Agency establishments meant that the windows couldn't be opened. They were afraid that the Russians, communists or any other of the enemies of Western "democracy" to which they had devoted their efforts would overhear the secret conversations and assassination and terrorist conspiracies planned there.

King mopped beads of sweat from his forehead from time to time and fanned himself with a file in an attempt to alleviate the heat. He had before him fresh information from agents who had radioed messages from Cuba on the situation after Castro's victory over the brigade of Cuban exiles at the Bay of Pigs.

Everything had ended in failure. To a certain extent it wasn't his responsibility, as Bissell — the great strategist — had designated Jack Esterline to head the operation. However, he had advised on various occasions that things were not as simple as his superiors thought, and that Cuba was no Guatemala. The Assault Brigade 2506 had been defeated in less than 72 hours by the Cuban forces; the internal front that had cost so much to construct was in pieces, many of the best agents had been captured, and Castro had rubbed the nose of the US government in its own defeat.

King believed that Kennedy bore a lot of responsibility for what had happened. The president did not want to commit the US armed forces when the brigade called for help from the Cuban beaches. The president was weak, pusillanimous and too receptive to the ideas of liberal advisors who talked to him of democratic change in Latin America. The Russians were taking advantage of the occasion to gain ground. With the Bay of Pigs defeat they had consolidated a beachhead in the Americas.

After the debacle, Kennedy formed a government commission headed by General Maxwell Taylor[1] to investigate the causes of the defeat. It had been leaked that the commission had orders to find "guilty parties," and blame was sure to fall on the CIA, as everyone was aware of Kennedy's animosity towards the Agency.

With those thoughts in mind, he sent for various officers waiting outside his office. They included David Phillips, James Noel, Frank Bender, and Karl Hetsh.

The objective of the meeting was to seek alternatives to the crisis that would be unleashed as a result of the Taylor Commission, which they anticipated would hold them responsible for the defeat. If possible, they might also be able to take revenge for the blow by making Castro pay for his audacity.

"We have to act rapidly," King stated, looking in Bender's direction and inviting him to report back.

"We have an important network in Cuba that has not been discovered by G-2," Bender said. "This is the AM/BLOOD group, composed of trustworthy agents including Tito, Ernesto, Brand, Javier and 2637. In addition, there are various underground groups that weren't damaged by Cuban security operations, and within them, decisive men of absolute confidence. I think we have an opportunity to do something. Remember, they were involved in Operation Patty at the Guantánamo naval base. Unfortunately

---

1.   Maxwell Taylor: general of the US armed forces, who would later become chief of staff and finally ambassador to Vietnam. A military theorist, he designed the scheme of low- and medium-intensity warfare used to combat national and revolutionary movements.

Rogelio González was arrested, but it would seem that nobody squealed, as our people have not been picked up by G-2.

"We shouldn't lose our heads," King said. "We still have some cards to play, we just need a good plan; but this time we'll do it alone. Nobody will hear about it in Washington, and when it takes place, they will have no option but to follow our directions.

"I agree," interjected Phillips, "but I think that we should de-centralize operations, separate them out. We shouldn't put all our forces into just one undertaking. In the case of G-2 discovering one group, the others will still be viable. I remind you, Colonel, that we have the Grau Alsina[2] Rescate group and other individuals from Tony Varona's FRD [Revolutionary Democratic Front], all of them men of action who also have the weapons we infiltrated prior to the Bay of Pigs."

"Yes, that's an interesting idea, but how are we going to get in contact with them? I don't think they have their own means of communication and if they did, they would surely have lost them in the communist raids," King replied.

"We have the person for that," Phillips explained. "Rodolfo León Curbelo, the courier Tony Varona utilized to send the poison capsules to Cuba in March. He has good contacts with Caldevilla, an attaché at the Spanish embassy in Havana who works for us, and we can send instructions through him. They don't have the men for mass operations, but they would be excellent for an attempt on Castro."

At that point the telephone on the polished meeting table rang. King picked up the receiver, and after a brief conversation, hung up and explained to those present:

"Hunt reports that agent Tito has just arrived in Miami. He says he has talked with him for a number of hours, and that he's very depressed about the Bay of Pigs fiasco. He has expressed a desire

---

2.   María Leopoldina Grau Alsina and her brother Ramón were niece and nephew of former president Ramón Grau.

to come to Washington to talk with Agency chiefs to update them and find out what future awaits him in Cuba."

"That could be very good or very bad," Hetsh cut in. "If he comes here we can't keep him from the Taylor Commission and he could say things that would prejudice us."

"He's a man we can trust," Phillips put in, "and I think that it would be good for him to come and see for himself what the administration is devoting its efforts to while we are sacrificing our best men in his country..." After confirming the impact he had made on those present with his words, he extracted a bunch of papers from his file and explained: "I have here various messages from agent Luis reporting from Santiago de Cuba on the present situation among the counterrevolutionaries on the island:

"The failure of the Bay of Pigs invasion has caused confusion and desperation, but now they are beginning to react again. The lack of direction and action is impeding the activities of the civil resistance. Although he is a highly regarded man, Miró Cardona's council will not give people any inspiration whatsoever. In reality, they [the council members] do not identify with the people, they are figureheads rather than leaders. That is the reason for the lack of an open opposition..."

"We have to reflect before adopting a line of action," Bender stated. "However, I think we should act rapidly, or that son-of-a-bitch Kennedy is going to have us all by the balls."

King remained silent, meditating on what had been said. He realized that something had to be done and as soon as possible. He walked up and down the room, while the others observed him with growing interest. They knew him and understood that something was buzzing in his mind. Suddenly he stopped, sat down again at the table and with a gleam in his eye, proclaimed:

"Sirs, we have to stake our all, it's time to launch our men into the final combat. We have lost a battle but not the war. The only correct solution is to eliminate Castro and his closest supporters. That would plunge the communists into tremendous confusion and would be the ideal moment for an armed uprising by the groups we still have on the island. The president would have no option but to send in the marines to help the Cubans, because if he didn't, he would lose all authority. Bring Tito to Washington and initiate contact once more with the most capable agents operating in Cuba in order to send them the necessary instructions. Everything is not lost yet. I think that we can kill two birds with one stone..."

Operation Patty
Havana, May 1961. DSE[3] Headquarters

Alfredo Izaguirre de la Riva, alias Tito, a journalist and descendent of one of the richest families on the island, the Izaguirre-Hornedos, was recruited in 1959 by the CIA station in Havana, and lent it immeasurable services from that date.

With his collaboration various microphones were placed in the penthouse of the Rosita de Hornedo Hotel, in readiness for the Soviet embassy installing its offices there.

On two occasions — September 1960 and February 1961 — Izaguirre de la Riva went to the United States for espionage training, and he was instructed to organize a network on the island to supply weapons and explosives to counterrevolutionary groups for a subversive operation envisaged as a backup to the Bay of Pigs invasion. The intention was to create internal chaos by disrupting communications, eliminating revolutionary cadres, damaging electricity and water supply systems, and eventually provoking such levels of instability that the invaders would be received as saviors.

In March 1961, the CIA dropped a significant arsenal from a

---

3.   DSE: State Security Department, the name adopted by DIER after the establishment of the Ministry of the Interior in June 1961.

plane onto one of his farms in the vicinity of San José de las Lajas, Havana province. The materials included a bazooka with shells, 14 Garand rifles, five Thompson submachine guns, two .30-caliber machine guns, four Bar rifles and a large volume of munitions and explosives.

In that same month agent Jorge García Rubio, alias Tony, was sent to him as a radio operator to maintain communications. García also facilitated contact with other chiefs of agent networks undertaking labors similar to his own, including Emilio Adolfo Rivero Caro (Brand), José Pujals Mederos (Ernesto), Luis Torroella y Martín-Rivero (Luis), Javier Souto Álvarez (Javier), and Juan Manuel Guillot Castellanos (codename 2637).

The mission consisted of supporting the counterrevolutionary leadership that, headed by Rafael Díaz Hanscom and Humberto Sorí Marín, had infiltrated the country in the first half of March to direct the underground organizations in support of the planned invasion. But then came the Bay of Pigs debacle and they were left on their own with no contact with the internal front. Their US contacts went silent and the agents who escaped detention agreed that Tito should go to Miami to clarify the situation and the prospects for fighting. Alfredo Izaguirre de la Riva (Tito) reached Miami one sunny morning in the second half of May 1961.

After talking with various CIA officers, he asked for a meeting with the Washington chiefs and subsequently met with General Taylor, one of the administration hawks in charge of the Cuban case. It was not difficult for them to reach agreement. In a matter of days they had drawn up a new plan, this time bearing in mind the information contributed by those people who were at risk on the island, and when everything was in place, Izaguirre returned to Cuba.

As soon as he had ensured that nobody was suspicious of his brief absence, he initiated an intensive series of meetings with the main counterrevolutionary chiefs. He had to get their agreement in order to then communicate it to the United States, and if everything was approved, give each of them their new mission. The idea was to eliminate Fidel and Raúl Castro, taking advantage of their presence at events in Havana and Santiago de Cuba to commemorate the anniversary of July 26. At the same time, a unit of their men, with arms donated by the CIA, would attack the US military installation at Guantánamo with mortars and light cannon fire to provoke the troops stationed there. Believing they were under attack, these US troops would return fire and ask their government for support, giving it the option to intervene militarily in Cuba.

Everything was perfectly planned. Everything, except that they hadn't counted on the G-2 agents in Santiago and Havana who were informed of their plans.

On July 22, four days before the date scheduled by the conspirators, the Cuban security operation began. They were all captured, their weapons seized, and the plans uncovered down to the smallest detail.

The world would learn of the extent of the conspiracy in August 1961, at the conference of the OAS in Punta del Este, Uruguay, where *Comandante* Che Guevara exposed it in full.

Havana, July 1961.
Testimony of Alfredo Izaguirre de la Riva[4]

After the defeat at the Bay of Pigs, with the consequent demoralization and detention of contacts and counterrevolutionary leaders, you can understand the disorganization of the group involved... We received no word from the United States for two weeks. Finally they instructed us to go ahead and reorganize the groups, with no further explanation. This was for Ernesto and myself as we knew nothing at all about Brand. After various meetings between Ernesto

---

4.   This testimony is part of Izaguirre's account to his captors after he was detained for his terrorist activities.

and César (Octavio Barroso Gómez, another CIA agent), to whom Ernesto had introduced me as operative chief of the United Front along with Hipólito (Carlos Bandín, MRR coordinator), he brought me to Juanito from Liberation, who in turn introduced me to Justo, head of Liberation and the civil coordinator of the United Front. The Democratic Insurrectional Movement (MID) headed by Víctor (Raúl Alfonso García) came up with the idea that somebody had to go to the United States to find out why the Bay of Pigs operation had failed...

When I got to Miami, I met with CIA officer Bill Williams [Howard Hunt], who explained the plans they had drawn up awaiting Washington's final approval. In general terms the plans were to reorganize the navy and refit all the groups' vessels with artillery; to utilize the vessels to lay mines in Cuba's most important bays in order to blow up supply vessels; to organize attacks on Cuban objectives near the coast to raise counterrevolutionary morale; to obtain maritime and aerial control of the island through a rapid mobilization to take Cayo Coco (north of Camagüey province), which was out of range of the Cuban battery, to fill it with artillery to repel attacks, and to install a powerful transmission plant so as to install a provisional government and wear down the existing one; to continue supplying arms to the underground groups to provoke general destabilization in the country; and to eliminate Fidel Castro.

Hunt added that they had weapons to arm 50,000 men for this undertaking.

A few days later I left for Washington to meet with the CIA bosses, as per usual staying at the Mayflower Hotel in the city, and made contact with Karl Hetsh, aide to General Jim Bowdin, whom — as I was informed — was the Agency's politico in the Cuban case.

The next day, Hetsh took me to the Raleigh Hotel, where an apartment was reserved for me. Shortly afterwards, Bowdin appeared and explained that everything was on hold for the time being. When

I asked why the Bay of Pigs operation failed, he stated that, as he saw it, everything was well planned from the military point of view and that the failure was due to an executive error (on the part of President Kennedy). He explained that the Cuban government had halted the invasion with six or seven aircraft that could have been destroyed in a second bombardment, and thus had been able to hold the beachhead that the brigade had taken at Girón long enough for what subsequently occurred.

We had a lengthy discussion on the situation in Cuba. Bowdin explained the need to unite all the underground groups in one sole front in order to coordinate future operations.

We reviewed our contacts in the country: the MDC in Santiago de Cuba, directed from the Guantánamo naval base by El Zorro (José Amparo Rosabal), closely linked to Nino Díaz; the MID in Camagüey, headed by Víctor; Javier's group in Las Villas; and Ernesto, Brand and myself in Havana.

What he proposed was to create a "resistance unit" of all these groups and others that could be included to trigger a plan that would deal the final blow to the revolution.

That plan consisted of organizing a provocation at the US Guantánamo base with the Santiago de Cuba people through an attack on the installation by counterrevolutionaries disguised as Cuban troops; preparing an uprising of underground groups in all the provinces where we had contingents, for which they would send weapons and the necessary military hardware; and assassinating Fidel and Raúl.

I felt there were no great difficulties with the first two points. They would take care of informing the MDC people in Oriente (province) and I would send instructions to the Camagüey and Las Villas groups. Good communications already existed and various points on the coast had been selected to land the materials. Osvaldo Ramírez and Benito Campos, chiefs of the insurgency groups in Las Villas province, had been contacted and unity in terms of action was agreed.

However, the planned assassinations would be very difficult because Fidel and Raúl were not easy to pin down in a convenient place.

The MRR had an old plan to assassinate Fidel in Revolution Plaza and eliminate Raúl in his home on 26th Street in Vedado, shooting from the Chinese cemetery opposite.

I informed Bowdin of those plans and he asked me to study them and confirm things later by radio.

The next day I met with General Maxwell Taylor in his Pentagon office. There I explained the situation in Cuba after the Bay of Pigs and our ideas for moving forward. By then I had absorbed Bowdin's plan and put it forward as an idea of the "internal front."

One of the people at the meeting told me that we should forget it, that "the marines were going to make a surprise intervention in Cuba" to sort out the Cuban problem. "That depends on your people creating a situation allowing direct aid."

A few hours later I met up again with Bowdin and Hetsh in the hotel. They were very satisfied and brought congratulations from the CIA executive. The ideas discussed had been approved and would be initiated as soon as I returned to Cuba. The operation was codenamed Patty…

Santiago de Cuba, June 25, 1961.
DSE Provincial Headquarters

One of the counterrevolutionary leaders, José Amparo Rosabal, alias El Zorro, was concealed in the Guantánamo naval base coordinating the plans. He was head of the Ministry of Transportation in the early days of the revolution and an old collaborator of Carlos Prío and Tony Varona, in contact with the CIA through Nino Díaz, who got him into the intelligence service at the base. The plan consisted of placing armaments close to the perimeter of the base on the morning of July 17. Antonio Marra Acosta and Emilio Quintana González were in charge of picking them up from a US sergeant named Smith. When arrested, the counterrevolutionaries were found with the following armaments: two 57-millimeter cannons, four bazookas, 23 Garand rifles and several hand grenades.

Subsequent operations turned up other weapons from the US base including 35 Springfield rifles, a 60-millimeter mortar, a .30-caliber submachine gun, 12 M3 submachine guns, munitions, grenades and explosives.

Santa Clara, August 19, 1961.
DSE Provincial Headquarters

Investigations uncovered an operation being executed by agents José Ángel González Castro, Segundo Borges Ranzola, Miguel Pentón Alfonso and Javier Souto Álvarez.

These agents' plans involved uniting the different counter-revolutionary groups; illegally introducing paper money from the United States in order to bankrupt the country's economy; systematic sabotage attacks on production such as the poisoning of cattle; and acts of sabotage in the industrial sector, particularly on the Antonio Guiteras electricity substation.

In addition, military plans were aimed at organizing commando groups in the main cities and aiding insurgent groups, mainly those of Osvaldo Ramírez in the Escambray and Benito Campos in Corralillo. This was confirmed by the interception of coded radio message 124 requesting an arms shipment to Dutton Cay, north of Isabela de Sagua, consisting of 192 M1 carbines, 12 .30-caliber submachine guns, 24 pistols, 500 pounds of explosives, 200 pounds of incendiary material, three bazookas, three recoilless cannons and large quantities of ammunition. This shipment, which also included special weapons fitted with silencers for personal attacks, was requested for July 22.

Havana, December 22, 1961. DSE Headquarters

Through investigations that led to the arrest of Alfredo Izaguirre de la Riva, we discovered that he commenced his counterrevolutionary activities in the early months of 1959, trying to unite all the counterrevolutionary organizations under his command in response to CIA directives. This resulted in numerous meetings with the coordinators of such groups, including Carlos Bandín Cruz (Hipólito) of the MRR; Reynold González of the MRP; Raúl Alfonso of the MID; Octavio Barroso of the United Front... He was the principal advocate of actions planned for July 26, including those in Oriente province, which involved an attempt on the life of *Comandante* Raúl Castro, an attack on the Santiago refinery and a provocation at the Guantánamo naval base. Also planned were sabotage operations in Camagüey and Las Villas, and finally, an assassination attempt on *Comandante* Fidel Castro at the commemorative event in Revolution Plaza, using a mortar deployed in a house on Amézaga Street.

Havana, November 1993.
Testimony of Carlos Valdés Sánchez[5]

There were two alternatives for the attempt on *Comandante* Raúl Castro. One consisted of firing at him with a .30-caliber machine gun while he was speaking at the July 26 event; and if that failed, an ambush on the highway to the airport, where several men armed with submachine guns would attack him. The second option was based on the assumption that as soon as he knew about the attack on Fidel in Havana, Raúl would leave for the local airport, thus providing them with an opportunity. Meanwhile, a group of counterrevolutionaries dressed in Rebel Army uniforms would fire

---

5.   Carlos Valdés Sánchez: Cuban officer who acted in the investigation of Operation Patty.

mortars in the direction of the US base in Guantánamo, an attack that would give the signal to underground groups in Santiago and other eastern cities to initiate their subversive action.

In Havana, a group of men also dressed in military uniform would place a 60-millimeter mortar within 200 meters of the platform in Revolution Plaza. From there they would open fire on the Cuban leaders with the aim of assassinating Fidel Castro and his *compañeros*. In summary, that was the plan of Operation Patty, which Cuban security gave its own codename: *Candela* [Trouble].

A Perfect Target
Havana, May 1961

One day towards the end of the month, Rodolfo León Curbelo received a phone call from Jaime Caldevilla, press attaché at the Spanish embassy. The diplomat wanted an urgent meeting with him at the embassy office. León knew Caldevilla well and was aware that when such a request was made it was in connection with a message from the "Americans," so he dressed rapidly and took off for the meeting.

Jaime Caldevilla was a veteran CIA agent who used the Spanish embassy for his espionage activities, for which he was expelled from Cuba in 1965.

When León was comfortably seated in the diplomat's office, the latter explained that he had received instructions from the Agency to direct the assassination of Fidel Castro using two of the most trustworthy counterrevolutionary groups on the island. They had attempted this task some months earlier, in January, but the operation had failed when Cuban agent Félix Rodríguez could not be infiltrated. Nevertheless, they now believed that the conditions were ripe for Mario Chanes's and Higinio Menéndez's men to act.

Mario Chanes de Armas was a resentful, bitter man. He had fought against the Batista dictatorship, but after the revolutionary triumph, felt frustrated at not being given the position that he expected. He became involved in various conspiracies until he finally decided that Fidel was the cause of all his ills, and thus dedicated himself wholeheartedly to his elimination.

Higinio Menéndez Beltrán and his group had different origins; their political background was linked to the criminal gangs that had devastated the country in the 1940s. Menéndez had reached the same conclusion on his own account, and was offered the job of assassinating the revolutionary leader.

One attack was planned at a location in close proximity to a house Fidel often visited in the capital; the other plan was for a gangster-style shootout in one of Havana's main avenues.

Once he had given his explanation, the Spanish diplomat informed León that after committing the crime he should keep a low profile, or if he had family in the rural part of the island, stay with them for a reasonable period of time. Within a few days, León had passed on instructions to the selected assassins and each of them got down to the planning.

Carrying a Springfield rifle with a telescopic sight obtained in an earlier adventure, Mario Chanes would fire as soon as the target was in range. He was an accurate shot and had practiced a great deal.

The location was ideal: an apartment located above a grocery store on the corner of 11th and 12th Streets in Vedado, a few meters from the home of Celia Sánchez, executive secretary of the Council of Ministers and one of Fidel's close collaborators, who hosted him frequently at the house. They only had to wait for an opportunity to kill him. After various meetings, the conspirators selected the week July 19–26, 1961, as the time to execute the operation. They had reached the conclusion that prior to the events for July 26 Fidel would visit Celia's home at some point, to finalize details for the the commemoration of an event so important to the revolution. However, a few days before, on July 17, G-2 discovered the homicidal plot, captured everybody involved, and thus frustrated the assassination attempt.

Havana, November 1994.
Testimony of Florentino Fernández León[6]

I don't remember dates, but I think it would be in mid-1960 when I started to attend meetings of revolutionary combatants organized by Mario Chanes in the Puentes Grandes brewery club. I didn't have much of a friendship with him, but we had been *compañeros*-in-struggle against the Batista dictatorship.

At those meetings, Chanes expressed his displeasure at the direction being taken by the revolutionary government, because he felt he was underestimated and that he was more worthy than other people in important posts in the administration.

At one of those meetings I met a friend of Chanes called Orlando Ulacia Valdés. He was a kind of agitator who explained at the meetings how the real revolutionaries were being relegated, while others without merit, like those from the Socialist Party, were occupying important positions. Ulacia and I rapidly identified politically, and through him, I soon began to obtain knowledge of their conspiratorial activities and Mario Chanes's role as a leading figure in them.

Ulacia "recruited" me for these activities and we began to meet with some regularity. I had the credentials of having been detained for a few days for alleged counterrevolutionary activities. In reality that was a story prepared for me by a *compañero* from G-2, which had already become suspicious of the Chanes brothers' conspiratorial activities and was setting me up for the infiltration. In the early months of 1961 I went to a meeting in the Nela butter factory office where Ulacia worked. Two other individuals whose names I've forgotten were there. Ulacia explained that it was necessary to activate counterrevolutionary activities, concretely in reference to a plot to assassinate Fidel, whom he stated had to be physically

---

6.   Florentino Fernández León: a Moncada Garrison assailant who dis-
      covered this assassination conspiracy and informed the authorities.

eliminated. He sketched the corner of 11th and 12th [streets] in Vedado on paper, and pointed out the place from which they would shoot with a rifle fitted with a telescopic sight, taking advantage of one of Fidel's visits to *compañera* Celia Sánchez's home. Ulacia stated that he had checked Fidel's movements there from the balcony of a house on the corner where a family he knew lived. He said that when Fidel got out of the car, he usually went around the back of it and that then was the precise moment to shoot. He said that there would be a number of participants in the attack and a car with its engine running would be parked on the corner for a rapid getaway.

They held various other meetings elsewhere to fine-tune the plan, at a bar on Puentes Grandes Avenue close to the Pavo Real match factory and also in Ulacia's house.

At the beginning of July everything was ready, and we informed the *compañero* looking after us, who, after consulting with headquarters, explained that we couldn't wait any longer to move in. That was how these traitors were caught.

Havana, July 1961.
Testimony of Mario Morales Mesa

On July 17, I was working on the Pinar del Río case involving brothers Mario and Francisco Chanes and other characters.

We had been investigating these individuals for their counter-revolutionary activities from January of that year, and had discovered that they were in contact with CIA agents from that date and were planning to assassinate Prime Minister Fidel Castro during one of his visits to the house of *compañera* Celia Sánchez, located on 11th Street between 10th and 12th, Vedado.

Originally, they were to support a group of agents who were to be infiltrated from the United States to execute the action. When that operation failed, a commando unit consisting of the Chanes brothers and others was organized to assault the apartment on the upper floor of a grocery store on 11th and 12th, Vedado, barely 50 meters from the location of the target.

The operation included the 30 November Revolutionary Movement, People's Revolutionary Movement and the FRD counter-revolutionary groups. The date selected for the attempt was the week 19–26 July, 1961. All the conspirators were caught and their weapons seized.

The Suicides
Havana, May–June 1961

Higinio Menéndez and Guillermo Caula's group was fairly small. Its members included individuals from various underground groups hit by the DSE at various times. They were united by the common cause of their hatred for Fidel Castro, and had decided that the only alternative left open to them, after the defeats suffered, was to assassinate the prime minister in order to provoke a US intervention in Cuba.

They tried it on two occasions. Once during Fidel's visit to a densely populated Havana neighborhood and the other when the leader was dining in a well-known city restaurant. Both attempts failed, neutralized by the effective vigilance of his security guards.

However, after receiving the CIA message guaranteeing both its backing and a substantial sum of money, they got together and hatched up a new assassination scheme.

The idea was a simple one. The conspirators were counting on the complicity of the owner of an automobile service center at the intersection of Rancho Boyeros and Santa Catalina Avenues, an obligatory transit route for Fidel from the city center to the airport on the outskirts of Havana. They would lie in wait there for the approach of the leader's cars and then fire on them with a bazooka. The date selected was the first week of June.

A feverish bout of activity commenced to put the finishing touches on the plan. The bazooka and weapons were transferred and the men quartered. Everything was ready; the only thing that they had not foreseen was the action by the Cuban G-2, which, informed of the plan, decided to detain all those involved.

Havana, July 25, 1961. DSE Headquarters

Information was recently obtained that a group of individuals were periodically meeting in an establishment managed by Juan Bacigalupe Hornedo, located on the corner of Vento Highway and Estrada Avenue in the Casino Deportivo district. The most important participants were Higinio Menéndez Beltrán, Guillermo Caula Ferrer, Ibrahim Álvarez Cuesta, Augusto Jiménez Montenegro, Román Rodríguez Quevedo and Osvaldo Díaz Espinoza, individuals who maintained contact with ex-captains Bernardo Corrales and Santiago Ríos, both fugitives from justice. They also met in the service station on Rancho Boyeros and Santa Catalina owned by Carlos Pérez González.

Investigations revealed that the group had relations with members of the CIA and made frequent visits to the Guantánamo naval base where they received war munitions and instructions for effecting sabotage and assassination attempts on leaders of the revolution.

On June 14, 1961, the group met in the Casino Deportivo land sales office with an individual known as León (Rodolfo León Curbelo), sent to Cuba by the FRD with the mission of assassinating Fidel. In that meeting Juan Bacigalupe, Higinio Menéndez and Guillermo Caula were assigned to the job and given the necessary funds.

Those individuals were given the task of making contact with the chiefs of various counterrevolutionary organizations so that they could check out the places frequented by the leader of the revolution. On one occasion when Fidel went to the Cucalambé restaurant on Fifth Avenue and 112th Street, Higinio Menéndez was seen reconnoitering it with an individual named Antonio and one Josefa Delgado Piñeiro (Fina), who were constantly under the watch of State Security agents.

Through subsequent investigations it was discovered that during the conspiratorial meetings Carlos Pérez González and Augusto Jiménez Montenegro were given the task of checking the area located on the stretch of Rancho Boyeros highway between Santa Catalina and Vía Blanca, opposite land occupied by the Ciudad Deportiva.

On July 2 all those involved were arrested and two bazookas with their shells, three M1 carbines, three .45-caliber Thompson submachine guns, two crates of US fragmentation grenades, a radio plant similar to those utilized by the CIA and a large volume of ammunition were found buried in the Rancho Boyeros and Santa Catalina service station...

6 Operation Liborio: "Cuba in Flames"

1959 was a year of great emotion and profound disillusion for Antonio Veciana Blanch. When the revolution triumphed he was a public accountant working for sugar magnate Julio Lobo, with aspirations of becoming a prosperous businessman. However, measures taken almost immediately by the new government had frustrated his dreams. Those measures doubtless cast a disagreeable shadow over his economic plans, and so he began to link up with other people who were discontented with the new regime.

Many of them hoped that the Americans, as they had done before, would take the action needed to halt or derail the high-speed train that was the revolution and its socioeconomic changes.

Veciana had some interesting contacts. Rufo López Fresquet, minister of the treasury; Felipe Pazos, president of the National Bank; Raúl Chibás, president of the Rail Transportation Corporation; Manuel Ray Rivero, minister of Public Works, and others who, almost from the outset, recruited him to develop a dissident movement of malcontents within the government that would try to divide the revolutionary government, neutralize the radicals, and bring their program to a halt.

This proved harder than they anticipated. The revolution was growing more radical and Veciana's associates lost the little power they once held, and so the option they chose was to conspire against the regime. On the recommendation of Rufo López Fresquet, they decided to contact veteran CIA agent David Phillips, who operated from a public relations office near Havana's busy Rampa.

After several conversations, Phillips was convinced that Veciana possessed the ability to conduct acts of terrorism, given his marked inclination for violence. Thus they reached an agreement and a few weeks later Veciana started classes at a branch of the Berlitz Language School, but in subversion, not a foreign language.

The classes Veciana attended covered psychological warfare, sabotage, intelligence, the organization of underground groups and acts of terrorism. He passed the course with flying colors.

Originally, Veciana was instructed to work directly with Phillips, who in mid-1960 was organizing groups for intelligence operations, psychological warfare and subversion. Phillips would be a sort of mentor while Veciana acquired experience in the art of conspiracy.

It was in that period, towards the end of 1960, that they received an order from the CIA station in the capital to consider an assassination attempt on Fidel Castro at one of the public meetings he attended almost daily.

They discussed various locations: the university precinct, restaurants, public ministries, plazas, and finally the esplanade that stretched from the Presidential Palace to Havana's Malecón, which was at that time the location of many rallies.

The Palace had an irresistible attraction and they concluded that it was the ideal place. A line of buildings extended around the improvised popular plaza with a large park in its center. Several of those buildings were rented out as homes. Number 29, Misiones Avenue met all the necessary conditions. The meetings were conducted on the Palace's north-facing terrace, 50 meters from the selected building.

After various negotiations, Darling Hoost, an agent of US origin acting under contract, rented an apartment on the eighth floor. The main obstacle to the project — the location from which to execute it — had been overcome.

At that point, Phillips was recalled to general headquarters in

Washington to take charge of psychological warfare against Cuba on a continental scale; Veciana was momentarily without contact and had to postpone the plans.

While he was waiting, he joined Manuel Ray's MRP. At the time of the Bay of Pigs it was one of the most active counterrevolutionary groups, engaging in many acts of sabotage including the arson attack on El Encanto department store in which Fe del Valle, an exemplary worker, was killed.

After the defeat of the invasion, a new coordinator, Reynold González, took on the MRP leadership and appointed Veciana as its military attaché, in charge of all subversive and terrorist actions.

A few months later, in mid-1961, they heard about Operation Patty. After several talks with its leader, Alfredo Izaguirre, they evaluated its weaknesses and decided to keep their distance from it, so as not be to affected if it was discovered, which subsequently occurred.

For his part, Veciana continued with his own project. Week by week weapons were smuggled into the apartment at Misiones Avenue, and he could soon count on a bazooka, submachine guns, grenades and the uniforms the assassins would use when the order was given, which came when it was least expected — just when he had come to the conclusion that his patrons to the North had thrown the plan into the waste basket.

Death Terrace
Washington, July 1961. The Mayflower Hotel

One day at the end of July 1961, CIA agent José Pujals Mederos was called to Washington by his bosses. He had arrived from Cuba a few weeks earlier to report on the progress of Operation Patty and thus had avoided being arrested when the plot was dismantled by the Cuban security forces.

Karl Hetsh, his case officer, was waiting for him in the hotel room to which he had been summoned with another American called Harold Bishop (David Phillips), who needed to instruct him on a new mission.

In perfect Spanish, occasionally tinged with a certain South American accent, Bishop explained that the task consisted of activating a new project to incite rebellion within Cuba. A large number of men, humiliated by the defeats inflicted upon them, were clamoring for revenge. That was why the mercenary was there.

His work would be relatively easy: he would direct the MRP group headed by Reynold González and Antonio Veciana to conduct extensive sabotage and terrorist operations in the country's main provincial capitals and to assassinate Fidel on the north terrace of the Presidential Palace. This was part of a coordinated plan whereby key elements of the international press would announce to the world that Cuba was plunged into civil war and that the United States would intervene to impose peace.

The remaining task was a little more delicate: it consisted of serving as contact for a small espionage network located in the Cuban air base at San Antonio de los Baños, where a squadron of Soviet-manufactured MIG-15 aircraft about to arrive in Cuba were to be installed. After Phillips explained the details, an animated conversation began among those at the meeting:

"I don't foresee any difficulties in executing either task, but I think that the harder one will be the operation against Castro," José Pujals emphasized.

"Veciana should already have the necessary men," responded Phillips. "He is in contact with the Rescate people and they will facilitate what he needs. Your mission is to give the orders, supervise the operation and coordinate the infiltration of the necessary equipment. Afterwards you can concentrate on information concerning the aircraft."

A few hours later, on July 28, José Pujals, now the principal CIA link in Cuba, infiltrated the island at a point off the northern coast of Havana province in the immediate vicinity of Puerto Escondido.

Havana, Early August 1961

Two days after his entry and a short, well-earned rest, Pujals met with Reynold González and Antonio Veciana and gave his orders with a wealth of detail.

According to his subsequent accounts, González didn't like the project. He was displeased at the latest failures and believed in conserving the organization, using it only for propaganda work in expectation of better times when the Americans decided on definitive action. Right now, he felt that the Americans were manipulating the MRP so that it would provide the cannon fodder; it was his *compañeros* who would be detained or shot.

On the other hand, Veciana proposed direct action to damage the regime at its weakest points. In the end, after much discussion, they couldn't agree and entrusted the decision to an extraordinary meeting of their terrorist organization's national leadership.

Pujals did not want to get involved in the dispute. He knew that it wasn't his terrain and he was very clear on the orders he had received. Veciana could take charge of solving the problem. Meanwhile, he would meet up with Octavio Barroso, alias César, one of his most important collaborators, who had recruited a dentist lieutenant at the San Antonio de los Baños airbase where they were beginning to arm the MIG-15 combat aircraft they had recently received from the Soviet Union. Thus he would fulfill one of the priorities earmarked by the CIA.

The meeting of the MRP national directorate went ahead on a farm belonging to a group member called Amador Odio,[1] outside Havana in the small town of Wajay. Various leaders spoke, some in favor and some against the plans put forward. Finally, Veciana's

---

1.   Amador Odio: husband of Sara del Toro, who was one of the organizers of Operation Peter Pan, which took more than 14,000 children out of Cuba without their parents. Their daughters Silvia and Ana were linked to Lee Harvey Oswald shortly before Kennedy's assassination.

proposal won the day. Everybody knew where the order had come from and nobody was prepared to stand up to that. Moreover, Veciana confirmed that he had the necessary men and nobody anticipated any direct risk to themselves. Visibly annoyed, González withdrew and let Veciana take care of the details.

"The plan is simple," Veciana explained to the people present. "The idea is to sabotage department stores: Sears, Fin de Siglo, J. Vallés and Ultra; and to blow up the Havana aqueduct and the National Paper Store."

Various teams were organized to engage in these actions by placing explosive devices in the stores selected, particularly in locations with inflammable material. In the case of the paper store and the aqueduct, the Rescate group had men working in those places who would lay the charges. Finally, the operation was divided into two stages: the first stage would encompass the acts of terrorism led by José Manuel Izquierdo, alias Aníbal; and the second stage, led by Veciana, was the assassination attempt. This division was based on the supposition that after the planned acts of sabotage and terror had been executed, Fidel would convene a mass meeting at the Presidential Palace as he had done previously, providing the occasion to eliminate him.

González's secretary, María de los Ángeles Abach (Mary), who took the minutes of the meeting, asked when the operation would commence and what it was to be called. Veciana told her that the codename was "Cuba in Flames" and the acts of sabotage would commence on September 20, 1961.

Havana, August 8, 1961

The day dawned cloudy, and Pujals, convinced that it was going to rain, dressed slowly. He had returned from the United States 10 days earlier and planned to take advantage of his position at the head of all the agents to take control of the internal counterrevolution at the appropriate moment. Then, he would be one of the agents that the Americans would have to take into account.

One of his first tasks — activating Operation Liborio or "Cuba in Flames" — had been accomplished. That operation only affected him indirectly, as it meant giving the order to the group headed by Reynold González and Antonio Veciana to undertake the planned actions; after that, it was only a matter of periodically reporting on progress. The only things that bothered him were the constant meetings he was obliged to attend with the underground leaders, because when the acts of sabotage began, G-2 would come down hard on them.

Pujals left the Miramar house in which he was hiding and walked down to Fifth Avenue to wait for a taxi, which arrived quickly. In fact, the vehicle's prompt arrival surprised him; taxis weren't usually so forthcoming at that early hour.

"Where to, sir?"

"19th Street between Paseo and A in Vedado, please."

The taxi swiftly moved in that direction.

Pujals absently watched the passing landscape. Many of the mansions he saw belonged to old friends of his, now in exile. He recalled how the government had confiscated his farm in Santa Cruz del Sur. "These communists have done away with everything," he thought, "and they still want the Americans to leave them alone. They all have to be liquidated, even their kids, to ensure that their ideas totally disappear from the Cuban scene."

At some point he stopped thinking of the past and returned to the events of the last few days.

Phillips had impressed him more than any other CIA officer he knew. His command of the Spanish language was perfect, and judging by his questions, it was easy to guess he had spent a long time in Havana. A gentle cadence was imprinted on his voice; his approach was direct with a hint of affection and understanding. Nevertheless, he knew how to impose his authority when necessary, and then his expression changed like that of an experienced actor.

He was diverted from his meditations when the taxi pulled up at his destination. After paying the fare, Pujals walked for a few blocks as a security measure and then turned back on himself, heading for an apartment building that he entered, going up to the second floor. Waiting for him was Octavio Barroso — César, the man with the most valuable military information at that moment, concerning the assembly of the Soviet MIG-15 aircraft recently arrived in Cuba and the state of training of the Cuban pilot crews.

"Ernesto, punctual as always! You must have German ancestors," César said, only half joking.

He made a joke of his extraordinary punctuality, but he had learned to never arrive late for a clandestine meeting. The two of them went out onto the terrace, while César's mother prepared coffee. The subject of the meeting was the activity of two recently recruited agents, Cadet Francisco Crespo and the dentist Lieutenant José Muiño, who were passing information on the preparation of the Soviet aircraft. The planes were still crewed by Russians, but Muiño had noted that a group of Cuban pilots were about to return from training in Czechoslovakia. Within two months, they calculated, the first MIG-15 squadron would be in full combat readiness.

A knock at the door sent them into hiding in a corner of the terrace. It was a housing inspector in search of information from Barroso's mother. A few minutes later, when Pujals was explaining to his host the need to devote himself solely to the network of military agents so as not to expose himself in other kinds of conspiratorial activities, another knock at the door forced them to conceal themselves again. It was the same housing inspector, who had returned to emphasize to Barroso's mother that she needed to put all her housing documents in order so as to benefit from the Urban Reform Act.

Havana, September 1993. Testimony of Alberto Santana[2]

That morning, August 8, 1961, I recall that our chief, Blanco "El Flaco" [The Thin One],[3] gave us a work order: to locate CIA agent Octavio Barroso. The only detail we had on him was his mother's address. Around 10:00 a.m. I arrived at her apartment and introduced myself to the lady as a housing inspector, asking her for documents. I was able to observe that there were two men on the terrace who attempted to hide, so after looking at the documents I left, explaining to the lady that the building was going to be confiscated and she shouldn't pay any more rent until she received fresh instructions.

I went out into the passage and veered around by a window looking onto to the wing of the building. From there I could see that one of the men was the individual in the photo I had been given; the other had a holster at his waist. That was the man I was looking for. I left the building and asked for backup. Shortly afterwards a G-2 patrol came to my aid and we all went up to the apartment. I knocked again, and when the lady answered I explained that I had to ask her some further questions about her housing. She opened the door. We raced to the terrace and detained the two subjects, who turned out to be Octavio Barroso and José Pujals, a spy just infiltrated into Cuba. They had a Colt .38 that they were unable to use.

Pujals immediately confessed to his main mission. He gave details of the meeting with Reynold González and Antonio Veciana and the objectives of Operation Liborio; he only held back the dates and locations of the meetings. From that point we were faced with a veritable nightmare, and we met every night to review any new

---

2.   Colonel Alberto Santana Martín: DSE official operative who detained terrorist spies Pujals and Barroso.
3.   Lieutenant Colonel Gustavo Blanco Oropesa: former head of Cuban counterintelligence.

information. Soon several leads were found, and finally the group was arrested and the attempt frustrated. Barroso and Pujals also named the military spies, who were quickly detained.

Havana, September 1961

September 15, 1961, was the date picked by Antonio Veciana to pass on the latest instructions to the command in charge of assassinating Fidel Castro. He had called them to Apartment 8A, 29 Misiones Avenue, beside the Presidential Palace.

Present were José Manuel Izquierdo (Aníbal), Bernardo Paradela (Angelito), Raúl Venta del Mazo (Chiquitico) and Noel Casas Vega (El Pelao). They were all men of action, some from the MRP and others from Rescate and the Second National Front of the Escambray.

"This is the bazooka that will ensure our success," Veciana explained to his *compañeros*.

Raúl Venta del Mazo, who had been trained in the Dominican Republic during the struggle against Batista, got up from his chair, took the bazooka, and approached the window, which offered a view over the northern terrace of the Presidential Palace. Placing himself in a firing position, he covered the entire objective with the sight: it couldn't fail. The distance was sufficiently short to make impact with the first shot.

After returning to his seat, Venta del Mazo asked: "And when do we have to get in position? We can't be here indefinitely until there's a public meeting."

"Chiquitico," Veciana replied, "Our people are going to carry out acts of sabotage all over Havana, which I assure you will provoke a meeting. Your task is to fire the bazooka and to then launch some grenades from the window onto the avenue. The grenades will explode in the middle of the mass demonstration, causing terrible confusion and chaos. That will be the moment to flee, dressed in the militia uniforms that we have here. We can't fail!"

"And when do we take up position?" Angelito repeated.

"The operation commences on September 20 and you must all be in your assigned positions. On the 25th the complete group will be here; Aníbal will be the last to arrive because he has other tasks to carry out. Then we'll see if the mouse falls into the trap."

Havana, November 1961. DSE Headquarters

September 29 was the day picked to unleash the terrorist plan. José Manuel Izquierdo (Aníbal) was in charge of distributing the materials to be employed. María de los Angeles Abach (Mary) was appointed to sabotage Fin de Siglo, and would be taken there by Ernesto Amador del Río.

Co-conspirators Dalia Jorge Díaz, José Manuel Izquierdo and someone known as "Kike" went to Mary's house in the morning to distribute the C-4 explosive packs. Alina Hiort was designated to sabotage the Ultra department store, but was unable to execute the plan, being arrested beforehand. A couple from Rescate, who have not been identified, were selected for J. Vallés and La Época. The Capri Hotel sabotage was to be carried out by Joaquín Alzugaray, who was given two packs, while other acts of terrorism involved two bombs, incendiary devices and "live phosphorus," handed over to Raúl Fernández Rivero who was to distribute them within the student sector.

On that day, September 29, Dalia Jorge was arrested at 5:50 p.m while placing the explosive charge in the Sears store, as a consequence of the vigilance of employee Élida Salazar.

Havana, November 1994.
Testimony of Raúl Alfonso Roldán[4]

According to our investigations, in mid-1959, Antonio Veciana Blanch — a public accountant and employee of the former Financiero National Bank owned by magnate Julio Lobo — was recruited by David Phillips, a CIA agent located in Havana. That officer, who some years later occupied a high-level CIA post, entered Cuba in 1958 and operated under the cover of David Phillips Associates, a public relations agency located at Office 502, 106 Humboldt Street, Vedado. He lived with his wife and four sons at 21413, Avenue 19A, Nuevo Biltmore, Marianao.

After his recruitment, Veciana received intensive training from Phillips in the following subjects: counterintelligence observation, explosives, communications, sabotage and propaganda.

The initial tasks carried out by the recently graduated agent were related to psychological warfare actions.

In late 1960, Veciana joined the recently formed MRP counter-revolutionary organization. Phillips had instructed him to penetrate the group so as to be part of the political bloc that the CIA wanted to promote in the United States under the command of Manuel Antonio de Varona.

After joining the MRP, Veciana became its military coordinator, operating from that point under the pseudonym of Víctor. From that date the MRP group's terrorist activities increased with a large number of sabotage operations, including the placing of incendiary devices in La Epoca department store, the Ten Cents stores on Monte and Obispo, the Puentes Grandes paper factory, and an arson attack on the El Encanto department store.

In mid-1960 Phillips left Cuba, having been recalled by his chief to take over the propaganda operation against Cuba. He left

---

4.   Raúl Alfonso Roldán: instructor in the investigations into this plot.

Veciana in contact with Colonel Sam Kail, military attaché at the US embassy in Havana.

Before leaving, Phillips put his trainee in charge of a delicate mission: an assassination attempt on *Comandante* Fidel Castro. To that end he was given weapons and Apartment 8A, 29 Misiones Avenue, beside the Presidential Palace. This apartment was in the name of US citizen Darling Hoost until November 1960, and was then transferred in December to Cuban Caridad Rodríguez Aróstegui, Antonio Veciana's mother-in-law.

The arms to be deployed in the attack were carefully concealed in the false wall of a closet in this apartment.

After the failure of the Bay of Pigs mercenary invasion, Phillips sent an envoy, José Pujals Mederos, to activate the assassination plot, which involved a series of sabotage attacks throughout Havana to prompt a public demonstration at the Palace that would provide an opportunity to commit the crime.

Pujals was arrested during those operations and provided us with initial information on the plan, codenamed Operation Liborio.

On September 16, G-2 commenced an operation that led to the capture of a group of MRP members who were trying to circulate a false governmental decree throughout the island, declaring that parents were to lose custody of their children to the state.

As a result of security measures taken in the capital's main department stores, Dalia Jorge Díaz was arrested while attempting to place an incendiary device in Sears, whereupon she confessed and gave the location of José Manuel Izquierdo.

At that time President Osvaldo Dortícos's[5] return from a tour of the socialist countries had been announced, and he was to be received by the capital's residents on the esplanade to the north of the former Presidential Palace. That was the occasion agreed for the attack.

---

5.   Osvaldo Dortícos: Cuban president 1959–76.

Izquierdo and other accomplices were arrested. Veciana fled the country, abandoning the group in the Misiones apartment before we occupied it. A bazooka, various Czech Model 25 submachine guns, fragmentation grenades and militia uniforms were discovered in that location.

A few days later the main leaders of the MRP, including its national coordinator, Reynold González, were captured and a weapons arsenal seized from a safe house occupied by the underground group at 2117, 202nd Street, Siboney. The following materials were confiscated there: a 60-millimeter mortar with eight shells, a .30-caliber machine gun, seven Garand rifles, four Thompson submachine guns and a large quantity of explosive material and munitions.

That was the end of Operation Liborio.

7 Task Force W: "A Chocolate Milkshake"

The buildings housing the CIA general headquarters were known as Quarters Eye and were located in close proximity to the Lincoln Memorial in Washington. They had belonged to the navy and in the 1950s were fitted out for espionage activities. Many of the buildings had restricted access, particularly those occupied by the chiefs, and the guards at the entries to each block who checked functionaries' and officers' passes were backed up by a modern surveillance system.

However, everybody knew that the new buildings in Langley, Virginia, where the CIA was constructing its permanent headquarters, would soon be ready. Large rooms, spacious offices, sophisticated security systems, radio installations to link up with agents operating in enemy territory, cafés and spacious parking lots promised even the most demanding individuals enviable conditions in which to dedicate themselves fulltime to their activities. This had been made possible by two men, who at that time were about to be booted out of the Agency by the president: Allen Dulles and Richard Bissell.

A Special Charm
Washington, November 1961. CIA Headquarters

It was a shame, thought Bissell, heading for his office on that cold morning, that he wouldn't be able to enjoy the building that they had designed.

With his university professor's ambling gate, Bissell strode along the glossy corridor to his office. Some of the officials he knew well greeted him reverentially. The new ones, who had heard of his upcoming enforced retirement, gave him the slip so as not to compromise themselves. Such was the bureaucratic optimism of those who thought they would ascend in the shadow of John F. Kennedy, the youthful president.

He pushed open the door to his office and greeted William Harvey, who had been waiting for him for few minutes in the ante-room. With a quick wave Bissell invited him in, and after depositing various papers that he had under his arm on the desk, sat down in his revolving chair.

"Harvey, I have some news for you. Everything seems to indicate that after Dulles is replaced, I'll be the next victim and I want to leave the main issues in good hands. Richard Helms is to replace me and we thought you could be responsible for a new task force, with the mission of reorganizing the Cuba project now that Washington has realized that it cannot escape unscathed from the Bay of Pigs business."

"I don't understand what this purge is about, when right now an operation is being planned at state level to liquidate Castro," Harvey replied.

"The president wants to purge the CIA of his enemies and is taking advantage of the Bay of Pigs. He was solely responsible for the disaster because he halted the second bombardment of Cuban airports that would have destroyed Castro's air force. And then he wouldn't give the go-ahead to our naval forces in the area to support the Assault Brigade 2506. The rope always gives at its weakest point and so it's Dulles and me, but the Agency is in safe hands. The chiefs might change but it is you, the most long-standing officers, trained in this lengthy war against communism, who make policy and execute operations."

Bissell bent over his desk, and picking up some papers, began to explain the new plans. He hoped to remain the CIA second-in-command for a few months during the handover to Helms, and that would give him enough time to organize all pending matters.

"Operation Mongoose is the codename of the campaign to be initiated to overthrow the Cuban regime. In line with General Maxwell Taylor's proposal, it will be a state war within the context of the Cold War strategy on communism at the international level. You will reorganize the Cuban task force at headquarters and at the JM/WAVE base that directs actions from Florida. In your own right, you will belong to the general staff directing Mongoose under the command of General Edward Lansdale, a Pentagon expert on irregular warfare and Taylor's protégé. You'll have to be careful with him, as he's a fantasist hankering after a position in our country's intelligence complex. But I repeat, our top priority is Fidel Castro's elimination."

"I'm ready for the mission," Harvey replied. "I have met with the participants in the Bay of Pigs operation and I understand their experiences and their errors. I've also met with Edwards and O'Connell to study the reasons for the failure of the Roselli and Varona poison capsule plan. You can be sure that I'll approach this task just like the ZR/Rifle operation."

And with an affectionate handshake, Bissell concluded the meeting. Harvey had understood. He was sure that even being out of the Agency for a long time, he and Dulles would continue to wield influence.

Washington, November 1975, US Senate.
Report of the Church Commission

The inspector general's report divides the gambling syndicate operation into Phase I, terminating with the Bay of Pigs, and Phase II, continuing with the transfer of the operation to William Harvey in late 1961. The distinction between a clearly demarcated Phase I and Phase II may be an artificial one, as there is considerable evidence that the operation was continuous, perhaps lying dormant for the period immediately following the Bay of Pigs...

Harvey's notes reflect that Bissell asked him to take over the gambling syndicate operation from Edwards and that they discussed the "application of ZR/Rifle program to Cuba" on November 16, 1961. Bissell confirmed that the conversation took place and accepted the November date as accurate. He also testified that the operation "was not reactivated, in other words, no instructions went out to Roselli or to others... to renew the attempt, until after I had left the Agency in February 1962." Harvey agreed that his conversation with Bissell was limited to exploring the feasibility of using the gambling syndicate against Castro.

Richard Helms replaced Bissell as DD/P in February 1962. As such, he was Harvey's superior.

Washington, November 1961. CIA Headquarters

Harvey took one of the elevators in the central building and then walked along one of its large, illuminated corridors until he reached a door labeled Office of Security. He knocked gently and waited for a few seconds until a guard opened it. After a routine identification check, he passed into the spacious office of his colleague Colonel Edwards. Approaching Harvey, Edwards explained that Bissell had already brought him up to date on the new missions, and that he was at Harvey's service. In a fawning tone, he stated:

"I congratulate you on your assignment as the head of Task Force W, and as far as the reactivation of the capsules operation goes, everything is ready to hand over the contacts from my office to yours."

Harvey didn't like this individual. His military bearing and his show of efficiency turned Harvey's stomach. Edwards had had the plan to poison Castro in his hands for over a year and had done very little. On various occasions Harvey had tried to pull

Edwards out of the operation but his close relations with Colonel King prevented that. "Now everything will be different," Harvey thought. He was commanding the Agency's most important unit, directly subordinate to the DD/P, with resources within the United States itself, which nobody had been able to count on previously in the entire history of the CIA. He was chief of an army that was to initiate a clandestine war that never had a name.

Harvey needed O'Connell, who had all the contacts with the gambling syndicate men that he wanted to manage the business through. He was thinking of pulling Giancana and maybe Trafficante out of the project. Roselli knew Varona and could resolve things directly with his people. He wanted to send one of Varona's men to Cuba to reorganize the Rescate group and transform it into a large intelligence network that would facilitate the communication needed to execute the plan. Moreover, that group had recruited many military men from the Carlos Prío government who could organize an armed uprising at any given moment if they were well organized. He and Helms had the idea of organizing Castro's elimination in combination with a program of internal subversive action that would give the Pentagon boys a pretext to effect a military intervention.

Edwards agreed. Colonel King had already informed him of the plans underway. He reached out his hand to pick up the phone and called O'Connell, who he quickly updated on the mission.

They spent some time discussing certain details. O'Connell had talked with Dr. Gunn, one of the Agency scientists responsible for manufacturing the items to be used against Castro. The first poison capsules that they had sent to Cuba just before the Bay of Pigs were difficult to handle and slow to dissolve, but the lab had found a new formula for the manufacture of synthetic botulin in tablet form, with improved qualities. The new version would dissolve in any liquid and was easier to handle.

The only detail missing was a reliable way of getting the capsules to Cuba. The men were against them being sent via an infiltration group. Those people often suffered setbacks, and even if everything went well, they would have to jump ship near the Cuban coast and that could affect the capsules. In addition, the regular journeys between Havana and Miami had been suspended since the Bay of Pigs.

"Let's see if Mr. Varona, who resolved the matter last time, can come up with a proposal," O'Connell suggested. "Another matter worrying me is Mr. Roselli. I would like you to bear in mind, Mr. Harvey, that this man doesn't work for free. He doesn't want money, but protection against prosecution from Attorney General Robert Kennedy. He's been threatened with deportation on various occasions and that's bothering him a lot."

"Don't worry," Harvey replied. "This is a matter of national security with top priority assigned by the president himself, who will have to control his little brother."

Edwards got up, indicating that the meeting was over. Harvey and O'Connell agreed to meet the following week in the New York Plaza Hotel, where they would meet with Roselli to finalize details.

The new chief of Task Force W left Colonel Edwards's office feeling satisfied. There were many things to do to take charge of the whole Cuban operation; however, one of the main actions was already underway. In the next few days, he would meet with Roselli and establish the rules of the game very clearly with him.

When he returned to his office he telephoned Ted Shackley, chief of the JM/WAVE base in Florida, to hear how the actions against Cuba were progressing, and in passing, to arrange various meetings with exile leaders. He would have a good opportunity to study Tony Varona up close and find out what kind of person he was. In Harvey's opinion, the Cubans, like all Latinos, were casual and untruthful. They claimed to have hundreds of men, but it subsequently would turn out they had barely a few dozen.

Later, when night had fallen on that cold winter's day at the end of 1961, he got in his car and drove to his favorite bar, the Parade, for some drinks with the sweet girls who made the place enjoyable.

Everything was running smoothly, he reflected, and a little distraction would do no harm before he immersed himself in the new war.

Miami-Havana, January 1962

Norberto Martínez had been a lifelong supporter of former president Ramón Grau San Martín and a loyal man to his successors in the [Authentic] Party, Carlos Prío and Tony Varona. He went into exile with them when they realized that Fidel Castro would not include them as part of his government and that the Moncada program was a Cuban form of communism. In Miami he enrolled in the Assault Brigade 2506, but his political mentors advised him to enlist in one of the groups that the CIA was training for commando operations. The Bay of Pigs defeat traumatized him. He had dreamed of an important position in the government that Prío and Varona would head, but everything collapsed in an instant when the brigade was annihilated. Nevertheless, he continued within the CIA commandos and was not surprised when, one afternoon in January 1962, Robert, his CIA case officer, called him for an important mission. He was to infiltrate the island to reorganize the Rescate group, whose members he knew very well.

The point selected for his infiltration was Santa Lucía in the north of Pinar del Río province. It was a safe place. There he could rely on Pedro,[1] a charcoal miner who had a small boat that would pick him up at sea and bring him in to land.

A few days later he was in Havana. Alberto Cruz Caso, the head of Rescate, had met him and hidden him in the house of María Leopoldina Grau Alsina (Polita). Once established and equipped

---

1. Pedro Fernández Díaz: detained in 1964 for his participation in a CIA network supplying agents in Cuba.

with a sound story so that the Comités[2] wouldn't suspect him, he met with the group's principal leaders.

At the meeting were Polita Grau and her brother Ramón (Mongo), two founding members of the organization; ex-colonel Francisco Álvarez Margolles, a nationalized Spaniard who had made a career in the army in the Prío period; Rodolfo León Curbelo, the CIA courier; Manuel Campanioni Souza, a former dealer in the gambling room of the Sans Souci cabaret owned by Santos Trafficante; Dr. Carlos Guerrero Costales, who was Prío's physician; and other characters trusted by the group.

"I have instructions from Tony and the CIA to reorganize the group," Norberto began. "The American government is preparing a final offensive against Castro and we need to create the conditions to ignite the country when that time arrives. Colonel Margolles is to tour the island to organize the interior of the country, creating a sector in each province and providing the leaders with means of independent communication. Thus, each one can coordinate his own supplies with a minimum of risk. Here, you need to unite the most trustworthy groups, preferably those from genuine origins. As soon as everything is organized in line with these instructions, the CIA will start to send supplies." Alberto Cruz and the others were in agreement. They all thought a change of tactics was necessary in the wake of the Bay of Pigs failure. The Cuban G-2 had learned a lot and had penetrated the underground organizations with much success.

After detailing each person's tasks, Martínez asked Alberto Cruz and Polita Grau to stay behind to discuss another matter.

"Do we still have the Havana Libre Hotel people?" the spy asked.

---

2.   Comités: a reference to the Committees for the Defense of the Revolution (CDRs), groups created by Fidel Castro on September 28, 1960, as a popular response to the aggressive actions of the counterrevolutionary organizations.

"Yes, three trustworthy members of the organization are working there," Alberto replied.

"Good, the Agency wants to activate the poison capsules plan to get Fidel out of the way. According to our information, he still frequently visits the Havana Libre, especially with foreign guests, and that could present an opportunity. Who are those men?"

"We have Santos de la Caridad Pérez in the café, and Bartolomé Pérez and José Saceiro in the banquet hall. One is a maître d' and the other an assistant. Any one of them could undertake the mission," Polita Grau affirmed.

"There's only one detail left to work out," Martínez said. "How are we going to bring the capsules from Miami?"

"I reckon that Vergara[3] could bring them," Polita interjected. "He's a person we can trust, a diplomat at the Spanish embassy working under Caldevilla's orders, and can travel normally to Miami, collect them and hand them over to me in the embassy. As you know, I'm often there and my visit wouldn't be seen as suspicious."

And so Norberto Martínez's second and most important mission was arranged. A few days later the spy communicated with his headquarters and a CIA vessel picked him up in the same area in Pinar del Río and took him back to the lair.

New York, April 1962

The Savoy Plaza in New York was a luxury hotel with spacious lobbies and several bars and restaurants to satisfy the demands of its regular clients. Attentive and efficient employees took care of a variety of meetings of businessmen or amorous couples, who chose the place for its discretion.

---

3.   Alejandro Vergara Mauri: information attaché at the Spanish embassy in Havana from July 1960 to January 1964 and a CIA agent.

Such discretion was the reason why William Harvey selected that hotel as an ideal venue for his meeting with John Roselli, the notorious Chicago Mafia man. Jim O'Connell, the CIA officer, and Robert Maheu, the Mafia contact man, were also to be there, so the meeting had to be private.

Each of them booked in separately and at the agreed time gathered in the comfortable conference room they had booked. There they had a minibar and soft armchairs so that they could comfortably discuss the CIA's prospective plans.

O'Connell was the first to arrive, so that he could check that everything was in order. A few minutes later Roselli appeared with his friend Maheu, and finally, like the star of the night, Harvey turned up in his crumpled dark suit, a pistol in his armpit and a cynical expression on his face.

Harvey quickly took the floor to make his leadership of the group clear:

"Mr. Roselli, the businessmen that I represent believe that the time has come to reactivate the operation to liquidate Castro before the US government effects its plans to overthrow his regime. I can assure you that my representatives are very influential people and are prepared to pay for this job in whatever manner required."

With his actor's face, the dark glasses he never removed even at night, and that salesman's smile, Roselli got up from his chair, and taking a few paces about the spacious room, replied:

"As you are aware, money doesn't interest us. Perhaps some favor at the appropriate moment, but that can be seen to when necessary. Your word is enough. In terms of the job, I can see various problems. The capsules you gave us last time were very dangerous to handle and they didn't dissolve in any liquid. They will have to be improved if this undertaking is to be successful. Another matter that requires attention is the selection of the men involved. As you know, we have the group of Mr. Antonio de Varona, currently one of the vice presidents of the political front that you operate. Certain privileges would have to be given to these people, and above all, we must provide assurances that their political ambitions will be satisfied once Castro is eliminated. If those details can be resolved, I don't see any problems with executing the contract."

Harvey gave the guarantees that the gangster sought and advised him to leave his associate Sam Giancana out of the conspiracy as well as Florida capo Santos Trafficante, if that was possible. Roselli couldn't make any promises. He knew it was impossible to act in the territory of a "family" without its consent, but he decided not to divulge that fact to the Agency men. The final agreement was that they would meet up in Miami with Varona on April 21, 1962, to finalize all the details of the operation.

Washington, November 1975, US Senate.
Report of the Church Commission

In early April 1962, Harvey, who testified that he was acting on "explicit orders" from Helms, requested Edwards to put him in touch with Roselli. Harvey stated that he brought Helms up to date by detailing the proposals before making his first contact with Roselli, and also informed Helms of the results of the meeting with Roselli. Harvey stated that subsequently he kept Helms regularly informed regarding the situation of Operation Castro...

Harvey, the support chief and Roselli met for a second time in New York on April 8–9, 1962...

Harvey recalls having left Washington for Miami on April 19. He thinks that he picked up the capsules handed over by Dr. Gunn before leaving. Gunn does not recall handing them over on that date. He noted that he had given four capsules to J.C. on April 18, 1962; he believes that this was Jim O'Connell...

The pills were passed to Harvey, who arrived in Miami on April 21, and found Roselli already in touch with the same Cuban [Tony Varona] who had been involved in the pre-Bay of Pigs pill passage. Harvey explained the way in which the lethal substance should be introduced into Castro's meal, detailing a Varona contact that had access to somebody in a restaurant frequented by Castro...

The Cuban requested arms and equipment as a *quid pro quo* for carrying out the assassination operation. With the help of the CIA's Miami station which ran covert operations against Cuba (JM/WAVE), Harvey procured explosives, detonators, rifles, handguns, radios and boat radar costing about $5,000. Harvey and the chief of the JM/WAVE station [Ted Shackley] rented a U-Haul truck under an assumed name and delivered the equipment to a parking lot. The keys were given to Roselli, who watched the delivery with the support chief from across the street. The truckload of equipment was finally picked up by either the Cuban or Roselli's agent.

Harvey and Roselli had a telephone communication system through which Harvey was kept up to date on events. Using a pay phone, Harvey could call Roselli at the Los Angeles Friars Club at 1600 hours. Roselli could call Harvey at home during the night. Roselli informed him that the capsules were in Cuba and in the restaurant regularly visited by Castro.[4]

Havana, September 1993.
Testimony of Mario Morales Mesa

Operative officers Marcos and Ramón worked on the case in the period when *compañeros* Demetrio and Eduardo were their chiefs.

The main suspects were brother and sister Ramón and María Leopoldina Grau (Polita); José Luis Pelleyá Jústiz, Prío's former lawyer; Dr. Carlos Guerrero Costales; Manuel Campanioni, Trafficante's old gambling friend; and several other individuals.

At that time, the activities of the CIA and the counterrevolution

---

4.   Senate Select Committee (Church Commission), *Alleged Assassination Plots Involving Foreign Leaders* (Washington: US Government Printing Office, 1975), 83–84.

were very strong and we used the method of penetrating the subversive groups and networks, but only arresting the main leaders and terrorists, leaving the rest of the conspirators on the streets to allow us to keep up a penetration that would permit us to discover new enemy plots in time.

In September 1962 various leaders of Rescate were captured, including its military coordinator Francisco Álvarez Margolles, an ex-colonel in the Batista army who was plotting with other counter-revolutionary groups to execute a subversive plan on a national scale. However, we let Polita, her brother Ramón and Alberto Cruz slip out of the net. Not without reason, we thought that through their contacts with the CIA and Tony Varona we would obtain news of planned operations against Cuba.

By that period the group was already using various means of communication with Miami, including a RR44 radio receiver and encoded letters. They also had access to the diplomatic bags of the embassies of Spain and Italy, as diplomats and CIA agents Alejandro Vergara and Jaime Caldevilla worked in the former, and Massimo Muratori in the latter.

During 1962 the Rescate group divided into various subversive networks made up of handfuls of people with independent means of communication and specific tasks, although the links among the groups were so strong that they frequently met at the Graus' house to discuss the work they were doing or to ask for aid in a particular task.

In August 1962 the group reunited, disobeying CIA orders in relation to the division they were supposed to maintain, for a "counterrevolutionary uprising" planned for that date with Álvarez Margolles as one of its leaders. After its failure, everyone returned to their normal activities, without suspecting that we were on their trail.

In early 1963 we lost the agent we had within the circle of close associates of the Grau siblings, an agent who was one of our main sources of information on the conspirators' activities.

In July 1964, thanks to an error within the CIA, one of our agents established contact with the group of spies communicating through José Luis Pellayá Jústiz, who worked as a representative for the Mexicana aviation company.

We already knew that Pellayá Jústiz had a specially built communications system, known as AT-3, which transmitted coded messages in just a few seconds, and were also aware of his contacts with other CIA collaborators including Henri Beyens, first secretary at the Belgian embassy; Clemente Inclán Werner; and Julio Bravo Rodríguez.

Through the investigative work carried out the pieces of the puzzle came together and we uncovered various networks that the CIA had organized in Cuba.

In January 1965 headquarters took the decision to capture all the conspirators, and through the patient labor of the operations section, the plot to assassinate *Comandante* Fidel Castro was also discovered.

This had been initiated in March 1961, and despite its failure just before the invasion of the Bay of Pigs, it was reactivated the following year.

In April 1962, the CIA dispatched more poison capsules via Spanish diplomat Alejandro Vergara, this time concealed in a Bayer aspirin bottle.

By that date, the whole group was already divided into small intelligence and subversion networks. One of the agents, Manuel Campanioni, offered to find the men to attempt Fidel's assassination.

That was how Havana Libre Hotel employees Santos de la Caridad Pérez, Bartolomé Pérez and José Saceiro were recruited. One was an assistant in the café and the other two worked in one of the restaurants. The poison capsules were handed over to the three of them.

The plot against Fidel had begun. In June 1962, Polita Grau, desperate because Fidel had not gone to the hotel, proposed an alternative plan. It was to poison *Comandante* Efigenio Ameijeiras[5] so that the revolutionary leader could be targeted while attending his funeral.

They consulted with CIA headquarters by radio and the plan was approved; two pistols with silencers to be used in the attack were dispatched via CIA agent Massimo Muratori of the Italian embassy.

A command composed of various former soldiers and headed by ex-colonels Álvarez Margolles and Miguel Matamoros Valle picked the site of the ambush on 4th Street and 23rd Avenue in Vedado, along the route that they supposed the funeral cortege of *Comandante* Ameijeiras would pass.

Everything was ready, but the days were passing. August 30, 1962, the date for the planned counterrevolutionary uprising was approaching, and they all understood the importance of decapitating the revolution — but something unexpected occurred. After committing himself and accepting the lethal capsules, the person recruited to poison Ameijeiras — who worked in a café regularly used by the latter — changed his mind and moved to another province, thus depriving the group of its opportunity.

And so 1962 went by, and then the first months of the following year. One night, at the end of March 1963, when Santos de la Caridad Pérez was on duty at the Havana Libre café, he saw Fidel Castro arrive, accompanied by various people. They ordered a chocolate milkshake, and in the rush and the nervousness brought on by the moment for which he had prepared himself for over one year, he broke the capsule of poison while trying to pick it up, as it had stuck to the shelf of the freezer in which it was hidden.

---

5.   Efigenio Ameijeiras Delgado: founding member of the first July 26 Movement underground cell in Havana, expeditionary in the *Granma* voyage, combatant at the Bay of Pigs, international combatant and brigadier general of the Revolutionary Armed Forces.

He prepared the chocolate milkshake, which Fidel enjoyed, and despairingly observed him emerge safe and sound from the homicidal trap laid by the CIA and the internal counterrevolution.

The entire group was detained in January 1965 and its members confessed their criminal plans with a wealth of detail. Recalling that case, the phrase uttered by mafioso John Roselli at the Church Commission comes to mind: "Castro seemed to be wrapped in a special charm."

8 .375 Magnum

Richard Helms began his espionage career as a very young man. He was initially in the OSS during World War II, where he acquired fame as an efficient and professional operative. He trained under the tutelage of William "Wild Bill" Donovan, one of the OSS founders, taking advantage of a posting in London to assimilate from his British colleagues the knowledge and perfidy they had perfected over many years. Afterwards, with the creation of the CIA, he had various responsibilities, all of them related to covert action. At first he was Richard Bissell's aide, and subsequently he headed covert operations when Bissell was sacked by Kennedy after the Bay of Pigs fiasco.

Among his own kind, Helms was a figure of legend and controversy. All his sentiments, memories and experiences were related to the Agency. He had been made ambassador to Iran in 1973, at the moment when the Watergate affair was about to explode. If someone had asked him how many journeys he had had to make from Tehran to Washington to respond to questions from the Church Commission, he probably wouldn't have remembered. Finally, for refusing to answer to one of the committees investigating CIA participation in the coup against President Salvador Allende in Chile, he was given a $2,000 fine and a two-year prison term. The fine was paid by supporters who organized a public collection and the prison sentence was suspended.

Elegantly dressed, almost always in gray, and carefully groomed, at 40-odd years of age he was at the peak of his profession. Everyone regarded him as the logical successor when CIA head John McCone retired.

It was January 1963, and that morning Helms, as head of covert operations, had an important meeting in his Langley office. He had called in the main operatives on the Cuba case to discuss the new policy direction adopted by the administration after the October Missile Crisis. He also had to communicate to the units involved that William Harvey had been replaced by Desmond FitzGerald as the head of Task Force W — in charge of the Cuba case — which from that point was to be subordinated to the recently established Domestic Operations Division under the name of the Special Affairs Section (SAS).

In reality, that decision created an unprecedented force that we have called the "Cuban American Mechanism" of the CIA and the Mafia, which from that point would operate within US territory and even assume certain policing operations — and would grow until it controlled policy in Florida and obtained a quota of legislative and executive power in the United States.

One by one those summoned made their appearance: Colonel King, William Harvey, Desmond FitzGerald, Tracy Barnes, Ted Shackley, Samuel Halpern, Howard Hunt, David Phillips, James Angleton and various other officers. After everyone was seated in the spacious conference room, Helms took the floor:

"Mongoose has been discontinued. McGeorge Bundy, the security advisor, has convinced the president to rethink policy on Castro. The attorney general is not totally convinced, but for now he does not want to contradict the president's advisors."

Briefly he explained that the new task was to draw up strategies that could be adjusted to provide multiple ways of combating Castro. Tightening the economic blockade, developing covert and psychological actions to undermine the Cubans at vital points, and reorganizing the Assault Brigade 2506 for direct military action at a specific moment in time. Meanwhile, ways of forcing a split between Castro and his Soviet allies were being investigated as the Agency sought to take advantage of the conflicts that had arisen with Moscow in the heat of the Missile Crisis. If they could isolate Castro from the old Cuban communists and divide his regime, they might invade militarily or force Cuba to the negotiating table under favorable conditions. "That's the idea," Helms concluded.

He also took advantage of the opportunity to inform them that Harvey was to be replaced by Desmond FitzGerald as head of the operative force. It was an essential decision. Sometimes men represented specific strategies, and when these were concluded, they had to go.

Everyone looked at Harvey. They knew his explosive nature and understood how uncomfortable he felt. He was the sacrificial lamb, as Dulles and Bissell had been in their time. However, the ex-chief of the anti-Cuba force said nothing; he confined himself to lighting a cigarette. He clearly knew about the decision in advance and had already prepared himself for his demotion. In reality, he hadn't come out of it too badly. He had been made chief of the CIA station in Rome, and many of the people at the meeting knew of his relations with the criminal world, and in particular with John Roselli and Santos Trafficante. He would be a kind of dual-ambassador in Italy, given that he would be representing both the CIA and the Mafia in its country of origin.

When the meeting ended, Helms asked FitzGerald to stay behind for a few minutes. When they were alone he said:

"You have to take the necessary measures so that the operations underway continue on their course. Castro's elimination continues to be one of our top priorities. It will not be possible to achieve our strategic objectives in Cuba with him alive."

FitzGerald agreed. He understood what he was being told. In his long career as an operative it wasn't the first time that he had faced matters of this nature. He picked up his papers and took his leave of Helms.

Meanwhile, in the anteroom, James Angleton saw to it that he left at the same time as Harvey.

"You seem to be relieved at the way things have played out; your new destination is a reward. It's as if you are being paid to take a vacation in Europe for a couple of years…"

The tremendous effort Harvey had made to contain himself in the meeting was released like a tightly coiled spring. His accumulated rancor against President Kennedy and his disagreement with the administration's line erupted:

"After so much sacrifice, what are we going to say to the Cuban exiles? What are we going to do with all those people in the training camps? Are we going to tell them that from now on we're going to be friends with the Russians and that Castro's a good guy? What's going on, Jim, is that the president got scared over the Missile Crisis. I'm glad to be out of this operation, because at least I won't have to explain anything to the Cubans. Those people surrounding Kennedy: Bundy, Sorenson, Schlesinger, Salinger and co., are weak individuals, and they're the only ones allowed to give him advice. We're headed for failure, and if you like, go ahead and tell McCone what I think…"

"This guy's baiting me," Harvey reflected as he walked off down the long corridor in the direction of his office. "At least I told him what I thought so nobody can say later that they weren't warned."

A Caribbean Adventure
Miami, February 1963. JM/WAVE Base

The recognition of the new winds blowing through Washington in relation to Cuba dropped like a bomb on the community of US and Cuban spies at the JM/WAVE station in Miami. The resolution of the Missile Crisis in October 1962 did not please them in the slightest. When Kennedy discovered the rockets in Cuba everyone believed that a military invasion was inevitable, and they all made their preparations to return. But the crisis was averted through negotiation and it was rumored that Castro had obtained a promise from the United States that it would not attack the island militarily. Dejection spread through the exile community.

However, the exchange of the Bay of Pigs expeditionaries and President Kennedy's speech at the Miami Orange Bowl during their reception at the end of December 1962 had given the exiles new hope.

Plans started to move ahead at full steam in 1963. Robert Kennedy met with Manuel Artime, the political leader of the brigade, and guaranteed him US support for the formation of a new exile army based in Nicaragua, which in due course would attack the island again.

The attorney general also met with another CIA protégé: Enrique (Harry) Ruiz Williams, a Cuban American, former Bay of Pigs combatant, and Artime's right-hand man. He was to be in charge of organizing a strong paramilitary detachment from the Dominican Republic to initiate a guerrilla war in Cuba's easternmost province, where it could use the Guantánamo naval base as a safe rearguard.

In addition, a new commando group was being trained at a secret CIA base near New Orleans to replace the one captured in Cuba in the middle of the Missile Crisis . It was called the Mambi Commandos and would be responsible for extermination missions deep in Cuban territory.

Various radio stations were being activated to increase psychological warfare. The special missions groups, commando formations operating out of the JM/WAVE station, were being fortified with new agents and vessels to pursue their objectives of harassing maritime transportation, supplying subversive networks within Cuba, and destroying economic and basic energy targets.

Finally, there were plans to use various newly created terrorist groups, also based in the Dominican Republic, to attack Cuban representatives in third countries and foreign enterprises attempting to break the economic blockade.

The idea of forcing a split between Fidel Castro and the Soviets and possibly negotiating with Castro, even under favorable conditions, did not please the "covert warriors." They wanted to destroy the Cuban revolution totally. Desmond FitzGerald was pulled in to allay the fears of his men regarding a possible move to the negotiating table.

In his first meeting with the JM/WAVE leaders, FitzGerald employed his strongest arguments. He confirmed that the approved projects would go ahead, with the assassination of Castro as a priority. As he said this, FitzGerald noticed that the displeasure written on their faces had begun to moderate. He grasped that this was a vital issue for those at the meeting.

After stressing the need for compartmentalization of the new projects being discussed, FitzGerald detailed an ingenious plan to eliminate the Cuban leader.

The plan had two variants. The first, to persuade James Donovan, the lawyer who negotiated with Fidel Castro for the exchange of the Assault Brigade 2506 prisoners, to give the Cuban leader a diving suit impregnated with poisonous chemical substances. The second, to place a shell containing a powerful charge of plastic explosive to be placed in an area where the Cuban leader went underwater fishing.

The JM/WAVE chiefs were satisfied. They only asked if the president had given his approval, to which FitzGerald replied with a smile that they all interpreted as confirmation. This pacified the men. They could accept that the changes in the administration's strategy were merely cosmetic ones for the benefit of public consumption.

FitzGerald also had another trick up his sleeve: he had information on the existence of a powerful underground organization in Cuba that was ready to act against the Fidel Castro regime. They had sent a message explaining that they were preparing to assassinate the Cuban leader and then stage an armed uprising of all their members throughout the island. At least, that was what their emissaries claimed…

"It could be a good opportunity," he reasoned, taking his leave of the people at the meeting.

Langley, May 1967, CIA Headquarters.
Report of the CIA Inspector General

At about the time of the Donovan-Castro negotiations for the release of the Bay of Pigs prisoners a plan was devised to have Donovan present a contaminated skin diving suit to Castro as a gift… Desmond FitzGerald told us of [the plan] as if it had originated after he took over the Cuba task force in January 1963. Samuel Halpern said that it began under William Harvey and that he, Halpern, briefed FitzGerald on it. Harvey states positively that he never heard of it.

According to Sidney Gottlieb, this scheme progressed to the point of actually buying a diving suit and readying it for delivery. The technique involved dusting the inside of the suit with a fungus that would produce a disabling and chronic skin disease (Madura foot) and contaminating the breathing apparatus with tubercle bacilli. Gottlieb does not remember what came of the scheme or what happened to the scuba suit. Sam Halpern, who was in on the scheme, at first said the plan was dropped because it was obviously impracticable. He later recalled that the plan was abandoned because it was overtaken by events: Donovan had already given Castro a skin diving suit on his own initiative…

Some time in 1963, date uncertain but probably early in the year, Desmond FitzGerald, then Chief, SAS, originated a scheme for doing away with Castro by means of an explosives-rigged sea shell. The idea was to take an unusually spectacular sea shell that would be certain to catch Castro's eye, load it with an explosive triggered to blow when it was lifted, and submerge it in an area where Castro often went skin diving.

The Conspirators
Guantánamo, Cuba, January 1963. US Naval Base

Ricardo Lorié was an experienced CIA agent who had commenced his counterrevolutionary activities in 1959, a few months after the triumph of the revolution. He was lucky, as since his initiation he had worked with people specializing in difficult tasks who, with the passing of time, had risen up the CIA ranks. Now he had been selected to work with the New Orleans group that, headed by Higinio Díaz, his former boss, was coordinating the trafficking of arms acquired by the Agency to the anti-Castro forces in Cuba.

They had recently sent him on a special mission to the Guantánamo naval base. His task was to link up with an underground detachment of the MRR operating in Havana under the orders of an unknown individual by the name of Luis David Rodríguez González. Through the influence of David Sánchez Morales and his Miami people, he was received with much deference at the base.

Rodríguez's group presented excellent credentials. According to his information, in June 1962 it had planned to assassinate Fidel Castro in Revolution Plaza with an 82-millimeter mortar located at a distance of 300 meters. The scheduled event in the plaza was suddenly switched to Santiago de Cuba and the plot was averted.

At the end of that year, Rodríguez constituted a "revolutionary unit," enlisting the most important groups in the country — including those operating in the Escambray mountains — which he referred to as the Anticommunist Civic Resistance (RCA). He then sent a communiqué to Miami to inform them of its existence, with the express desire to be kept in mind for any CIA plans. That was why Lorié's chiefs had decided to send him to the base, to wait for Manuel Cuza Portuondo, Rodríguez's envoy.

The meeting took place as soon as Cuza arrived at the base after a hazardous journey through the minefield surrounding the military enclave. A detailed analysis lasting several hours satisfied Lorié's curiosity, particularly in the context of a new plan to assassinate Fidel Castro at an upcoming public event. Afterwards, Cuza explained, they would activate their groups throughout the country and create the conditions for "the Americans" landing their troops to "pacify the island."

The CIA agent committed himself to sending the arms and explosives requested and handed over a hefty sum of US dollars and Cuban money to the "resistance" envoy. When he left, Lorié smiled. He had fulfilled to perfection his instructions, and at the same time, he was in possession of invaluable information: the approximate date of Fidel Castro's death. He could now alert the friends of Trafficante and Carlos Marcello, who would duly pay him for his information. As he saw it, in reality Luis David Rodríguez's only demand was the post of government minister in the cabinet to be formed after the collapse of revolution, and his friends would agree to that.

Havana, January 1963

The meeting took place in a relaxed atmosphere. The location selected lent itself to that: the back room of La Sierra service station, located in the populous Luyanó district of the Cuban capital. The individuals meeting there were giving the final touches to plans to overthrow the revolution in the next few weeks. They were: Luis David Rodríguez, chief of the MRR; Ricardo Olmedo, leader of the Montecristi Group; Juan Morales, representative of the Escambray insurgents; Enrique Rodríguez Valdés, military chief of the MRR; Jorge Espino Escarles, head of the National Liberation Army (ELN); and Samuel Carballo Moreno, a CIA agent recently infiltrated to supervise and coordinate the plans.

Ricardo Olmedo detailed the action proposed to execute Castro:

"Everything is ready. The .44 Magnum rifle, has been hidden in a house in Cotorro by the FUG (United Front of Guanabacoa) people. The plan is to take over an attic in one of the buildings facing the university stairway. We think that D-Day should be March 13, because as everybody knows, that is the date of the commemoration of the deaths of José Antonio Echeverría and the other Presidential Palace assailants. As always, Fidel will be there, undoubtedly he will speak at the event, and that will be the opportune moment to shoot him. Our men will be wearing khaki and when G-2 arrives to see what has happened, it will all be over."

Luis David Rodríguez, who was listening attentively, stated:

"So, that will be the moment to trigger the actions. Each one of you must prepare your men bearing in mind the plan that has been drawn up. What is fundamental is to seize some strategic positions in Havana and the provincial capitals, have the Escambray people cut off the central highway, and ensure that the CIA organizes a good publicity campaign on what is happening in Cuba. That's the pretext that the Americans have asked us for in order to intervene."

Everybody agreed. They were not ignoring the dangers they would face, but with support from the US government, the project should be successful. When the men had left, Olmedo stayed behind to talk with Carballo. He wanted to firm up certain details for the future and thus asked him:

"Carballo, you know that I'm going for the big time. I betrayed Fidel and if we're caught there's no pardon for me. You have contacts with the CIA and Luis David and I have contacts with the former American casino owners. They want the city's most important hotels to be left standing. That's where their interests lie and they want to recoup them. That will be one of my military objectives and I want you to guarantee that, when the Americans arrive, they won't get involved with my affairs."

"Don't worry Ricardo. My chiefs are already informed of this. The basic matter now is to eliminate the man and I'll take charge of the rest. It doesn't even matter if the uprising isn't so large; the basic issue is to have a big shoot-out in Havana in which a good few people die. The scandal's going to be huge. The OAS will intervene and finally it'll be over."

Havana, November 1994. Testimony of Roberto Fernández[1]

A number of operative units worked on this case and I headed one of them. We were responsible for investigating the MRR and had information on the moves of Luis David Rodríguez González, together with Jorge Espino Escarles, to form a new counterrevolutionary unit. They planned an attack on the *Comandante* with an 82-millimeter mortar on July 26 of that year in Revolution Plaza, to be handled by Braulio Roque Arosamena, but the plot was foiled when the venue for the day was switched to Santiago de Cuba.

The constitution of the RCA, made up of the MRR, ELN, Triple A, the Montecristi Group, the Agramonte Resistance, Revolutionary Unity, the FUG, the National Central Council and the Second National Front of the Escambray, was signed on September 15, 1962.

On November 5 of that year, in the midst of the Missile Crisis, Luis David traveled to the Escambray and met with Tomás San Gil, chief of the bandits operating there, obtaining his integration into the counterrevolutionary bloc.

Through Manuel Cuza Portuondo he reestablished contact with the CIA via the US naval base in Guantánamo, and agreed to a plan of action that included an uprising by all the counterrevolutionary groups in Cuba, and Fidel Castro's assassination.

To that end, in line with the plan adopted by the RCA, Ricardo Olmedo's group organized an attempt on the Cuban leader on March 13, 1963, when Fidel was to speak from a platform on the university stairway.

The weapons had been smuggled into Cuba in March via various infiltrations coordinated by Samuel Carballo Moreno, a CIA agent involved in the operation with Luis David and Olmedo.

A number of our agents had penetrated the outfit, and given

---

1.   Roberto Fernández: case officer for the Cuban operation against the RCA.

the imminence of the actions, headquarters decided to operate the case on March 9. The principal conspirators were detained and Luis David was shot after killing *compañero* Orlando López González when the latter attempted to capture him.

Three weapons arsenals were seized. One at 42 Amenidad Street in Havana, another in El Cotorro neighborhood, and the last in a house in San Miguel del Padrón, a Havana district. They included two guns fitted with telescopic sight, one of them a .375 Magnum used in elephant hunts; various M3 submachine guns equipped with silencers; radio equipment; a bazooka with shells; and dozens of other weapons.

Nevertheless, not all the counterrevolutionaries were caught and one group, commanded by Enrique Rodríguez Valdés, activated an alternative plan to assassinate the *comandante-en-jefe* in El Cerro baseball stadium.

The final game in the national baseball series was on April 7, 1963, and the conspirators knew that Fidel would be there. A group of nine men, four of them wearing military uniform and situated in the area where the leader generally sat, would be responsible for throwing hand grenades at him.

The homicide team was composed of Orestes Valero Barzola, Ricardo López Cabrera, Guido Valiente, Esteban Ramos Kessell, Alfredo Farah, Orlando Tacarona, José Cervantes, Honorio Torres Perdomo and Enrique Rodríguez Valdés.

The group was captured before they could execute the attack.

It appeared that the principal counterrevolutionary groups had been neutralized, but a few days later, during the second half of May, one of our agents informed us of the existence of an 82-millimeter mortar that had not been seized in any of the earlier raids.

It turned out there was a highly compartmentalized MRR cell operating in the area of the Monte Street market and headed by Luis Montes de Oca, alias El Campeón [The Champ]. In complicity with Braulio Roque Arosamena, an expert mortar operator trained years earlier in the Dominican Republic, this subject was planning to reactivate the assassination plot of the previous year, firing on the platform of the central event for July 26, which this time was to be held in Revolution Plaza.

The dangerous mortar was seized and all the group members were detained, with the exception of Roque Arosamena, who went into hiding for some months until he was captured the following year. This ended the history of the RCA and an assassination conspiracy in which the CIA and the Mafia combined in a joint effort to murder Fidel Castro on four occasions. This operation also signified the dismantling of one of the last counterrevolutionary blocs directed by the CIA in its plans to defeat the Cuban revolution.

Washington, 1978, US House of Representatives. Report of the House Select Committee

In 1971, Jack Anderson (a US journalist linked to the Mafia media and the CIA) once again published information supporting the revenge theory (that the Kennedy assassination was linked to conspiracies against the Cuban leaders) in two articles dated January 18 and 19. These articles provided further details, noting that before being detained, various criminals had attempted to assassinate the Cuban prime minister from an attic located at a distance that made Castro a perfect target. Anderson stated that this had occurred at the end of February or the beginning of March 1963, that Robert Kennedy had at least tolerated the CIA-Mafia plans, and that John Roselli had dispatched poison capsules to a contact in the Miami Fontainebleau Hotel on March 13, 1961, to be used to assassinate Castro.

9 An "Autonomous Operation"

Mario Salabarría Aguiar was one of the most active chiefs in the National Police during the 1940s while Ramón Grau San Martín[1] was in power. Under his command, the monstrous Group for the Repression of Enemy Activities (GRAE), a police outfit created in the heat of the Cold War, was a key element in President Grau's efforts to annihilate the workers' and revolutionary movements in Cuba. In those years, positions in the police force and other repressive forces became highly sought after among elements of the national Mafia who were disputing the markets for gambling, drugs, contraband goods and prostitution.

In fact, all the gangsters had their territory staked out, but the moment arrived when disputes for new markets began; in particular the necessary public positions that could offer protection. Salabarría, a police commander at the time, was determined to preserve and protect his businesses, and in competition with others of his kind, unleashed a war among the main gangs. This war reached its zenith in an infamous battle in the peaceful neighborhood of Orfila, in Marianao municipality.

The Orfila battle occurred in 1947 and was the result of an attack by Salabarría's group on one of his sworn enemies, Morín Dopico.

---

1. Ramón Grau San Martín: president of Cuba 1944–48.

Dopico was also a police commander, and taking refuge in his home, he put up such strong resistance that the National Army had to intervene to stop the warring parties.

Mario Salabarría was sentenced to a 20-year prison term and only after the revolution was his case reviewed by the courts. He was given parole on account of the time he had served and his good conduct in prison, as prescribed by law.

After leaving prison, Salabarría tried to reinitiate his gangster activities; however, he found himself in an unfamiliar Cuba. Almost all of his old friends had emigrated to the United States and the new Cuban regime had cleared the public institutions of corrupt individuals, gangsters and embezzlers, cut the drug trafficking routes, and closed down the casinos and brothels. He found himself alone and then concluded that the only way open to him was to conspire against the revolution that had given him his freedom.

Operation Rafael
Havana, May 1963

His battle against the revolution was what led Mario Salabarría to agree to meet Alberto Cruz, chief of the Rescate group, whom he knew from his days as a member of Congress in the Ramón Grau San Martín government.

Alberto Cruz had heard of the gangster's situation and had in-depth knowledge of his history as a hired killer and his lack of scruples. Thus, when the demands from CIA headquarters to find a way to assassinate Fidel Castro were stepped up, he thought of Salabarría.

He met with his closest people, including Polita Grau and her brother Ramón, and everyone agreed to offer the killer a large sum of money to carry out the job. So they summoned him that May afternoon to the Graus' old mansion on Fifth Avenue and 14th Street in Miramar district.

They got down to business. Both men were used to dealing with the most delicate subjects in a direct way and without unnecessary circumlocutions.

"Mario, you know that I've been against this government from the start," Cruz stated. "Tony Varona is our leader and representative in exile. The organization has worked hard in the last few years against Castro's regime, but it's getting harder and harder to bring together all the forces to combat the communists. G-2 and the CDRs are making life impossible for us. Recently an envoy from Varona informed us that the CIA was going to take over directing our group and work has been done on a new project to bring down the government. The idea is simple: liquidate Castro and then, using the people we still have within the government, try to take control of it, and if that proves impossible, organize an uprising of all the underground groups in the country. The Americans have assured us that they will intervene with the navy, if we provide them with an internationally acceptable motive. They've guaranteed there will be no repeat of the Bay of Pigs. So we thought of you. What do you think?"

Mario Salabarría understood what was being asked of him. It had come up a few days earlier in a conversation with Polita Grau. He had nothing to lose, he reasoned. If the plan was successful, Tony Varona and his boss, Carlos Prío, would remember him and he might even become the next chief of the Cuban police. So he responded without hesitation:

"Alberto, you can count on me for anything. I'll need some cash and a rifle with a telescopic sight, if possible fitted with a silencer. I'll take care of the rest."

The two men made a deal. Alberto Cruz would give Salabarría a few thousand pesos and would ask CIA headquarters for the weapon with the requested specifications.

Miami, May 1963. JM/WAVE Base

David Sánchez Morales was in his new office in the buildings occupied by JM/WAVE, located on land adjoining the University of Miami. He had been made chief of special operations on Cuban territory and the major subversive plans were his responsibility. "El Indio," as everyone called him, was aspiring to destroy the Havana regime through a direct, unrelenting war, taking advantage of the thousands of exiles under his orders and the vast resources at his disposal in that emporium of terrorism, espionage and subversion.

However, the task was not an easy one. It was becoming steadily clearer that the administration's policy was leaning towards pressure and containment and that they were only being utilized for the former, through the approval of selective sabotage. He had thought that after the Missile Crisis the Kennedy brothers might acknowledge the existence of a communist state in the Caribbean as a definite fact. But it seemed that if Castro was to distance himself from the Russians, the White House intellectuals would probably be prepared to pardon Cuba and seek a rapprochement.

In addition, the new SAS chief, Desmond FitzGerald, who had very good relations with the attorney general, wanted to control everything and was starting to subject every plan to his approval, which meant that Morales had to constantly appeal to Tracy Barnes, head of the Domestic Operations Division, to help him. There was no doubt, he reflected, that the bureaucracy would end up diluting the effectiveness of the war, thus endangering the authority and prestige of the United States.

That was one of the reasons why Morales decided to take some of his own initiatives. He secretly met with John Roselli and Santos Trafficante, Mafia leaders from Chicago and Florida. They had been the Agency's "fellow travelers" in various adventures against Cuba and were individuals that could be counted on for an undertaking that would not appear in the CIA annals. According to rumors running through the Agency, the president was highly grateful to Sam Giancana, the godfather of La Cosa Nostra, on account of Giancana's contribution to the campaign that took him to the White House. "If they're good enough for the president, why not us?" he reasoned.

One of the actions that Morales had recently taken at the request of the mafiosi was the creation of a new "political front," which would sideline the CRC headed by José Miró Cardona. The CRC had been discredited after the fiasco of the Bay of Pigs when Miró had prematurely claimed victory. Now — using Mafia money — Morales had set up the Junta of the Cuban Government in Exile (JGCE), presided over by Carlos Prío and controlled by an obscure junior gangster called Paulino Sierra. Those two were soon joined by the most combative exile leaders, including Orlando Bosch, Antonio Veciana and Manuel Artime.

It was a classic autonomous operation. The objectives were fixed, the resources handed over, and they would come up with the goods. When the results became public, the Agency would not be implicated in any way.

However, the Mafia did not want to run unnecessary risks and made its help conditional on the direct participation of one of its captains, John Roselli, who was installed in one of the training camps in the Florida base with his associates. They were discreet and efficient people who could be counted on at the right moment.

That moment soon presented itself. Through one of his agents, Norberto Martínez Díaz, who had recently arrived from the island, Morales heard of the plans of the Rescate group, headed by Alberto Cruz, including an attempt on the life of Fidel via a hired killer. He quickly got in touch with Roselli and Prío, who were interested in the plan and decided to back it.

Everything had to be properly covered. Nobody could suspect that the CIA or any other US government agency was backing the conspiracy. Thus a meeting was organized on a small tourist island in the Bahamas called Bimini, which John Roselli would attend.

The JGCE leaders would be waiting for him there and it would be an agreement between them, although various case officers would supervise all the details of the operation.

When the meeting was fixed, Morales phoned the Luces, owners of *Time* and *Life* magazines, and former ambassador William Pawley, who were all involved in the anti-Cuba crusade, and informed them of the details of the plan. They would spur the mass media into a huge campaign to discredit Kennedy's policy toward Cuba, and would use their influence in the Republican Party to support the new organization of Cuban exiles as a viable structure for the next government in Cuba when Castro was defeated.

Bimini Island, Bahamas. May 1963

Robert Plumlee, an experienced CIA pilot, landed his light aircraft on the runway of the little airport serving Bimini Island, in the vicinity of southern Florida. On board was Carlos Prío, the former president of Cuba (1948–52), who was the last of the characters to arrive in that holiday paradise. John Roselli, the Mafia capo; William Carr, aide to Colonel J.C. King; and case officer Robert (Bob) Rogers had preceded him.

These men were there for an important meeting with only one item on the agenda: the assassination of Cuban Prime Minister Fidel Castro. When everyone was settled on one of the sunny and deserted terraces of the hotel where they were staying, Carlos Prío spoke:

"We have received important news from Havana. One of our underground groups, also operating under the orders of our friends in the CIA, has found the opportunity and the personnel to eliminate Castro. As a result of earlier failures, our Agency friends proposed this meeting to coordinate the details of the operation with the participation of the interested parties."

Thus he explained the information available to him and why Alberto Cruz's group had not used normal CIA channels to transmit the message. They wanted only the "upper echelons" of the Agency and the people fundamental to the operation to be in-the-know. G-2 had many agents in Miami and that was one of the factors that had led to the discovery of earlier plots, so secrecy was essential.

"We need to remember certain things," William Carr stated. "It is vital that the CIA or any other US agency should not appear to have any involvement in this matter. Acting on our behalf, our friend Roselli will have the resources required to execute the operation."

"That's correct," Roselli replied. "We have the human resources that can give Mr. Cruz what he needs."

"In this way we can decentralize the operation," interjected the case officer, "some providing the action and others handing over resources and acting as backup. It's an innovative way of avoiding penetration and information leaks. I propose that we give this operation the codename Rafael."

The sinister meeting concluded with whiskeys and coconuts filled with rum.

Havana, Early July 1963

The supply tasks were successfully completed. The M1 rifle with a telescopic sight was smuggled in through the Spanish diplomatic bag, and the money for the assassination was brought in by CIA agent Arturo Varona Hernández, who handed over 10,000 pesos, two 9-millimeter pistols fitted with silencers, two .375 Magnum revolvers and two portable radio transmitters to Mario Salabarría.

From that moment, acting alone, Salabarría began to set in motion the plan he had carefully drawn up. When he agreed to take on the operation, he thought of using the flat roof of the National Library for the attack. Later, when it became a solid proposition, he visited the place and found that it wasn't difficult to gain access to the roof, which overlooked the whole of Revolution Plaza, and confirmed that he could position himself there in order to fire on his victim during one of the regular mass rallies in the square. There was always the inconvenience of having to neutralize the security guard, but that was something that could be overcome.

When everything was ready, in line with the instructions he had received, he asked for a meeting with Arturo Varona to inform him of the details. They agreed to meet in the Havana Amphitheater at the entrance to the capital's bay. Some children were playing with a brightly colored ball while their mothers, keeping them in sight, strolled along a pathway lined with beautiful flowers. There, in the afternoon sun, the two conspirators talked animatedly:

"I think that the best day to execute the plan is July 26, when there will be a celebration in the plaza. I've got everything worked out. I'll park the car close by the library the day before. Then, I'll go up to the roof, as I've done on various occasions, and hide there until the next day. When the security guard arrives I can neutralize him using the pistol with the silencer and I'll have enough time to aim at our man and liquidate him. What do you think?"

"Fine," Varona replied. "There's only one thing that worries me; how are you going to escape after the shooting? Don't you need backup?"

"No, it's better to do things alone," the other man answered. "When the shooting happens there'll be tremendous confusion. Nobody will guess where it came from, as the weapon is pretty quiet. I already tested it and it hardly made a sound. There will be all the racket of the people marching and rousing speeches from the platform. When security reacts, I'll be far away!"

Havana, August 1965. DSE Headquarters

Our investigations have revealed the following:

From mid-1963 to date, through its agents in Cuba, the CIA has attempted to assassinate our Prime Minister Fidel Castro on four occasions. The aforementioned CIA agents participating to a greater or lesser degree in this plot were: Mario Salabarría Aguiar, Alberto Cruz Caso, María Leopoldina and Ramón Grau Alsina, Miguel Matamoros Valle, Arturo Varona Hernández, Rafael Quintana Castellanos, Bernardo Milanés López, Roberto Caíñas Milanés, Eduardo Llanes García, Roberto Sabater Cepero, Pedro Fuentes Milián, Mercedes de la Paz, Joel Trujillo, Antonio Fernández Rodríguez, Magalys Reyes Gil, Enrique Díaz Hernández, Juan Soto Rodríguez, Félix Rodolfo Valdés Cabrera. Also involved were Antonio de Varona Loredo, Carlos Prío Socarrás, Joaquín Sanjenís and Julio Salabarría Aguiar, all Cubans resident in the United States, and two CIA officers known as Henry and Bill.

The four plots referred to were to be executed at:

- Revolution Plaza, at the 1963 commemoration of July 26, when the conspirators planned to fire on our prime minister Fidel Castro from the roof of the National Library, an action neutralized by security measures which prevented detainee Mario Salabarría's access to the building selected.

- The Potín restaurant on Línea and Paseo in Vedado, where the conspirators planned to fire on *Comandante* Fidel Castro during one of his occasional visits.

- Between Línea and 23rd Street on Paseo Avenue, where the conspirators planned a three-car ambush to cut off the vehicle in which Fidel was traveling and fire on it with submachine guns.

- A Fifth Avenue intersection in Miramar, where an ambush was planned utilizing a telephone company truck with a .30-caliber machine gun in the back to fire on Fidel's car.

Three CIA subversive networks participated in the execution of the conspiracy described: the one headed by Alberto Cruz Caso; the one led by Arturo Varona Hernández; and the one organized by Dr. Bernardo Milanés López.

The CIA, which planned the project from the outset, periodically exerted control over it. Thus, after Arturo Varona fled to the United States, it recruited Dr. Milanés López in Madrid to act as backup for Operation Rafael, because it needed a man close to Mario Salabarría Aguiar who could exercise effective influence over him. To that same end, in January 1964 CIA agent Joaquín Sanjenís and the US officers known as Henry and Bill gave instructions and provided the means of communication to retain control of the operation, reiterating to Salabarría the order to assassinate *Comandante* Fidel Castro.

In various searches related to the detainees the following weapons were seized: an M1 carbine, four .375 Magnum revolvers, two 9-millimeter pistols fitted with silencers, two portable radio transmitters and a number of bullets...

10   AM/LASH

Immersed in a voluminous file, Desmond FitzGerald was still in his Langley office a little after 9:00 p.m. Working late had become a habit since he took command of Cuban affairs, and that day he was deeply preoccupied at losing an operative codenamed AM/LASH, the Agency's most important man in Cuba for the last two years.

The previous day he had received an urgent message from agent AM/WHIP, a former jeweler of Italian descent who had lived in Havana until the revolution came to power. He explained that AM/LASH was currently in Porto Alegre, Brazil, and that he planned to travel to Paris and defect from Cuba.

AM/LASH was one of FitzGerald's main cards against the Havana government: a *comandante* in the Rebel Army, a student leader and former government minister, with access to the top revolutionary leadership.

FitzGerald meditated on his man's history and searched among the files on his desk until he found the one he wanted. With a label stating "FitzGerald Only," the dossier contained all the information on the case that was occupying his thoughts. He opened it and began to read one of the documents:

> In 1953 he became friends with AM/WHIP, when the latter was the proprietor of La Diadema jewelers on a main commercial street in the Cuban capital. At that time he was involved in activities against the Fulgencio Batista government, and he participated in 1956 in the

assassination of Colonel Antonio Blanco Rico, head of the Military Intelligence Service (SIM).

In early 1957 the FBI located him in Miami, in the Trade Winds Hotel belonging to José Alemán,[1] a close friend and also a Bureau informant. There he reestablished relations with AM/WHIP and it was through these sources that tabs were kept on the revolutionary activities of AM/LASH and his group.

In early 1958 AM/LASH returned to Cuba with a revolutionary expedition that set up a base in the Escambray mountains, where they commenced guerrilla activities, linking up with Che Guevara's troops at the end of the campaign against Batista.

A few months after Castro's victory, AM/LASH suffered a depressive illness. According to him, he was pursued by the ghost of murdered Colonel Blanco Rico, and José Alemán, who was in Cuba, found a psychiatrist to help him recover.

In April 1959 information was received from an agent close to AM/LASH, who had told him that he had talked with Fidel Castro and explained his displeasure with the situation in Cuba. According to the agent, AM/LASH told him that he was so fed up that if he didn't leave the country soon, he'd kill Castro himself. Around that time he traveled to Europe and made contact with AM/WHIP who, in conjunction with another agent and with the intention of recruiting him, detailed an international communist plot to take over Cuba.

In June of that year AM/LASH took over the post of deputy government minister, which he used to help Santos Trafficante — detained in a camp for undesirable foreigners — to attend his daughter's birthday celebrations, and subsequently collaborated in the latter's release.

In October 1959 he was elected president of the Federation of University Students (FEU) and in that position traveled to a student congress in Mexico in early 1961.

In Mexico he made contact with AM/WHIP, who traveled to that city with a case officer to complete AM/LASH's recruitment process.

---

1. José Braulio Alemán Gutiérrez: son of José Alemán, ex-minister of education in the Ramón Grau government who embezzled $20 million from his institution at the end of his term and established himself in Miami.

After various conversations between AM/WHIP, the case officer and AM/LASH, it was decided that the latter could support the action planned by Juan Orta Córdova,[2] whom he knew from Havana and who had received some poison capsules from the Agency to eliminate Fidel Castro. The details of the plan were not revealed, but he was directed to get in contact with Orta, from whom he would receive instructions at the appropriate moment. The idea was that with his authority within the government AM/LASH could assume control after Castro was gone.

In the case of failure, or of AM/LASH being unable to impose himself on the communists, the idea was to get him and Orta out of the country. Initially the operation was scheduled for the last days of March 1961, prior to the Assault Brigade 2506 invasion.

The elimination plot collapsed when Orta took refuge in a Latin American embassy, and the exfiltration did not take place. In mid-1962, AM/LASH traveled to Helsinki as part of a Cuban delegation attending the World Festival of Youth and Students, an event organized by the Russians, where he was contacted and his recruitment consolidated, with AM/LASH agreeing to undertake the intelligence tasks agreed…"[3]

Desmond FitzGerald closed the file without reading it in full. To date, nothing had happened. It was true that the 1962 Missile Crisis had resulted in unforeseen consequences for Fidel Castro's enemies. Many people had thought that the United States would attack the island and finally overthrow the Havana regime. However, none of that occurred and the latest government measures to restrict the activities of the counterrevolution in Cuba had discouraged many people, who had come to the conclusion that there was no solution to the Cuban problem.

FitzGerald got up from his chair and paced around the room. The case still looked promising, as AM/LASH continued to be an important figure in the Cuban government. According to the files, it seemed that his predecessors had treated AM/LASH very superficially. Perhaps he should meet with him personally,

---

2.   Juan Orta Córdova: secretary of the prime minister's office in 1959.
3.   Excerpts from the 1967 report of the CIA inspector general.

FitzGerald reflected. The plan to eliminate Castro and stage a military coup attracted him.

Returning to his desk, he pulled out the note with the information on AM/WHIP and wrote: "Have our man contact him in Paris and sound out his state of mind. We need AM/LASH to be available for the upcoming operation we are preparing."

Langley, May 1967, CIA Headquarters.
Report of the CIA Inspector General

5–8 September 1963. Cubela attended the Collegiate Games in Porto Alegre, Brazil, as a representative of the Cuban government. He was met there by [Censored][4] and [Censored]. Also participating was [Censored], a Spanish-speaking case officer from headquarters, who thereafter acted as case officer for Cubela…

Cubela discussed a group of Cuban military officers known to him, and possible ways of approaching them. The problem was, he explained, that although many of them were anticommunist they were either loyal to Fidel or were so afraid of him that they were reluctant to discuss any conspiracies for fear they might be provocations. Cubela said that he thought highly of [Censored] [AM/TRUNK], who was hiding [Censored]. [Censored] had been sent to Cuba by the CIA to recruit [Censored] in place, and had done so.

16 September 1963. Cubela (in Paris) wrote to [Censored] (in New York): "I don't intend to see (be interviewed by) your friend again," which you should tell them, "so they don't make the trip. I want get away from politics completely…"

3 October 1963. [Censored] arrived in Paris for meetings with Cubela.

---

4.   [Censored] indicates where data was deleted from the report.

11 October 1963. [Censored] cabled that Cubela was insistent upon meeting with a senior US official, preferably Robert F. Kennedy, for assurances of US moral support for any activity that Cubela under took in Cuba.

17 October 1963. [Censored] cabled the results of a meeting with Cubela and [Censored]. Cubela, in a private conversation with [Censored], reiterated his desire to speak with a high-level US government official. [Censored] said that basically Cubela wanted assurances that the US government would support him if his enterprise was successful.

29 October 1963. Desmond FitzGerald, then Chief, SAS, who was going to Paris on other business, arranged to meet with Cubela to give him the assurances he sought.

The contact plan for the meeting has this to say on cover: "Fitzgerald will represent self as personal representative of Robert F. Kennedy who traveled Paris for specific purpose meeting Cubela and giving him assurances of full US support if there is change of the present government in Cuba." According to Fitzgerald, he discussed the planned meeting with the DD/P (Helms) who decided it was not necessary to seek approval from Robert Kennedy for FitzGerald to speak in his name.

The meeting was held in [Censored]'s house in Paris on 29 October 1963. FitzGerald used the alias [Censored]. [Censored] acted as interpreter. [Censored] was not present during the meeting. [Censored] on 13 November 1963 wrote a memorandum for the record of the meeting. It reads, in part: "FitzGerald informed Cubela that the United States is prepared to render all necessary assistance to any anticommunist Cuban group which succeeds in neutralizing the present Cuban leadership and assumes sufficient control to invite the United States to render the assistance it is prepared to give. It was emphasized that the above support will be forthcoming only after a real coup has been effected and the group involved is in a position to request US (probably under OAS auspices) recognition and support. It was made clear that the US was not prepared to commit itself to supporting an isolated uprising, as such an uprising can be extinguished in a matter of hours if the present government is still in control of Havana. As for the post-coup period, the US does not desire that the political clock be turned back but will support the necessary economic and political reforms which will benefit the mass of the Cuban people."

FitzGerald recalls that Cubela spoke repeatedly of the need for an assassination weapon. In particular, he wanted a high-powered rifle with telescopic sights or some other weapon that could be used to kill Castro from a distance. FitzGerald wanted no part of such a scheme and told [Censored] to tell Cubela that the US simply does not do such things… FitzGerald says that when he met with Cubela in Paris he told Cubela that the US government would have no part of an attempt on Castro's life.

14 November 1963 [Censored] met with [Censored] in New York City on 14 November. [Censored]'s contact report reveals Cubela's reaction (as told to [Censored]) to his meeting with FitzGerald.

> The visit with FitzGerald, who acted in the capacity of a representative of high levels of the government concerned with the Cuban problem satisfied Cubela as far as policy was concerned, but he was not at all happy with the fact that he still was not given the technical assistance for the operational plan as he saw it. [Censored] said that Cubela dwelt constantly on this point. He could not understand why he was denied certain small pieces of equipment which promised a final solution to the problem, while, on the other hand, the US government gave much equipment and money to exile groups for their ineffective excursions against Cuban coastal targets. According to [Censored] Cubela feels strongly on this point, and if he does not get advice and materials from a US government technician, he will probably become fed up again, and we will lose whatever progress we have made to date.

19 November 1963. Memorandum for the record prepared by [Censored]: C/SAS (FitzGerald) approved telling Cubela he would be given a cache inside Cuba. Cache could, if he requested it, include… high-power rifles w/scopes… C/SAS requested written

reports on AM/LASH operation be kept to a minimum.

20 November 1963. Samuel Halpern and [Censored] approached Dr. Gunn for assistance... What they settled upon was Black Leaf 40, a common, easily obtainable insecticide containing about 40 percent nicotine sulfate. Nicotine is a deadly poison that may be administered orally, by injection, or by absorption through the skin...

The plan reached the action stage when Halpern and [Censored] contacted Gunn again on the morning of 20 November 1963 and told him that the device for administering the poison (a ballpoint pen rigged as a hypodermic syringe) had to be ready in time for [Censored] to catch a plane at noon the next day... He succeeded in converting a Paper-Mate pen into a hypodermic syringe that worked. He said that the needle was so fine that the victim would hardly feel it when it was inserted — he compared it with the scratch from a shirt with too much starch. He delivered the workable device to [Censored] the following morning and retained two of the later prototypes.

22 November 1963. [Censored] arrived in Paris in the morning of 22 November and met with Cubela late that afternoon. [Censored] states that he showed the pen/syringe to Cubela and explained how it worked. He is not sure, but he believes that Cubela accepted the device but said that he would not take it to Cuba with him... Cubela said that, as a doctor, he knew all about Black Leaf 40 and that we surely could come up with something more sophisticated than that...

[Censored] reiterated the assurances given Cubela by FitzGerald of full US support if a real coup against the Castro regime were successful. Cubela asked for the following items to be included in a cache inside Cuba: 20 hand grenades, two high-powered rifles with telescopic sights, and approximately 20 pounds of C-4 explosive and related equipment. Cubela suggested the best place for the cache was on the *finca* (farm) managed by his friend, [Censored]... As they were coming out of the meeting, [Censored] and Cubela were informed that President Kennedy had been assassinated. Cubela was visibly moved over the news... The contact report does not state the time nor the duration of the [Censored]-Cubela meeting, but it is likely that at the very moment President Kennedy was shot a CIA officer was meeting with a Cuban agent in Paris and giving him an assassination device for use against Castro.

[Censored] states that he received an OPIM cable from FitzGerald that night or early the next morning telling him that everything was off. We do not find such a cable in the AM/LASH file. There is a record in the file that [Censored] was due to arrive back in Washington at 1810 hours, 23 November.

1 December 1963. FBIS [Foreign Broadcast Information Service] reported that Cubela returned to Cuba from Prague.

Washington, November 1975, US Senate.
Report of the Church Commission

CIA cables indicate that one cache of arms for AM/LASH was delivered in Cuba in March 1964 and another in June. An entry in the AM/LASH file for May 5, 1964, states that the case officer requested the Technical Services Division to produce, on a "crash basis," a silencer which would fit an FAL rifle...

Documents in the AM/LASH file establish that in early 1965, the CIA put AM/LASH in contact with B-1, the leader of an anti-Castro group. As the case officer explained to the CIA inspector general: "What had happened was that SAS had contrived to put B-1 and AM/LASH together in such a way that neither of them knew that the contact had been engineered by CIA. The thought was that B-1 needed a man inside and AM/LASH wanted a silenced weapon, which CIA was unwilling to furnish to him directly. By putting the two together, B-1 might get its man inside Cuba and AM/LASH might get his silenced weapon — from B-1."

A CIA document dated January 3, 1965, states that B-1, in a

lengthy interview with a case officer, said that he and AM/LASH had reached firm agreement on the following points:

1. B-1 is to provide AM/LASH with a silencer for the FAL; if this is impossible, B-1 is to cache in a designated location a rifle with a scope and silencer plus several bombs, concealed either in a suitcase, a lamp or some other concealment device which he would be able to carry, and place next to Fidel Castro.

2. B-1 is to provide AM/LASH with escape routes controlled by B-1 and not the Americans. The lack of confidence built up by the Bay of Pigs looms large.

3. B-1 is to prepare one of the western provinces, either Pinar del Río or Havana, with arms caches and a clandestine underground mechanism. This would be a fall back position and a safe area where men and weapons are available to the group.

4. B-1 is to be in Cuba one week before the elimination of Fidel, but no one, including AM/LASH, will know B-1's location.

5. B-1 is to arrange for recognition by at least five Latin American countries as soon as Fidel is neutralized and a junta is formed. This junta will be established even though Raúl Castro and Che Guevara may still be alive and may still be in control of part of the country. This is the reason AM/LASH requested that B-1 be able to establish some control over one of the provinces so that the junta can be formed in that location.

6. One month to the day before the neutralization of Fidel, B-1 will increase the number of commando attacks to a maximum in order to raise the spirit and morale of the people inside Cuba. In all communiqués, in all radio messages, in all propaganda put out by B-1 he must relate that the raid was possible thanks to the information received from clandestine sources inside Cuba and from the clandestine underground apparatus directed by "P." This will be AM/LASH's war name...

The Conspirator
Havana, November 1979. DSE Headquarters

Rolando Cubela Secades was born in 1932 in Cienfuegos; later he moved to Cárdenas in Matanzas province where he began his studies. On completing them he entered the University of Havana, where he played an active part in the struggle against the Batista dictatorship and became military chief of the Revolutionary Student Directorate (DRE), being detained on a number of occasions for activities related to that movement.

At the end of 1956, after participating in the execution of Blanco Rico, the dictatorship's Military Intelligence chief, he went into exile in Miami, taking refuge in the motel run by José Alemán, a friend from Havana who had become an FBI agent and who would have a key influence on his future conduct.

At the beginning of 1958 he returned to Cuba on an expedition to promote an uprising in the Escambray mountains, fighting there until the revolutionary triumph in 1959. He was promoted on account of his conduct to the rank of *comandante* of the Rebel Army.

In 1959 he was made deputy secretary of government and later, in October, he was elected president of the FEU after defeating his opponent, a right-wing candidate, in a hard-fought election.

Reckless and licentious behavior characterized his life that year. He constantly frequented bars and nightclubs, spending time with friends who began to criticize the revolutionary government's measures.

Cubela expressed his disagreement with the direction in which the revolution was going within that circle, verbally attacking Fidel Castro for being, in his view, the main protagonist of the country's misguided sociopolitical development.

Cubela was a voluble, unstable and ambitious man with a false concept of friendship that prevented him from seeing the defects of the people around him. Also inconsistent in his political ideas, which varied according to his emotional state, he turned against the revolution and its leaders.

His conduct and personal characteristics were known, but because of his revolutionary history he was not perceived as a danger and was able to act with relative impunity for several years, until in 1965 information was received corroborating his involvement in conspiratorial activities. An investigation was initiated that uncovered part of the plot, for which he was sanctioned the following year.

The information that activated our investigation came from Paris: on April 9, 1965, it was communicated by a reliable source that Rolando Cubela was conspiring against the revolution. It emerged that he was handling large sums of money, frequenting nightclubs and luxury restaurants, and had made a number of trips to Paris, Madrid and Switzerland, where he was constantly visited by Jorge Robreño and Carlos Tepedino, two CIA agents. The source insisted that Cubela was involved in a conspiracy to assassinate Fidel Castro.

Subsequently, the activities of Cubela and his close friends were monitored for nearly one year. It was established that he was in contact with Cuban exile groups in the United States, France and Spain, and it also emerged that this contact was linked to a CIA plan to assassinate Fidel Castro and defeat the revolutionary government in Cuba.

All the information at that time was related to the basic aspects of the plot reorganized by the CIA at the end of 1964, when a meeting was arranged in Madrid between Cubela and its agent B-1 — none other than Manuel Artime Buesa, head of a mercenary brigade being trained in Nicaragua to instigate a military coup once the Cuban leader was assassinated.

It was necessary to reconstruct the entire plot from its beginning in order to unravel the conspiracy. In the light of information declassified in the United States, the puzzle was gradually put together and we discovered a large volume of material in our files that had previously been unclear, or had not been seen as linked to the Cubela case up until that point.

In August 1960, during a visit to Switzerland, Cubela met with CIA agent Carlos Tepedino, an old friend from Havana, who invited him to spend a few days in Rome. On that occasion, while they were lunching in a restaurant, another acquaintance of Cubela's showed up — also a CIA agent — and gave him a detailed explanation of the communist penetration in Latin America and the related dangers for Cuba in that context.

At the beginning of 1961, Cubela visited Mexico to participate in a solidarity event. From there he got in touch with Tepedino again, and the latter turned up accompanied by a US officer, described by Tepedino as an expert on communism. The objective was to recruit Cubela, and there is evidence as to his possible participation in a conspiracy organized by the CIA and the Mafia to assassinate Fidel Castro prior to the Bay of Pigs invasion.

In March 1961, Rolando Cubela and Juan Orta decided to defect and requested help. CIA headquarters agreed to prepare an exfiltration operation for both of them, which was subsequently suspended because information reached them that G-2 was aware of it.

As head of the prime minister's office, Juan Orta was the person proposed by the Mafia to poison Fidel with capsules sent by the CIA.

Orta and Cubela knew each other from at least 1959 and both of them had been in contact with Santos Trafficante, the Mafia delegate in Cuba up until that year.

By that date Cubela was a recruited agent or one "in the process of being recruited" by the CIA: he had already affirmed his disposition to eliminate Fidel, which was known to the CIA; he had an important position within the revolutionary government; he was a commander of the army; and he was at the center of a group of resentful people prepared to follow him in any adventure against the Cuban regime.

Shortly after Cubela's return from Mexico — from March 20 to mid-May — he regularly visited Casablanca on the banks of the bay of Havana, even staying overnight on occasion in a boathouse there. Information given by different people on the movements of Cubela and persons in his company aroused suspicions that he was planning an illegal exit by sea.

After making some repairs, he left a vessel there, which according to one of the visitors "could get him to Florida in four hours." Concealed on board were various weapons, including Garand rifles. The people who frequented the place had long conversations with Cubela, who also received telephone calls from different provinces, particularly Las Villas. Cubela looked nervous, agitated, "as if he was waiting for something," according to one of the sources.

Finally, another unconfirmed piece of information from that time notes that on March 28 counterrevolutionary Margarito Espinosa, a fugitive from justice, stated that "Cubela was one of the men he was counting on to overthrow Fidel."

The interest in exfiltrating Orta and Cubela at the end of March 1961 could have been related to the assassination plot concocted by the CIA and the Mafia to decapitate the revolution before the mercenary invasion. They probably realized that Cuban State Security was aware of their plans, because the exfiltration was aborted and Orta took refuge in a Latin American embassy.

Then it became clear that the only reasonable motive for getting Cubela out of Cuba had to be his involvement in something very important that would make his exfiltration worthwhile right after his return from Mexico. Only a conspiracy that placed him in imminent danger could have warranted a plan of that nature.

On September 8, 1962, Cubela traveled to Paris where he stayed for one week, meeting with Carlos Tepedino who, as always, offered his protégé a well-earned vacation with all expenses paid.

A few weeks after returning to Cuba, Cubela visited a mountainous area in the Escambray region of Las Villas province with a group of 20 men. He stayed there for two or three days and then left, leaving behind his entourage, whose members remained in the area for two weeks without incident, despite the fact that it was frequented by insurgent bands.

That was not the only time that Cubela had visited the region, which was the former theater of his guerrilla actions, where he enjoyed a degree of support from the campesino community.

In mid-June of that year Cubela left Cuba for Helsinki to attend the World Festival of Youth and Students. Shortly before his departure, Cubela sent a message to Tepedino arranging to meet up with him in Europe.

On July 30 Cubela met with Tepedino and his case officer in Helsinki and informed them that he intended to defect. The officer persuaded him to return to Cuba to direct a US-backed plot to overthrow the Cuban government.

However, a semantic error by the recruiter almost led to the collapse of the undertaking. When he proposed the "assassination" of Fidel Castro, Cubela rejected the idea. He was not opposed to the act itself, but the choice of the word. For discussion purposes, "eliminate" was a more acceptable expression.

There were further meetings in the following days, held in Copenhagen and Stockholm to conceal Cubela's relationship with the CIA from the other members of the Cuban delegation, who remained in Helsinki. During that period, a plot was agreed to that included various sabotage operations against strategic objectives in Cuba as well as the assassination of veteran communist leader Carlos Rafael Rodríguez, the Soviet ambassador, and "Fidel and Raúl, if necessary."

Cubela stayed in Paris with Tepedino from August 14 to August 23, 1962, in order to receive training in various fields, including two of supreme importance: secret writing techniques and demolition.

New talks on the assassination of Fidel took place between Cubela and his case officer and the officer reported, as quoted by the CIA general inspector: "Have no intention give Cubela physical elimination mission as requirement but recognize this something he could or might try to carry out on his own initiative." Cubela remained in Paris until August 29, 1962, when he returned to Havana.

A few weeks later Cubela went to the Dos Arroyos area of the Escambray and visited the city of Placetas in the foothills of the mountains. There he met with various campesinos, former collaborators with his guerrilla force.

In October 1962 he left the Rebel Army. After his detention he said of that period: "I was beginning to feel unstable again and tried to seek refuge by traveling abroad, as I had done on previous occasions. But this time my intention was more definite as I was thinking of remaining in France."

In 1963 he began to work as a doctor in the Comandante Manuel Fajardo Hospital in Havana, and in August, as he had planned, he prepared a journey to Brazil which he viewed as a permanent departure.

He had been invited to the University Games in Porto Alegre in Brazil and there he made contact with Tepedino, to whom he voiced his desire to emigrate and establish himself in France. Some days later he was visited by "a Spanish-speaking case officer" who tried to persuade him to continue within the conspiracy. He failed to bring Cubela around, but they agreed to another meeting in Paris for a more detailed review of the matter.

While Cubela was in Brazil in September 1963, JM/WAVE was executing an important operation in Cuba under the codename AM/TRUNK. It consisted of recruiting various officers from the Rebel Army that the CIA believed it could hook. Among them was ex-commander Ramón Guín Díaz, one of Cubela's closest friends, who would subsequently be an active participant in the CIA plans to assassinate the Cuban prime minister.

That same September José Luis González Gallarreta arrived in Madrid as a diplomatic attaché. A few weeks later, he was recruited by James Noel, head of the Madrid CIA station. Gallarreta, who came from a bourgeois Cuban family that owned a liquor import company, was one of Cubela's men, who had studied in the United States and then at the University of Havana, where he had linked up with Cubela.

According to Cubela's statement, when he arrived in Paris in September 1963 he met with Tepedino — who was waiting for him — and reiterated his idea of remaining in France, but the latter convinced him to talk with a "second Spanish-speaking officer, because if he wanted to enter and live in the United States, that person could help him."

This new "Spanish-speaking officer," subsequently identified by Cuban security as David Sánchez Morales, was then second in command of JM/WAVE, the largest CIA operative base in the world. He was also David Phillips's officer when the former was working as an undercover agent in Havana at the end of the 1950s.

According to his statement, on that occasion Cubela insisted that he was not prepared to waste his time on uncertain future projects, and that if he was to continue in an operation of that nature he needed backing at the highest level from the United States. He proposed a meeting with Robert Kennedy, the brother of the US president.

Morales traveled to Washington to consult and there Richard Helms, deputy director of the CIA, decided that Desmond FitzGerald, chief of the SAS, should meet with Cubela using the cover of a US senator representing Robert Kennedy, and offer him the guarantees he wanted. On October 29, FitzGerald, Morales and the first Spanish-speaking officer[5] attending the case met with Cubela in Paris and discussed the future with him. The conspirator was flattered and satisfied by the guarantees offered and finally agreed to get involved in the conspiracy again.

---

5.   Possibly Néstor Sánchez, who is quoted in the CIA inspector general's report. When Cubela identified David Sánchez Morales in his statement, he explained that another Spanish-speaking officer attended him who he thought was Puerto Rican.

The plan had two parts: the first, the assassination of Fidel, and the second, a coup d'état instigated by Cubela's collaborators, backed by a US mini-invasion conducted with a brigade of Cuban mercenaries who were training in Nicaragua under the command of Manuel Artime.

Cubela insisted on the need for resources to effect the plan. He wanted a telescopic sight and a silencer (for a FAL rifle that he owned) deposited in Cuba, as well as other weapons and money. Finally they made a deal and FitzGerald assured him that his request would be met. They would send what he had asked for through Ramón Guín, agent AM/TRUNK, who had a farm on the northern coast of Matanzas province. The meeting was over.

From that point there was a period when, without any apparent justification, for one reason or another Cubela was prevented from returning to Cuba. He had booked a flight to Havana via Prague for November 19 but a fresh request from the officer made him put off his journey. The officer explained that he needed to consult with Washington in order to confirm certain details related to the deposit in Cuba. Finally, Cubela was called in for a meeting in the late afternoon of November 22.

The case officer was waiting for him, and according to Cubela's statement, tried to give him a fountain pen that could fire projectiles, another with a needle for injecting poison, and a radio transmitter. Disconcerted, Cubela categorically rejected the items, explaining that they were not what was agreed, as he had always emphasized that any attempt he made on Fidel had to be effected at a prudent distance in order to preserve his life. It was at that precise moment that a phone call came through informing the case officer of the death of John F. Kennedy, president of the United States.

Cubela was traumatized by the news and the officer explained to him that Kennedy's death could change all the plans, and that Cubela shouldn't return to Cuba until he had checked things out with Washington. They made their farewells and a few days later, disobeying the order, Cubela decided to return to Havana via Prague on November 28, 1963. The abrupt departure of his case officer had plunged him into uncertainty in relation to the project's viability. Nevertheless, a few weeks later, the CIA reestablished contact through Ramón Guín, and offered him the necessary guarantees. Two consignments of weapons and military equipment were sent to him via infiltration groups that smuggled them into Cuba.

The plan Cubela was trying to set in motion was the same: to organize an ambush for Fidel Castro at the summer residence of the Council of State in the resort of Varadero. He would wait for Castro there in order to assassinate him, and afterwards would attempt to take control of the new government that would be formed, or at least play a significant part in it.

The months went by and the plot failed because Fidel Castro did not fall into the trap. Cubela despaired and sought another opportunity to escape from Cuba and relocate to Europe.

That opportunity presented itself when, in November 1964, he was invited by the International Union of Students to a meeting of its executive committee in Prague. From there he traveled to Paris on November 25, where he made contact with Carlos Tepedino, to whom he confided his wish not to return to Cuba. The same episode was to be repeated: the same Spanish-speaking officer appeared and, with Tepedino, convinced Cubela to continue being part of the plot, this time with a new variant: the CIA proposed to formally disassociate itself from the assassination of Fidel Castro.

The new plan was that Cubela should meet with Manuel Artime and the two of them would coordinate the plans: one the assassination, and the other, in the midst of the predicted chaos created by the leader's death, an invasion of the island and the installation of a provisional government that would request US and OAS aid, thus legitimizing a military invention aimed at overthrowing the Cuban government.

That meeting finally took place in Madrid at the end of December. On one side, Cubela and Tepedino, and on the other, Artime, Howard Hunt — his case officer — and James Noel. Various CIA agents connected to both as aides and confidants were also present, including Jorge Robreño, José Luis González Gallarreta, Alberto Blanco, Cucú León and Bichi Bernal.

Cubela and Artime met on various occasions in the Spanish capital, where little by little the plan was consolidated. Cubela was to prepare a new ambush in Varadero and Artime to initiate a naval campaign on Cuban coastal targets to "raise the people's morale" until the crime was effected; afterwards Artime and his men would take Punta de Hicacos, the peninsula where the Varadero resort is located. Several Central American countries had committed their support to Artime in the event of Cubela and himself forming the government junta that would seek aid and assistance. The plan was to be initiated in June–July 1965.

Once again Cubela asked for the telescopic sight and silencer for his rifle. Artime mobilized the specialists in JM/WAVE to acquire the sight and manufacture the silencer, which were finally handed over.[6] Everything was agreed on and everyone was left to implement their part in the plan.

Cubela returned to Cuba on February 28, 1965, with the accessories he had requested for his rifle. He had agreed that Robreño would remain in Madrid as a link with Artime, while Blanco and Gallarreta would return to the island some weeks later to act as his aides in the execution of the assassination attempt. Several weeks went by; May arrived, and none of Artime's promises had materialized.

That was the month scheduled for the attacks on Cuban coastal targets. Cubela maintained contact with the CIA through AM/TRUNK and on various occasions insisted on the need for Artime to fulfill his part of the contract; meanwhile, he and his aides positioned themselves in the house they had selected in the Varadero resort, from where they would target their victim. They had prepared a story that Cubela was on medical leave due to stress and needed a

---

6.   The silencer was tested on wasteland in Miami by Anis Feliafel, one of Artime's aides.

prolonged vacation. Thus his lengthy stay in that place would not arouse suspicions.

In June — given the imminence of the attack — CIA headquarters circulated a telegram to its European stations explaining that for security reasons they should suspend all contact with Cubela's group, which was not to be trusted on account of numerous indiscretions it had committed.

It also silenced radio messages sent to agent AM/TRUNK so that when the assassin compromised the United States there would be no evident connection with the crime and no compromising documents. In any event, the telegram could explain to anyone interested that, effectively, Cubela was a contact who had been abandoned due to his co-conspirators' indiscretions.

With that cable, which Cubela and his group never knew about, everything was concluded. It was an internal matter, only to exist in the archives in case it had to be utilized one day. A mechanism of "plausible denial" was set in motion.

Cubela's ambush failed again. Fidel Castro only rested when he could, not when he wanted to. The months went by and Cubela and his group drew up another alternative for the attempt. An important date was approaching: the commemoration of the 1957 assault on the Presidential Palace by a revolutionary group attempting to execute Batista. Fidel attended the event every year and was usually the final speaker. That would provide an occasion on which they could shoot him. The conspirators had an apartment at 455 N Street on the corner of San Lázaro, from where the platform erected on the university stairway was perfectly visible. Thus, everything was agreed: March 13, 1966, would be the date for the assassination of the prime minister.

After that decision was made, Cubela sent a message to José Braulio Alemán Gutiérrez in Miami, asking him to inform the CIA of the change of plans and activate US backing for the plan.

However, Cubela omitted some important details. He made no mention of abandoning the coup d'état plan and the insurrection in the Escambray mountains. He had arranged his own escape by recruiting a fisherman on Jaimanitas beach in the west of the capital to take him to the United States after effecting the crime.

The days went by rapidly for the conspirators, who were unaware that the authorities were following their every move.

On February 28, exactly 12 months after his return from his last trip abroad, Cubela was arrested along with all his co-conspirators. Operation AM/LASH — an attempt to assassinate Fidel Castro and overthrow the Cuban revolution spanning more than five years — was dismantled.

The detention of Cubela and his group marked the conclusion of one of the most extensive and important subversive actions planned by the United States against the life of the Cuban leader and the revolution.

This plan displayed all the ingredients that have characterized US aggression against our country over more than 40 years: attempted assassinations, terrorism, mercenary invasions, planned coup d'états and psychological warfare.

11 The Condor in Chile

David Phillips was waiting impatiently outside Richard Helms's office. He had been urgently summoned for a meeting with the director and presumed that it was related to an important mission. He reflected that he had come a long way from the day when he was recruited as a covert agent in Chile and from his time as a spy in Havana working under the cover of a publicity agency.

Responsibilities in Mexico and then the Dominican Republic, when it was decided to oust the Constitutionalists under Colonel Francisco Caamaño Deñó, trained him as a highly qualified professional within the Agency.

Despite their best efforts, the CIA had not met with the success that they had anticipated in their fight to contain communism in Latin America. The region's geopolitical map in that year of 1970 did not accord with the efforts they had expended. In spite of rigid US policies and the fact that soldiers trained in the United States controlled many national governments, in the Southern Cone — in Chile to be precise, where Phillips had begun his career — social instability was growing. The Socialist Party senator Salvador Allende was once again a candidate in the presidential elections and intelligence estimates gave him a slight majority. The Chilean left was very powerful and could actually win this time.

The secretary interrupted his thoughts: "The director says that you can go in," and a few seconds later he was facing the chief.

A conceited man with a cold and penetrating look, immaculately dressed and courteous, he was a CIA legend, having commenced his activities as a spy in the far-off days of World War II in London, where he acted as a link between the OSS and the British MI6.

The conversation between the two men moved directly to the issue that had prompted the meeting. Helms wanted Phillips to take charge of the task force being formed to prevent Salvador Allende winning the Chilean presidential elections that year. He would not have to give up his responsibility at the head of the Cuba section because, without a doubt, the Cubans and their leader Fidel Castro were backing the communists throughout the hemisphere, especially in Chile. Allende was the socialist leader who had contested elections on several occasions at the head of a left-wing coalition. He was also a consistent friend of the Cubans; it was Allende who received the survivors of Che Guevara's guerrilla force in his country when they crossed the border from Bolivia. He was likewise the principal instigator of solidarity campaigns with Cuba. Informants confirmed that one of the first measures he would take if he won the election would be to reestablish relations with Cuba.

Phillips understood his orders. However, he thought they had come very late in the day. Washington's strategies had led to much lost time and in reality, at this stage only a coup d'état could prevent a left-wing triumph. He had predicted it on various occasions. Given that he had spent his youth in Chile, he was well placed to grasp the direction in which Chilean politics was hurtling, but he couldn't turn down the task and thus assured Helms that he would do everything possible to block Allende's presidential aspirations.

Some hours later, in his office, Phillips mentally reviewed the troops he could count on for his new mission. The Cuban exiles would have to be the cornerstone of the plan: the Operation 40 group was in Miami, captained by Joaquín Sanjenís. Then there were Orlando Bosch's men, who had created a new political front to combat "Castroism" on a continental level. Luis Posada Carriles, Orlando García, Ricardo Morales Navarrete and various associates were in Caracas holding important positions within the political police, and his veteran agent Antonio Veciana had been in Bolivia since the war on Che Guevara and his army of internationalists, and was currently in charge of the psychological warfare program that the CIA had drawn up against the revolutionary movement in the Americas.

In addition, Phillips had excellent relations within the Chilean right-wing press, which would be needed to create a base for the subversive project through a solid campaign of psychological warfare to discredit the Popular Unity party that had nominated Salvador Allende as a candidate, to put pressure on the armed forces, and to prevent the triumph of the Marxist left.

Meditating on the responsibilities that had befallen him, a shiver ran down his spine when he realized that averting the possibility of a second Cuba in the hemisphere depended on his mission. Fidel Castro would certainly not let the opportunity to support Allende go by, and Chile might even become the first Latin American country that he would visit. Phillips got up from his armchair and contemplated the darkness of the night through the window. If that visit occurred, Chile would become Castro's tomb. On various occasions in the past he had prepared assassination attempts on the Cuban leader, but for one reason or another, they had all failed. In Chile it would be different. Maybe he would be unable to prevent Allende's triumph, but one thing he was sure of was that if Allende did win, it would provide the long-awaited opportunity to eliminate Fidel Castro.

Phillips began to call his agents in the various Latin American capitals, summoning them to a meeting to receive his instructions. He would send the Operation 40 group to Argentina to direct the commando groups responsible for unleashing war against leftists in the streets and communities on the border with Chile. The Caracas groups could offer training for the political activists and terrorists who would go on the offensive against the communist party, and Veciana's men could take care of the anti-Allende propaganda directed at Chile and its neighbors, explaining the threat to regional peace and stability implicit in a leftist victory.

A sense of power invaded him. He was about to enter into combat and this time he could depend on a president, Richard Nixon, who would not be daunted by the Russians and international communism.

The Flight of the Condor
Miami, Spring 1971

Phillips's men were meeting again, this time in a safe house in Miami. After being convened by Phillips they had worked hard, but had been unable to prevent Salvador Allende's electoral triumph. Despite all their efforts, including their [October 1970] assassination of General René Schneider, chief of the army, in an attempt to provoke an intervention by the armed forces, Allende had done it.

It was the first time since 1959 that an openly socialist, left-wing politician had won a general election, albeit with a small majority, and this set a precedent that had to be destroyed, even if the US government had to risk all its authority and prestige in achieving this. Ways of destabilizing the new Chilean government had to be found. All available resources would be mobilized, campaigns would be organized at the continental level, and the communist threat would by played up to the full.

As usual, David Phillips chaired the meeting. The rest settled themselves around the table. Antonio Veciana, Joaquín Sanjenís and Frank Sturgis were on his left, and on his right, Luis Posada, Ricardo Morales and Orlando Bosch.

After a brief description of the Chilean political scenario, he highlighted President Nixon's decision to defeat the constitutional government and, in addition, to take advantage of a possible visit to that country by Fidel Castro — Phillips had confidential information that it was going ahead — to eliminate him.

Everybody had assumed that would be the US approach from the day Allende assumed the presidency. His statements of solidarity, his visit to Havana, and above all, the recent presence of a Cuban security agent — associated on other occasions with Fidel Castro's security — at the Cuban embassy in Chile, all pointed in that direction. This confirmation was what they had been waiting for, and all of them rushed to propose options for the assassination.

Phillips had to intervene to call the meeting to order. The CIA had a plan, which consisted of taking advantage of two of the most insecure points of the visit. The first, when Fidel Castro would emerge onto the balcony of La Moneda Palace to address a crowd that would undoubtedly acclaim him, providing an opportunity to fire on him from one of the rooms of the Hilton Hotel, whose balconies faced in that direction. This plan was somewhat similar to the attempt planned years before on the northern terrace of the Presidential Palace in Havana.

If the opportunity did not present itself then, Fidel Castro would undoubtedly give a press conference at the end of his tour and could be shot at that point. They had thought to conceal a revolver inside a video camera. Two duly accredited journalists could smuggle it into the room with the complicity of police officers on guard at the venue, and use it to kill him. Afterwards, the same Chilean police agents implicated in the operation would detain the assassins, get them out of the place, and prevent Castro's agents from executing them.

The idea seemed like a good one to everyone. However, Veciana wanted to go over certain details. It seemed improbable to him that anyone could escape from the action at the press conference, and moreover, he considered the assassins' escape unnecessary. "Wouldn't it be better to make an agreement with the police to kill the assassins so as to cover up any possible traces?" he asked.

Phillips regarded him with a satisfied expression. Antonio Veciana was one of his first-rate agents. Phillips had recruited him in the early years after the revolution in Cuba, and since then he had become one of his finest instruments. Intelligent, passionate and calculating, he was always at hand when a frontline operative was needed.

He couldn't hide from those men the most interesting details of his plan. It had another component: Posada Carriles's group would fabricate a file to remain within the Venezuelan Police Department that would reveal the two men selected for the attempt on Castro as informers for Soviet intelligence. When the assassins were killed — and he looked at Veciana with a smile — the Chilean conspirators would initiate an investigation that would lead directly to Venezuelan police archives, thus exposing Fidel Castro's assassins as Soviet agents.

Caracas, Venezuela. September 1971

Luis Posada Carriles was a successful man. After the Bay of Pigs fiasco he enlisted in the US forces to participate in another invasion of Cuba set for mid-1962. He was sent to a training camp and there was selected to move on to Fort Jackson, where he took an intelligence course. Along with other Cubans, he was to be part of the new secret police that would clear the island of communists while the US troops set about conquering towns. However, that plan failed when Kennedy negotiated a way out of the Missile Crisis at the end of that same year, leaving him jobless. The boys of Operation 40, as his group was called, didn't abandon him and thus he established himself in Venezuela.

The skills he had acquired soon led him to investigative activities and he began to work in Venezuela's Directorate of Intelligence and Prevention Services (DISIP). Of course, none of that was by chance. His friends in the Caracas CIA station gave him the backing he needed and thus he rose to become one of the chiefs of that repressive agency by 1971.

His field of action was related to the communist movement and the activities of the Soviet and Cuban intelligence agencies. In particular, he took on the case of a Soviet press correspondent accredited in Caracas who appeared to be a KGB representative.

His relations with the émigré Cuban community were solid and from time to time he did small favors for his former *compañeros*-in-arms. On various occasions he had concealed the presence in Venezuela of persons wanted by the US courts for having "served justice" on an individual who had publicly expressed a desire for an improvement in relations between Cuba and the Cuban community in the United States. The exile movement, especially in Miami, could not be allowed to soften and be penetrated by Castro's influence, he reflected.

One of his closest friends was Cuban American Lucilo Peña, an important businessman who had been recruited to the terrorist training camp in the Dominican Republic in 1964 when the CIA decided to form a team of men to execute the Agency's dirty work in its war on Cuba.

In the end, all the terrorists had become businessmen, as in one way or another they wound up heading cover enterprises that the CIA had organized in order to carry out its Latin American activities. All of them had become rich. That had been one of the results of the "holy war" they had waged for more than 10 years. Some of the businesses were questionable; but it was a fact that they facilitated resources to continue the battle against communism.

Drug trafficking was at the hub of those flourishing enterprises. In 1968, Antonio Veciana became an important advisor to the Bolivian national bank. That gave him the cover to gain access to coca leaf producers. For his part, Posada controlled all the air traffic from a phantom CIA company operating in South America. It was easy to use that channel to smuggle drugs into the United States and everyone benefited, including the Agency chiefs. It was drug trafficking that had provided the money for the anti-Cuba campaigns on the continent and for advising various police agencies anxious to dismantle revolutionary organizations in their respective countries.

For those reasons, when Phillips proposed the mission to assassinate Fidel Castro in Chile, Posada and Veciana were happy to oblige. If the Cuban leader died the revolution could not be sustained and would rapidly collapse, and that would give them the possibility of converting the island into a transit point for drug trafficking to the United States. Business and political interests could advance hand in hand.

Fabricating the supposed Soviet agents who were to assassinate Castro in Chile was the responsibility of Posada's group, whose members commenced the task with their usual efficiency. Agents' reports, doctored photos and instructions supposedly received from the Soviets would be planted in the rooms the patsies occupied in Caracas en route to Chile, which would help the DISIP to demonstrate in its subsequent investigations that the Cuban assassins were agents of Moscow. The idea was similar to that utilized in the assassination of President Kennedy, when a huge propaganda operation was mounted to demonstrate that Lee Harvey Oswald was a Cuban and Soviet agent.

The Posada group was also in charge of seeking accreditation for the two assassins as Venevisión journalists, a task that was easily done. The complication lay in fitting the revolver into the video camera that they would carry, with which they would make the mortal shot. However, through Lucilo Peña's contacts the job was satisfactorily accomplished. When Phillips, Veciana, Frank Sturgis, Gerry Hemming, Félix Rodríguez, Orlando Bosch and Joaquín Sanjenís arrived in Caracas for the final decisions, everything was ready. They had heard through a reliable source — a general in the Chilean police — that Fidel Castro was to visit that country in early November of that year.

La Paz, Bolivia. Late October 1971

The city airport was unusually busy. That day the national folklore ensemble was returning to the country after a successful international tour and many fans had turned up to welcome them home. In one of the halls, a tall, slim man with a close-trimmed mustache, aged around 40, was waiting expectantly. The Caracas-constructed video camera fitted with a revolver and other arms including a powerful rifle with a telescopic sight and a silencer were also due in on that flight.

The idea was Antonio Veciana's. His contacts in Bolivia had made it possible to load the equipment in Caracas, the folklore ensemble's last stopover, and pick it up in La Paz with the aid of the customs authority, which had lent itself to tasks more complicated than this one on many other occasions.

The plan was ready. He was in charge of coordination on the ground. Two alternatives had been planned for the assassination of Castro and the room in the Santiago de Chile Hilton had been reserved. The Cubans would themselves take care of the press conference when it was called. Nevertheless, he would also take advantage of the assassins' accreditation to seek alternatives. The task could perhaps be moved forward. To that end, he directed the fake journalists to join the press caravan accompanying Fidel Castro throughout his visit. Whatever the case, this would be useful as they would get to know the bodyguards, who might let them get close enough to shoot when the moment arrived.

The most complicated detail was the execution of the assassins once they had shot the Cuban leader. The first plan was to pick them up in a car once they had done their job and then kill them in a safe place, giving credit to the efficiency of the national police force. In the alternative plan, their security agent contacts within the Chilean police force could take them out in the press conference room itself, thus frustrating certain action on the part of Castro's security.

One very important aspect was the need to not arouse the

suspicions of the killers. They were no novices in their field, and the slightest suspicion could result in their desertion.

These thoughts were running through Veciana's mind that morning in the Bolivian airport when a man approached him and muttered a few words. Both of them walked in the direction of the parking lot. There they found the weapons deposited in a van. Everything was ready and he would soon be transporting them himself on the highway to Santiago, where he would leave them in a previously arranged safe house. Then he would wait for the killers and inform Phillips, who was coordinating the operation from another safe house. Phillips was in contact with the Chilean police and had responsibility for the execution of the phoney journalists when they had completed their task.

Santiago de Chile, November 10, 1971.
Prensa Latina Report

Tonight Cuban prime minister Fidel Castro greeted Chilean workers and affirmed that his encounter with President Salvador Allende was a great victory for the peoples of Chile and Cuba, and thus for Latin America.

The Cuban leader spoke with a group of national and foreign journalists who managed to enter the front garden of the residence of Mario García Incháustegui, the Cuban ambassador to Chile, a few minutes after Fidel, accompanied by President Allende, had arrived from the airport.

Comandante Fidel Castro spoke informally on various international problems and replied to questions related to Peru, Bolivia and Uruguay.

When he was asked what significance he attributed to his visit to Chile, he said: "It has to be analyzed from a moral and revolutionary standpoint, and from that point of view it has great significance. Our two countries have engaged in many struggles and have both been dominated by imperialism. The meeting has importance not because of us, the protagonists, but on account of its historic value."

And he added: "This is a victory of the peoples of Chile and Cuba and thus of Latin America. One already has the sense of a revolutionary America. History is beginning to change in a distinctive manner. Perhaps this meeting can be best evaluated by the US imperialists themselves..."

The prime minister said that he didn't know how long he would be in Chile, and expressed his desire to meet with workers in the saltpeter, copper and charcoal mines and other campesino centers. He added that his interest in these sectors was personal and social as well as political.

In conversation with the journalists, the revolutionary leader had words of praise for Chile and the Chileans. At the end of his first statement on Chilean soil, *Comandante* Fidel Castro commented that he also had invitations to visit Algeria, Hungary, Bulgaria and the Soviet Union in the near future.

While it has not been confirmed, the Cuban leader is expected to offer a press conference tomorrow after a visit to President Allende in the Government Palace.

Havana, November 1979. DSE Headquarters

Through our investigations we discovered that from the end of 1970 the CIA was planning to assassinate *Comandante* Fidel Castro when he visited Chile. According to information we received the operation had a budget of $50,000 and its leaders were Cuban counterrevolutionaries Antonio Veciana Blanch, Luis Posada Carriles, Orlando Bosch, Lucilo Peña, Joaquín Sanjenís, Marcos Rodríguez, Diego Medina, Secundino Álvarez and Félix Rodríguez, as well as Frank Sturgis, Gerry Patrick Hemming, a Bolivian resident called Nápoles, and US officer David Phillips.

The homicide plot originally contained two alternatives that could be carried out in Chile, plus two further attempts in Lima, Peru and Quito, Ecuador, given the stopovers programmed for *Comandante* Fidel Castro's return to Cuba.

The assassination plot was hatched in meetings in the cities of Miami, Caracas, La Paz and Santiago; the first option was to effect the attack from a room in the Hilton Hotel adjacent to the Government Palace, the venue for the first of our prime minister's appearances in that country.

When that plan failed due to the participants' cowardice, the second option was put into action. Earlier, in Caracas, journalist credentials from the Venevisión channel had been given to Cuban counterrevolutionaries Marcos Rodríguez, from Orlando Bosch's group, who had very short, graying hair, olive skin, glasses, and was of regular height; and Diego Medina from the Second National Front of the Escambray, who was short, with thick hair, well-manicured nails and olive skin.

Both were trained in precision shooting and to handle the television camera that contained the .38-caliber revolver with which they would fire on Fidel in his final press conference in Chile.

This latter attempt failed because the assassins pulled out, perhaps realizing that they would not get out of the place alive. In fact, Rodríguez and Medina obstructed the plot from the outset. Medina claimed that a cousin of his who lived in Cuba was part of Fidel Castro's bodyguard and might recognize him at any moment, while Rodríguez simulated acute pain that doctors diagnosed as possible appendicitis. This led them to hospitalize him, thus giving him an excuse to back out of the action.

In fact, one of the principal reasons that the plot was neutralized was due to the strict security measures taken by our men, who demonstrated to the enemy at all times — as they later affirmed — that any attempt on the life of the *Comandante* would be fatal for the individual who risked it.

Investigations confirmed the complicity of the Chilean police corps. According to our informant, General José María Sepúlveda was in charge of facilitating the assassins' entry into the venue of Fidel's press conference. He was also responsible for executing the assassins once the fatal shot had been fired.

We also knew that counterrevolutionaries Luis Posada Carriles and Lucilo Peña, both resident in Venezuela, had thought up a scheme to fabricate false evidence linking Marcos Rodríguez and Diego Medina to Soviet intelligence officers in Caracas. The objective was to make it seem that the assassination of our prime minister had been the work of the Russians, acting to remove Fidel from the regional scenario out of their displeasure with his support for the revolutionary movements in Latin America.

Before the failure of the Chile plot, through counterrevolutionary Amaury Frajinals in Miami, Phillips and his group contracted Eusebio Ojeda, ex-captain of the Second National Front of the Escambray, to position himself on the terrace of Lima airport in Peru with two explosives experts known as Horacio and Marcelo. They were to wait for the arrival of Fidel's delegation on its return from Chile in order to attack it with two grenades. After agreeing to the plot, the two experts disappeared and could not be found. For that reason, Posada Carriles volunteered to assassinate Fidel when he landed at Quito airport in Ecuador on the final stopover of the flight to Cuba.

This last plot involved recruiting brothers Guillermo and Roberto Verdaguer, proprietors of an Ecuadorean airline, in order to have them conveniently place one of their planes in the terminal area, providing cover for Posada Carriles and another accomplice by the name of Osiel González to fire on Fidel as soon as he appeared at the door of his aircraft.

The plan failed when the Verdaguer brothers refused to carry out the action, arguing that they would be discovered and their business ruined.

One significant detail of these criminal plans is the origin of the weapons to be used. In all cases they were supplied by a contact in Dallas, Texas. That was where Veciana coordinated the transfer of weapons on various occasions through a Cuban woman called Hilda…

12 New York, New York

In 1979, 20 years after the triumph of the revolution in Cuba and 19 years after his first visit to New York, Fidel Castro was returning there to participate in the 34th session of the UN General Assembly, this time as president of the Non-Aligned Nations Movement, an organization that had recently concluded its Sixth Summit in Havana. Cuba's prestige and authority had grown in spite of the US blockade and the aggression and hardships suffered. Likewise, the stature of Fidel Castro had gained in dimension. He was the undisputed leader of the Third World nations.

The news of Castro's visit shook the counterrevolutionary émigrés to the core. Cuba's triumphs embittered them, the image of a combative Fidel Castro reminded them of the Bay of Pigs disaster, and the Cuban leader's visit to the United States was a provocation that they were not prepared to endure.

The years had passed, but for Antonio Veciana, Castro continued to be an obsession. Castro had destroyed his life and that of the men of his generation. The battle against him had consumed Veciana's youth. Before he escaped from Cuba in the 1960s he had attempted and failed to assassinate him. Later, when Castro visited Chile, he failed again, but on this occasion, Castro would be in the United States itself, on Veciana's own territory, and he would not escape.

Veciana was in his comfortable house located in the area of Miami known as "Little Havana." Before him was a letter informing him of Fidel's visit, and for a few minutes his thoughts went back through the years to the last day that he met his case officer, David Phillips, in that greyhound stadium parking lot on Flager Street. Phillips was very annoyed because somebody had informed on the cocaine racket that the two of them had been running from Bolivia to Colombia for a number of years. He recalled how, with a piercing stare, Phillips had explained that the police were about to arrest him and that he, Veciana, must take full responsibility so as to avoid involving the Agency in the scandal. Phillips invoked the services Veciana had lent and his loyalty to finally convince him that they wouldn't abandon him. Things had already been arranged with the relevant authorities so that he would only serve a few months of the prison term imposed, for which he would receive a payment of a quarter of a million dollars. At the end of the day, he had no other option if he wanted to stay alive, as Phillips couldn't predict the reaction of the Mafia associates who would inevitably be arrested if Veciana confessed.

Then, as if in a movie, he recalled the days of Watergate, of the Church Commission, and finally, when he was interrogated in 1978 by the House Select Committee investigating the Kennedy assassination. His statements had almost cost him his life.

It was a slip-up, he thought, confessing the existence of Phillips to investigator Gaetón Fonzi,[1] even under the cover of the pseudonym Harold Bishop. He fell into an acute depression then; the CIA was highly discredited by the Congressional exposé of many of their dirty dealings. The investigators' threats to include him in investigations into the assassination of the US president and the long months in prison on account of the drugs venture had finally loosened his tongue.

---

1.   Gaetón Fonzi: investigator with the 1978 House Select Committee and author of *The Last Investigation*.

Since then, he had discreetly distanced himself from his counter-revolutionary colleagues, claiming that the FBI was watching him and that his movements in Dade county were restricted, which was in fact true.

Still, everyone respected him in the Cuban émigré community. Andrés Nazario Sargén, the leader of Alpha 66 — the organization Veciana had founded when he arrived in Miami — always consulted him before taking any action, and that satisfied his vanity. That was why he thought of Sargén for the new idea that was circulating in his mind. He would call him, Veciana thought. "Now let's see if the old guy can hang onto his pants."

The Softball
Miami, September 1979

There were two covered armchairs in the little room, one in green and the other in red. Blown-up individual photos of smiling young people adorned the walls. The chairs were separated by a small table, at which Antonio Veciana, the host, was having an animated conversation with Andrés Nazario Sargén.

"Our friends have sent me a letter informing me of Fidel's upcoming visit to New York. They're sure that after his victory in the Non-Aligned Nations Movement meeting he'll come to the United States to rub their faces in it," Veciana explained.

"They always have reliable information. Anyway, the prediction is a logical one. Still, I wonder why they're persisting with the idea after such a long time. The CIA people have been hit hard and Carter has put a chief admiral in there, who, as I've heard, favors technical rather than human sources."

"Nevertheless," Veciana went on, "our people still hold key positions. They're getting ready for the elections, when Carter is going to get a kick in the ass. And something happening to Fidel on US territory would hasten Carter's exit: a president who can't even offer security to a foreign leader. It's also obvious that they don't want to be seen to be involved, and that's why they've passed the information onto me. They want us to do their dirty work as usual. What's happening is that our interests are converging again. Imagine if Fidel were to be blown into a thousand pieces in the middle of New York."

"What have you got in mind," asked Sargén.

"Nothing concrete for now. I'm just thinking that it would be good if you could get hold of a sufficient quantity of C-4 explosive through your contacts and maybe think about some of our *compañeros* who might be prepared to park a car along Fidel's route from the Cuban embassy to the United Nations. We could so something along the lines of Orlando Letelier; remember Allende's foreign minister who the Novo Sampol brothers and that little American CIA guy blew away in the middle of Washington?"

A smile lit up Nazario Sargén's face.

Havana, September 1979. DSE Headquarters

The prospect of this trip put everyone on edge. It was a period of escalating terrorism against Cuban representatives and officials located abroad, particularly on US territory, where the Cuban mission to the UN had been the target of many bomb attacks and constant threats on its personnel. By that time there had been more than 20 acts of terrorism in the New York area against the Soviet and Venezuelan missions to the UN, six attacks of the same kind on the Cuban mission, and the murder of Eulalio Negrín, a Cuban American who was advocating the normalization of relations. One year later Cuban diplomat Félix García was assassinated and an attempt on the ambassador Raúl Roa Kourí was foiled.

Those terrorist acts stemmed from the counterrevolutionaries' desperation and reflected their decline, although that didn't make them any less dangerous. In fact, they continued operating on US territory with a high degree of impunity and these groups' historical links with the CIA provided them with sophisticated training in subversion and access to arms, explosives and superior technical means for their actions. According to reports from the FBI itself, at that time the Cuban counterrevolutionary groups were the most dangerous network operating in the United States. Moreover, they were linked to organized crime, drug trafficking, and intelligence agencies that, as in the case of the Chilean National Intelligence Directorate, utilized them to eliminate their opponents in the United States itself.

Various specialist security teams traveled to New York to study conditions in the venues to be used and the routes the Cuban president would probably have to take, and to organize the necessary arrangements with the UN and US authorities in charge of protecting foreign statesmen.

In the midst of all this hectic activity, we received information that the counterrevolutionary organization Alpha 66 was planning to attack Fidel in New York. This group, set up by the CIA in 1962, had devoted itself for a number of years to attacking Cuban vessels and those from other countries trading with the island. In fact, they operated as armed pirates until international pressure forced their decline. Then they decided to terrorize sectors of the Cuban community in the United States that didn't share their position and to maintain a line in blackmail that served as a source of enrichment for the leaders. The CIA also used Alpha 66 on many occasions as a psychological resource to divert the attention of Cuban security and force it to invest resources in averting possible attacks that never materialized. It was originally thought that this projected attack was part of that strategy. Nevertheless, following our principles of professionalism, a plan was drawn up to verify the information.

One of our officers located in Miami received the mission to make contact with the person who had given the information. As the source was not considered entirely trustworthy, it was decided that our agent would approach the woman on her way to work so as to effect a surprise encounter, while taking special security measures. In his report on this operation the official stated:

> I located myself at a convenient café that afforded me control of the exit of her building and the parking lot through the window, as I didn't know whether she would leave on foot or in a car and my idea was to follow her in my car if she did the latter. It wasn't difficult to identify her because, as you say, she's a beautiful woman who attracts attention. I saw her open a red VW but she appeared to have forgotten something and went back into the building, which allowed me to approach her in the parking lot. That seemed to be a quieter and safer place to park alongside her car and when she arrived, I gave her the password in a totally natural way. She was clearly shocked and her reply was that we were crazy; laughing I said I guessed that wasn't her reply. She smiled and said: "Go to hell!" We went in her car because I didn't want it left there in case the family saw it and got worried about her, and neither did I want to leave her alone at any moment, so I indicated a route that gave me a chance to countercheck and detected no sign of enemy activity…
>
> She says that she got the information from her father, who Nazario had approached for money, telling him that it was for an attempt they were going to make on Fidel in New York and that they needed explosives. She also talked about it with one "Robertico," last name unknown, a new guy in Alpha 66 who arrived from Cuba not long ago and says that he was in prison. This Robertico is in love with her and told her that the explosion was going to be heard in Miami. She doesn't give much credence to this man because he's a bragger, but she is worried by a comment her father made along the lines that this time it's for real, which is unusual because he doesn't have any faith in Nazario and avoids him because he spends his whole life hitting people up for money. I directed her to sound out her father with the excuse that she was worried about innocent people dying and him being linked to something like that, and to approach Robertico to find out his real participation in it. She was a bit reluctant about the latter because she says that the guy's a sleazy idiot, and she's not prepared to have a thing with him. I clarified that nobody was asking her to do that; that she should reject him sexually as she has done up to now, but not totally cut off ties, and encourage his bragging. I insisted on the importance

of her mission and the responsibility with which she should assume it, went over with her the guide that you sent, had her learn it off by heart, and destroyed it in her presence so that she would realize the serious nature of things and acquire good habits. She asked me how she could get in touch with me and I told her that if she had anything urgent she should call Eastern Airlines and reserve a flight to Caracas in the name of María Portales on the 20th or the 27th of this month, and then I would locate her. I know it's a risk but I had no other alternative. She seems to be an immature but well-intentioned girl and came across as sincere and intelligent. I am going to direct G-24 to check out this information in depth and communicate with you. I will approach her again by surprise next week even if there's no urgency.

G-24 was an experienced agent with a number of contacts in various counterrevolutionary groups. He had his own means of communicating with Cuba and duly sent the results of his investigations through that channel:

I talked with Nazario and effectively they are preparing an attack, in which they will launch a grenade at the car taking Fidel from our embassy to the UN building. It would seem that it is not being organized by Alpha, although Nazario is asking for money on all sides and wants to claim success for it if it comes off. Alpha is possibly supplying the men and the car they will use. Nazario told me of a man and a woman living in Union City, which would let them avoid using Miami people. I suppose that the car would have a New York or New Jersey license plate for the same reason and would have to be hired with false documentation, a stolen car or one of those old cars bought for cash that don't need many papers. Nazario told me that they had economic problems in terms of buying the explosives but I doubt that's the case, he's saying that to get money. I told him that I could get him a clean car through a friend, thinking that if we had control of the car then we can control the operation. He said he thought Veciana already had one but if there was any need he'd call me. I don't believe that we have sufficient control via Nazario because Veciana is compartmentalizing things. I don't have any pretext to see Veciana directly but I will talk to [...] about what Nazario told me to see if he'll introduce me to Veciana. [...] must know something because of his access to explosives and his relationship with Veciana; it's important to see him because if he's in the know, then so is the CIA. I know for a fact that Nazario has talked to various people about this, so I don't think there's any problem in transferring the information to the US secret services so that they can neutralize the operation.

In the context of the visit, it was decided implement the planned move of the Cuban mission to the UN from its old mansion on 67th Street and 15th Avenue to a building on Lexington Avenue and 38th Street. This building offered the possibility of putting up the delegation more cheaply and with better security conditions. Located just a few blocks away from the UN building, in the center of downtown Manhattan, this area is one of the most central, populated and busy areas of the city. The consequences of blowing up a car loaded with explosives in a place like that were unimaginable. It would have killed Cuban officials and security personnel accompanying the delegation and also dozens of US secret service and police officers, together with many of the thousands of citizens passing through the area who would inevitably wait out of curiosity to see the Cuban president's convoy pass by. No political rationale could justify such an act; even for the Cuban security professionals who had confronted the counterrevolutionary groups' wildest plots and had witnessed arson attacks on stores full of people, attacks on humble fishing vessels and even the sabotage of a passenger plane in full flight, the idea was incredible. This plan went beyond the conceivable, but it was a fact. Something had to be done... and it was done.

Havana, January 1995

I was working in my office when a friend called to tell me that two Cuban journalists from the weekly *Juventud Rebelde* magazine had recently returned from a visit to Florida, where they had made a study of the Cuban community there. The study was sponsored by the Center for International Policy at the Johns Hopkins University, headed by Wayne Smith, the first chief of the US Interests Section in Cuba.

Journalists Hedelberto López Blanch and Ignacio Hernández Rotger spent almost three weeks in Miami and interviewed various personalities in the Cuban exile community. My conversation with them flowed easily. I explained the work that I was doing and they told me of an interview they did with Antonio Veciana, with whom they struck up a casual conversation in a restaurant. The journalists told him that they were from Cuba and were interested in facts rather than motives, and he told them his story. Of course, he told them only part of it: nothing in relation to the CIA, his case officer David Phillips, acts of terrorism against Cuban targets in third countries, expeditions against the island, drug trafficking, the adventure in Bolivia, or all the counterrevolutionary activities in which he participated during more than 30 years. It was a kind of sterilized, sweetened story but one that contained portions of the truth, and for that reason, we decided to include it here as a way of concluding the history in this book, in which he played a major role.

This account will allow readers to have not just our version of events, but also that of the enemy.

Miami, October 1994.
Interview with Antonio Veciana

I already sensed that the revolution was very strong and as a practical man I knew that we weren't winning, so my strategy was to kill Fidel, and I tried to do so on three occasions.

First: I rented Apartment 8A on Misiones Avenue before the Urban Reform Act was proposed. I needed a special weapon and I went to the US embassy to ask for it. Sam Kail was chief of intelligence. I told him who I was and that he could check me out.

He asked me what I was after and told me that he was going to the United States and when he returned he would give me an answer. When he came back he told me that he couldn't and didn't want to have anything to do with me. I told him that if Castro was killed the United States would be blamed anyway. He reaffirmed that he didn't want to know anything about it, and that his country couldn't be linked to the action. I told Bernardo Morales[2] about it and he told me he had a bazooka. At first I put my mother-in-law in the apartment, although I never told her what I was planning to do. The attempt failed, as the people who had to do it thought I was crazy or stupid. I had placed two men in the apartment, one was Bernardo Paradela. He thought that the gas produced by the bazooka might lead to an explosion in the apartment, and the operation failed because the others also backed out using the excuse of the gas, although originally around 50 to 60 people were prepared to do it. Orlando had obtained uniforms and machine guns.

Second: Chile. Somebody within the Chilean government who I still can't name told me six months beforehand that Fidel was going to Chile. I trained two individuals, both dead now: Diego Medina, killed in Santa Marta (Colombia) for peddling drugs, and Marcos Rodríguez. We trained them in Venezuela as photojournalists. I was a boxing entrepreneur and stole passports from various boxers. The training lasted for about three months. They went to Chile a month beforehand and managed to get the credentials to enter La Moneda Palace. The equipment was bought from the Venevisión channel; you know that money can buy anything. The plan was to kill him at a large press conference of around 30 journalists with the idea that the person who did it would become a hero in the international press. That scenario was selected because Castro's agents couldn't operate there and it had to be a moment of less tension. There were two of them, but only one of them was supposed to fire. Both the

---

2.   Bernardo Morales: possibly David Sánchez Morales.

guys involved asked for life insurance for their families in the event of anything happening to them and that was granted. Soon after Fidel arrived in Chile, Diego Medina ran away to Peru, but the other guy could and should have done the job. Marcos Rodríguez attended Fidel's first press conference, but as planned, to give Fidel's security people more confidence in him, he didn't carry the weapon. After that Marcos got himself admitted to hospital claiming that he had appendicitis. When I went to see the doctor, he told me that although the patient was suffering from chronic appendicitis, it wasn't a case for an urgent operation and could wait for months or even years. But Marcos insisted on an operation and after talking with him again, I told the doctor to go ahead with the operation and I'd take care of the cost. So neither of the two men attended the second press conference. They called me the "spider captain" because I was the one who supplied the weapons, found the locations, but by pure coincidence didn't take part in the actions. That time they didn't kill Fidel because they didn't have the balls.

Third: In Miami I met up again with Juanita, a crazy girl, but not too crazy. I remembered her from the underground movement because she saved my life once in Jaimanitas. I met up with her again in the United States, and we planned to eliminate Castro during his visit to the United Nations in 1979. I was the one who was going to check it out and follow Fidel's car right from the airport. I would do so with a walkie-talkie. We thought to use a contact detonator disguised as a softball with little Cuban and July 26 flags on it, when the crowd was gathered in the vicinity of the UN to receive Fidel. I would advise her of the car he was traveling in, and when he arrived, she would throw the ball. Given the crowd and the confusion, Juanita would easily be able to escape. But in this case there was an infiltration by the US secret service. They took me to an office and threatened to put me in the electric chair. They placed me under open surveillance to dishearten me. Then I thought that I could be the bait for the secret service and somebody else could execute my plan of action. That didn't work out because then Juanita, who should have thrown the ball, backed out at the last minute. I always tried to provide an escape route for the people who took part in those actions. If I had gone there would have been some action. I haven't been a man of exceptional valor, but of average valor. I'd prefer you to tell the truth. I was always arguing with the CIA and the FBI. They think they're more capable because they have far more resources, but some of the attempts they planned were really dumb, like the cigar and pen ones...

Epilogue

The war against Cuba continues and thus the enemies of the Cuban revolution are persisting in their plans to eliminate its leader. Just a few years ago a homicidal plot to be executed in Panama City during the Ibero-American Summit of Heads of State was averted. There, a group of CIA agents headed by arch-terrorist Luis Posada Carriles, the man who was responsible for the 1976 sabotage of a Cuban passenger plane in full flight where 73 people lost their lives, was discovered and taken prisoner.

A study undertaken in the early 1990s on plots uncovered and frustrated within and outside of Cuba exposes chilling figures. The plots were divided into two categories: those that were at the point of being effected and where the resources were seized, and those that were neutralized in the preparatory stage. The first are referred to as plots and the second as conspiracies. The final total is spectacular for one human being: 634 homicidal plans.[1]

By 1966, the internal counterrevolution had been decisively defeated through the disappearance of its support bases. Nevertheless, the plots and conspiracies intensified. Thousands of radio hours, written propaganda, rumors and every means of communication — in conjunction with sophisticated mechanisms specifically devised

---

1.   167 plots and 467 conspiracies.

for the assassination — were utilized to stimulate the physical elimination of Fidel Castro. Only popular vigilance, solidarity, the revolutionary leader's instincts and the protection provided by the Revolutionary Armed Forces and the Security Services prevented that occurrence.

Currently, with the United States acting as the universal sheriff and its anti-terrorist plans acquiring the dimension of international policy, US intentions toward Cuba remain the same. Without discounting the close-range shot, bomb or treacherous poison, Cuba's enemies have also tried to assassinate Fidel's ideals, ethics, authority and prestige. The CIA is returning anew to its past experiences, now with technological resources of incalculable proportions. Nobody could have imagined the dark forces unleashed after the September 11 strikes on New York and Washington.

It is the US intention to assassinate Fidel at any price, so that his example and ideas will disappear, and with them, the Cuban revolution. They continue to make the same error, and the history of Cuba, of this continent, is and will be witness to that.

Chronology of Crimes 1959–2000

This chronology includes two categories of homicidal plots: those which reached the stage of practical action before being discovered; and those which were neutralized at a preliminary stage.

The first category includes cases made public in the United States as a result of reports by the CIA and other agencies that have been declassified in recent years, and which were also investigated by the Cuban Security Services with the aim of expanding on and documenting the available information.

The result is a list of 167 homicidal plots whose authors were detained and punished by the courts or exposed before the relevant authorities in third countries, and 467 conspiracies which were uncovered in the planning phase, without counting those not made public or not uncovered by the Cuban authorities. There are no historical precedents for this.

Directly or indirectly, the United States has been responsible for all of the plots. On the occasions when they were not planned by US agencies, the hand or money of certain agents was often still present, and in those that occurred independently, the idea was fomented in the minds of the killers through propaganda campaigns from the United States urging the elimination of Cuban leaders. The information presented here demonstrates this and also shows that those criminal plots were an integral part of US plans to overthrow the Cuban revolution. Readers can see how both objectives — the assassination of Fidel Castro and the destabilization of our society — were pursued simultaneously within the anti-Cuban project. Attempts to destroy the revolutionary unity achieved over our years of struggle, which Fidel Castro has forged and guarded, are continuing. It is supposed that once Fidel has gone, that unity will collapse, thus facilitating the achievement of US objectives.

Readers of this book can discover the essential details of the 167 conspiracies uncovered by the Cuban Security Services in which weapons were seized and the conspirators sentenced by the Cuban courts, and of others uncovered through official reports declassified by the United States. We trust that this will serve to document irrefutably how the United States, the most powerful nation on Earth, has attacked our sovereign nation. We also hope that this exposé might help to eradicate actions of this nature from US policy and prevent such despicable acts being repeated in any other part of the planet to resolve conflicts or political disagreements.

1959

January: A plot to assassinate Fidel Castro in the Sierra Maestra, organized by FBI agents and the Fulgencio Batista dictatorship, was uncovered. US citizen Alan Robert Nye, captured December 25, 1958, by rebel combatants, confessed his intensions and named the instigators of the plot. His plan was to infiltrate the guerrilla movement and then ambush its leader. He was caught with a Remington .30-06 gun with a telescopic sight and a .38-caliber revolver. In early 1959 Nye was tried and sentenced by the Cuban courts.

March: On the initiative of Rafael Leónidas Trujillo, the Dominican dictator, and Fulgencio Batista, with the consent of the US authorities, Rolando Masferrer Rojas, an ex-chief of the death squads in pre-revolutionary Cuba, planned to assassinate Fidel Castro in an ambush in the vicinity of the Presidential Palace in Havana. The operative group consisted of Obdulio Piedra and Navi Ferrás, whom, on being discovered, fled the country for the United States.

Mid-1959: Frank Sturgis, an agent contracted by the CIA, planned to assassinate Fidel Castro by taking advantage of a meeting in the Cuban air force headquarters, which he had infiltrated. The conspiracy, approved by James Noel, head of the CIA station located in the US embassy, was to be executed with a bomb placed in the military installation. Pedro Luis Díaz Lanz, chief of the air force, and Gerry Patrick Hemming, a US mercenary, were also involved in the operation. The plot failed due to security measures in place at the selected location.

December: Colonel J.C. King, head of the Western Hemisphere Division of the CIA, proposed to his senior, Allen Dulles, the assassination of

Fidel Castro as the most expeditious means of defeating the Cuban revolution. A few weeks later his proposal was authorized by the CIA high command.

November 1959–February 1960: A counterrevolutionary group headed by Major Robert Van Horne, military attaché at the US embassy in Cuba, organized a plot to assassinate Fidel Castro during a visit to the residence of *Comandante* Ramiro Valdés, head of the Cuban Security Services. The plot was neutralized by security agents infiltrated into the group. The conspirators included US citizen Geraldine Shamman, Fernando López, Pablo Márquez and Homero Gutiérrez.

1960

April: On his return from an exploratory trip to Havana, Howard Hunt, a CIA officer assigned to the newly created anti-Cuba task force, proposed the assassination of Fidel Castro as the only way to defeat the revolution. In the same month a plot to assassinate Fidel Castro, directed from the United States by Manuel Artime Buesa, a protégé of Howard Hunt, was dismantled. On that occasion the plan was to shoot the Cuban leader at the University of Havana. The operation was commanded by Manuel Guillot Castellanos and Rafael Quintairos Santiso, who were arrested two years later for their activities in the service of the CIA.

August: Galo Martínez Chapman, Fernando Mancheco González, José Martínez Gómez, Alfredo Curí Abdo, Amancio Abeleiras Pérez and Reinaldo Ruíz Cortinas organized a conspiracy to provoke an armed uprising in the central region of Cuba in order to defeat the revolutionary government. To back that plan they agreed to effect an attempt on the life of Fidel Castro when the latter left his office in Havana, as well as various acts of sabotage, terrorism and subversion. All of them were detained when the plot was uncovered.

September: In conjunction with organized crime elements, the CIA planned on various occasions to assassinate Fidel Castro while he was in New York for the 34th session of the United Nations. The conspirators plotted to place a box of cigars containing a powerful poison in the hotel room the Cuban leader was to occupy.

When that plot failed due to lack of cooperation from the local police, they tried to put thallium salts in his shoes to cause his beard to fall out, and to induce him to smoke an LSD-impregnated cigar so that during a televised interview with the local media the drug would provoke uncontrollable laughter, thus affecting his prestige and charisma.

Finally, Walter Martino, a US gangster and brother of a casino operator in pre-revolutionary Havana, tried to assassinate Fidel Castro during an event in Central Park by placing a powerful explosive device under the speaker's platform, which was discovered and deactivated by the New York police.

October: Colonel Sheffield Edwards, chief of the CIA Office of Security, coordinated with Mafia capo John Roselli to send to Havana professional killer Richard Cain, who was to study the assassination of Fidel Castro on the ground. In the Cuban capital Cain contacted counterrevolutionaries Eufemio Fernández and Herminio Díaz, former henchmen of the Mafia capo Santos Trafficante, who were to support him in the operation. The plan was to shoot him from a moving car. After an exhaustive study of possible locations at which to execute the action, they cancelled it on account of the security measures provided for the revolutionary leader.

Counterrevolutionaries Indalecio Pérez, Rafael Pérez Campa, Carlos Rivero and Manuel Suárez were arrested while preparing an armed ambush of Fidel Castro in the vicinity of the Presidential Palace in Havana. The crime was part of a plot that included an assault on the 14th police precinct in Havana, as well as the unleashing of various acts of sabotage, and finally an armed uprising in the Escambray mountains.

A group of people incited by the US embassy in Havana were discovered organizing an attempt on the life of Fidel Castro in the vicinity of Revolution Plaza. The conspiracy was averted with the detention of Arturo Amaya Gil, Alfonso Armas Orozco, Alejandro Collazo Izquierdo, José García Lavado, Armando Junco Brizuela, Roberto Morffi González, Juan Nardo Echevarría and José E. Velasco.

November: An attempt on the life of Fidel Castro hatched by the CIA was averted with the detention of counterrevolutionaries Armando Cubría Ramos and Mario Tauler Sagué, who had infiltrated the island from Florida via Punto de Hicacos, Matanzas province, under the orders of CIA agent Eladio del Valle Gutiérrez. Weapons, grenades, a remote control device and six detonators were taken from them.

A plot to assassinate the Cuban prime minister in the vicinity of the National Institute of Agrarian Reform in Havana was hatched by Elpidio Brito Gómez, César Valdés Moreno, Ocilio Cruz Sánchez and

Luis Puentes Rodríguez, who were arrested and whose arms were seized.

December: A conspiracy to assassinate Fidel Castro on a bridge close to the Baracoa airport in Havana province was uncovered. On two occasions a group of men set up an ambush by placing a powerful dynamite charge to explode as the leader's car passed by, blocking the highway with a vehicle, and waiting with sawed-off shotguns to fire on their target. José A. Martí Rodríguez, Francisco Pujols Someillán, Javier Someillán Fernández and Roger Hernández Ramos were arrested.

A counterrevolutionary group was captured preparing to ambush Fidel Castro's car near the Presidential Palace. Orlando Borges Ray, Pedro René Hernández, Laureano Rodríguez Llorente and Emiliano Reinoso Hernández were detained and arms and explosives were taken from them.

Directed by the CIA station located in the US embassy, agent Vladimir Rodríguez — aka El Doctorcito — planned the assassination of Fidel Castro from a building on the corner of Línea and Paseo Avenues in Vedado. A gun with a telescopic sight was to be used to fire on the target when he entered the Potín restaurant, which faced the selected building. The plot was neutralized, the gun seized, and its author captured.

A team of CIA agents infiltrated from the United States was captured trying to place a powerful plastic explosive device in the drains of a central Havana avenue. The plan was to detonate it by remote control when Fidel Castro passed by. Julio Antonio Llebra Suárez, César Fuentes, Jorge Ulises Silva Soubelette and Ronald Condom Gil were arrested and the explosives seized.

1961

January: CIA agents Frank Sturgis and Marita Lorenz plotted to poison Fidel Castro as part of a conspiracy planned with US Mafia elements. The crime was to be executed in the Havana Libre Hotel, taking advantage of a visit there by the prime minister. According to Sturgis himself, the plot was abandoned on account of the danger to its executors.

Another plot to poison Fidel Castro was set in motion by Juan Orta Córdova, then head of the prime minister's office, who was an old associate of the Havana casino bosses during the 1950s and was responsible for recruiting CIA and Mafia elements. Orta Córdova was unable to carry out his plot, and on the eve of the Bay of Pigs aggression he took refuge in a Latin American embassy.

Guillermo F. Coloma, Ernesto Bordón Basconcillos, Francisco Salazar de la Aceña and other counterrevolutionary elements attempted to promote an armed uprising to defeat the revolution. Coloma and Bordón traveled to Miami and made contact with CIA agent Eladio del Valle, from whom they received money and precise instructions to assassinate Fidel Castro and commit other acts of terrorism. On returning to Cuba, they were arrested at José Martí International Airport and plans, photos and documents were taken from them.

March: A CIA-organized plot to assassinate Fidel Castro was dismantled. The plan was to ambush the leader in the vicinity of the home of Celia Sánchez, his secretary. Mario Hidalgo Garcel, Julio Berdote González and Carlos Suárez Roque were detained for this conspiracy, and arms and explosives were seized from them.

The CIA and the Mafia once again plotted to assassinate Fidel Castro, and in the framework of the military intervention they were planning, sent some poison tablets to Antonio Varona's group in Havana. The plan was to poison the Cuban leader during one of his regular lunches in the Pekín Chinese restaurant in the busy Vedado district. However, the executor, one of the chefs, took fright at the dangerous nature of the action and sought exile in an embassy. The principal conspirators included Alberto Cruz Caso, María Leopoldina Grau Alsina and Rodolfo León Curbelo, who were arrested some years later.

Rafael Díaz Hanscom, designated civil coordinator of the internal counterrevolutionary front set up to head actions in support of the mercenary invasion being prepared in Guatemala, was infiltrated into Cuba on March 13 in company with other agents. Díaz Hanscom's missions included unleashing Operation Generosa, a vast terrorist plot to attack the country's main energy installations, and — as a priority action — placing a powerful incendiary device in the National Housing Institute meeting room, given that a meeting had been called by Fidel Castro for March 27. The plot was frustrated with the capture of Díaz Hanscom and his accomplices and the seizure of their weapons.

May: Policemen José Álvarez García, Antonio Castro Cárdenas, Cándido Torres Pérez and Rafael Prío plotted to assault their own headquarters — that of the National Revolutionary Police. Subsequently, utilizing police patrol cars, they planned to position themselves on one of the access roads to the Presidential Palace to await the arrival of the Cuban leader, when they would throw a number of hand grenades. On being arrested, they admitted that they were influenced by radio broadcasts from the United States calling for the elimination of Fidel Castro.

June–July: Three criminal acts were plotted by a counterrevolutionary group acting under CIA instructions via veteran agent Antonio Varona, leader of the CRC, who ordered the following actions:

- An ambush in a residence located in the Biltmore district of Havana known to be regularly visited by Fidel Castro.
- An ambush in the Cucalambé restaurant in Marianao.
- If the earlier ambushes failed, another at the junction of Santa Catalina and Rancho Boyeros Avenues, firing from an open jeep with a bazooka and hand grenades.

Arms were seized and conspirators Juan Bacigalupe Hornedo, Higinio Menéndez Beltrán, Guillermo Caula Ferrer, Ibrahim Álvarez Cuesta, Augusto Jiménez Montenegro, Román Rodríguez and Osvaldo Díaz detained.

July: A conspiracy to assassinate Fidel Castro organized by the CIA in January 1961, in which notorious terrorist Félix Rodríguez Mendigutía was initially to participate, was set in motion. On this occasion, brothers Mario and Francisco Chanes de Armas selected two alternative locations for committing the crime: one in Santa María del Mar, east of the capital; the other was at the residence of Celia Sánchez. The first attempt failed given that Fidel did not go to there on the day selected for the ambush. A few weeks later, the second phase was set in motion when the assassins decided to forcibly enter a warehouse located 50 meters from the target residence and station themselves there with a gun equipped with a telescopic sight. A few days before the action, the weapons were seized and the executors arrested, including, in addition to the Chanes brothers, José Acosta, Orlando Ulacia, Ramón Laurent, Ángel Sánchez Pérez, Félix Tacoronte Valdés, Roberto Cosculluela Valcárcel and Alfonso Díaz Cosculluela.

Counterrevolutionaries José F. Díaz Quintana and Higinio Martín Castro were arrested preparing to fire on Fidel Castro from the Naroca building at the intersection of Línea and Paseo Avenues in Vedado. Both individuals had carried out various acts of sabotage in different parts of the capital.

The CIA planned to assassinate Fidel and Raúl Castro during commemorative events for the July 26 anniversary in Havana and Santiago de Cuba. This plan was connected to an act of provocation at the illegally occupied Guantánamo naval enclave in eastern Cuba, which would create a pretext for direct aggression by the United States. All the plotters were detained, including CIA agent Alfredo Izaguirre de la Riva, the main leader. Weapons and military equipment were seized in different parts of the country.

A counterrevolutionary group planned to assassinate Fidel Castro during the event commemorating the July 26 anniversary in Havana's Revolution Plaza. The action consisted of tossing several hand grenades at the platform when the leader was making his speech. Principal mastermind Alfredo Gómez was arrested and various weapons were taken from him.

August: Silvio Salvio Selva and Alberto Junco, two individuals belonging to the MDC, planned to ambush Fidel Castro during the latter's visit to a house in Vedado. They were detained and their weapons seized.

A plot was organized to assassinate Fidel Castro during one of his visits to the Ministry of Foreign Affairs. The plan was to fire on him from the window of an office opposite the selected venue. When this plan failed, another was drawn up to be executed at an event in Revolution Plaza. Plotters Julio Peón and Julio Díaz Argüelles were arrested and their weapons seized.

September: The Rescate group plotted the assassination of the Cuban prime minister during a public event to inaugurate several residential apartment buildings for workers in a district close to the capital. The plan was to launch hand grenades at Fidel. Francisco Álvarez Margolles, mastermind of the plot and an ex-colonel in the army of the dictatorship, was captured.

October: A major plot to assassinate Fidel Castro was set in motion by the CIA. From the previous year an apartment had been rented close to the northern terrace of the Presidential Palace, where the Cuban leader spoke in public meetings. Counterrevolutionaries secretly smuggled arms into the apartment and the action was decided for early October, taking advantage of a public welcome for President Osvaldo Dorticós on his return from a tour of the socialist countries. The operation was directed from the United States by CIA officer David Phillips and controlled in Cuba by his agent Antonio Veciana Blanch. The plot failed when its organizers fled the country. The weapons were seized and some of the conspirators detained, including Dalia Jorge Díaz, Manuel Izquierdo, Reynold González and others.

1962

January: A counterrevolutionary group tried to poison Fidel Castro with cyanide in the Carmelo restaurant in Vedado. All the conspirators were detained, including Pedro Forcades Conesa, Aldo Cabrera Heredia, Eduardo Pérez García, Rubén Fernández Florit, Rafael Llanos Rodríguez, Manuel Pérez Pérez and Eusebio Quesada López. The poison was seized.

March: Members of the National Liberation Front concocted a plan to assassinate Fidel Castro which consisted of placing an explosive device in the piles of the bridge over the River Quibú in Marianao. Heriberto Fernández Aguirre, Felipe González Cruz and Alberto Rodríguez Roque were arrested when it was discovered that they had access to the explosives.

Taking advantage of his job as a worker at the Baracoa air force base on the outskirts of Havana, aviation mechanic Humberto Noble Alexander tried to place a bomb in the aircraft used by Fidel Castro for his domestic trips. He was arrested and the criminal plot neutralized.

April: William Harvey, chief of Task Force W and responsible within the CIA for the "Cuban case," and John Roselli, a Mafia representative, handed over a bottle of poison capsules especially manufactured for the elimination of Fidel Castro to Antonio Varona in Miami. Utilizing Alejandro Vergara, the Spanish diplomat accredited in Havana, the capsules were sent to the Rescate group headed by Alberto Cruz Caso and María Leopoldina Grau Alsina, who were to give them to their accomplices in the Havana Libre Hotel so that they could poison the leader's meal on the first occasion that presented itself. The plotters had the capsules in their possession for more than 12 months while they sought an opportunity.

CIA agent Juan Guillot Castellanos plotted to eliminate Juan Marinello Vidaurreta, then rector of the University of Havana, in order to subsequently assassinate Fidel Castro at his funeral. The plot was neutralized with the capture of Guillot and the leadership of his organization.

Another armed ambush of the Cuban leader failed in the vicinity of Revolution Plaza. Detained in relation to the plot were Raúl García, Pedro Julio Espinosa and José García Vázquez, from whom a large quantity of automatic weapons were seized.

May: Under CIA directions from the US naval base in Guantánamo, the assassination of Foreign Minister Raúl Roa García was plotted with the aim of then eliminating Fidel Castro at Roa's funeral. The individuals involved were equipped with hand grenades and automatic pistols. The plot was linked to other subversive actions in the rest of the country. All of the conspirators, headed by Jorge Luis Cuervo Calvo, then grand master of the masonic lodge, were captured.

June: Under CIA supervision, a group headed by Bernardo Corrales, Elsa Alfaro and Servando Sánchez plotted to assassinate Fidel Castro by means of a bazooka fired from a building neighboring that of Celia Sánchez. The conspiracy failed due to security measures which made it impossible to smuggle in the bazooka.

July: A plot to kill Fidel via an ambush with fragmentation grenades in the vicinity of Revolution Plaza was halted with the arrest of Servando R. Ovies Fariñas, Abel Joaquín Costa Martínez, Felipe Becerra Espinosa and Rodolfo Montes López.

Directed by the CIA, Luis David Rodríguez, Ricardo Olmedo Moreno and Braulio Roque Arosamena attempted to assassinate Fidel Castro by firing at him with a mortar located near Revolution Plaza during the event commemorating July 26. The plot failed because the event was transferred to the city of Santiago de Cuba.

August: A bloc of counterrevolutionary organizations supported by the CIA planned a military uprising with the aim of destabilizing the country. The central element of the conspiracy was to assassinate Fidel Castro during an activity in Havana's Carlos Marx Theater. Guillermo Reyes Viaba, Tomás P. Ruíz Santana, Evelio Hernández Soto, Jesús Lazo Otaño, Otto Rodríguez Díaz, Félix Martín Nicerán, Félix Soto Sánchez, Leonel Hernández Mendez, Mario R. Estrada Alonso, Raúl V. Jorge León, José González Poladura, José M. Estrada González and Félix Sotolongo Morejón were detained for their part in the conspiracy.

Another attempt on the life of Fidel Castro was hatched by the RCA, which, under the direction of the CIA, plotted a general uprising by its groups in order to facilitate US intervention in Cuba. An ambush of the Cuban leader's car was organized in a central avenue of Havana. The plan was to hit the car with a number of fragmentation grenades. The operation was frustrated and the principal conspirators, Amaranto Torres, Ernesto Castillo and Ángel Custodio Portuondo, were captured.

September: Members of the Anticommunist Liberation Junta, Internal Liberation Front and the National Democratic Union plotted to simultaneously execute acts of sabotage, assaults on units of the Revolutionary Armed Forces, and an attempt on the life of Fidel Castro on a busy Havana avenue when the Cuban leader's car passed by. Delio A. Torres Hernández, Manuel Morales Jerez, Celio Armenteros Aruca, Eugenio Julián Jan, Ricardo González García, Mercedes N. López Fleites, Rafael Cruz Casio and Rafael Rojas Martí were arrested.

Various members of the 30 November Revolutionary Movement were caught plotting to assassinate Fidel Castro in the vicinity of Revolution Plaza. The detainees included Mario Ortiz Toledo, Manuel Pino Silva, Alberto Gálvez Alum, Elio Pardo Tabío and Heliodoro Grau.

Rafael Enrique Rojas Varela was detained by members of the commander-in-chief's bodyguard when he attempted to kill the leader on a public street.

End of 1962: Acting on CIA instructions, the Rescate group headed by Antonio Varona and Alberto Cruz planned to poison police chief Efigenio Ameijeiras in order to prompt Fidel's attendance at his funeral, when an armed commando group would assassinate him.

1963

First quarter: Desmond FitzGerald, CIA head of Cuban affairs, planned to assassinate Fidel Castro using a diving suit impregnated with bacteria. The plan was to use US lawyer James Donovan, who was doing business in Cuba and had access to Fidel. The plot failed when Donovan refused to cooperate. FitzGerald planned another homicide attempt that consisted of placing an exotic shell prepared with a powerful explosive charge in the area where Fidel went underwater fishing. The plot failed as they were unable to place it in the appropriate spot.

March: The RCA, directed by the CIA from Guantánamo, planned an armed uprising throughout the country to be initiated by the assassination of Fidel Castro at a March 13 activity at the University of Havana. The conspiracy was uncovered and all the participants detained, including principal leaders Luis David Rodríguez, Ricardo Olmedo Moreno and Jorge Espinosa Escarlés.

Members of the United Army in Arms planned to fire on Fidel Castro from an apartment close to the baseball pitch located within the DSE grounds in the Cuban capital. Evelio Montejo Quintana, Francisco Amigó O'Farrill and brothers Marcos and Delfín Martín González were arrested.

The Rescate group headed by Antonio Varona and Alberto Cruz had an opportunity to poison Fidel Castro with one of the capsules sent by the CIA when the leader went to the Havana Libre Hotel cafeteria while one of the conspirators, Santos de la Caridad Pérez, was working there. His task was to place the capsule in a chocolate milkshake, but he failed because the capsule broke when he removed it from the freezer where it was hidden.

April: A group from the MRR planned to assassinate Fidel Castro during a baseball game in El Cerro stadium in Havana. The operation consisted of throwing eight grenades at the leader. Arrested for that conspiracy were Enrique Rodríguez Valdés, Esteban Ramos Kessell, Alfredo Egued Farah and Ricardo López Cabrera.

May: The Revolutionary Anticommunist Front, directed from the United States, plotted an attempt on the life of Fidel Castro at the May Day event in Revolution Plaza. They were also to carry out various acts of sabotage on the Havana aqueduct, the El Naranjito electricity plant, La Rampa movie theater and other public buildings. Pedro Hernández Álvarez, Enrique González, Francisco Cepero Capiró and Indalecio Ferreiro Varela were detained.

June: The MRP plotted an attack on Fidel Castro with a street ambush as well as acts of sabotage and subversion at various key points in the Cuban capital. Detained were Carlos García Vázquez, Mariano Fernández Suárez, Pedro Julio Espinoza Martínez, Julio Hernández, José A. Marrero Frank, Horacio Arquímedes Ocumares Leyva and Armando Cuesto Constantino. Bars of C-3 explosive, homemade bombs, a .45-caliber submachine gun, fragmentation grenades and various pistols were taken from them.

July: The National Liberation Movement set up an ambush for Fidel

Castro when he visited a Havana residence where veterans of the Moncada attack were gathered for a modest ceremony to recall that event. Enrique Falcón Beltrán, Ramón Soria Licea, Eliecer Senra Ramírez and Antonio Senra Lugueira were detained.

Operation Rafael, a CIA-sponsored project to assassinate Fidel Castro during the July 26 Moncada commemoration in Revolution Plaza, was set in motion. The CIA sent the conspirators a gun with a telescopic sight and a silencer. Mario Salabarría and US intelligence agents Alberto Cruz Caso and Arturo Verona took part. The plan was frustrated by security.

A group from the MRR also planned to assassinate Fidel Castro at July 26 festivities in Revolution Plaza. Their plan was to fire an 81 millimeter mortar at the presidential platform from the patio of a neighboring house. Luis Montes de Oca and Braulio Roque Arosamena were arrested.

July–September: A homicide plot was hatched on US territory by Cuban terrorist Orlando Bosch and mafioso Mike McLaney, which consisted of bombing Fidel Castro's residence in Cojímar, east of Havana. The plan failed when the bombs were seized in a raid by the FBI and the subjects were detained. They were subsequently released as a result of CIA intervention.

August: A planned uprising by counterrevolutionary groups belonging to the Civic Resistance bloc was averted. The project included an assassination attempt against Fidel Castro, for which they had several high-precision weapons. Arrested in relation to this plot were Palmiro Bartolomé Santiago, Miguel Argueo Gallastegui Zayas, Gilberto Amat Rodríguez, Héctor Ballester Fernández, Honorio Torres Perdomo and others.

September: A counterrevolutionary group planned to attack Fidel Castro with hand grenades during a public event on the 28th to mark the anniversary of the CDRs in Revolution Plaza. The plan was frustrated and the conspirators arrested, including Ángel Mesa Puentes, Dositeo Fernández Fariñas and Roberto Porto Infanzón.

Another assassination attempt was frustrated during the CDR anniversary celebrations. Members of the so-called United Internal Revolutionary Front (FIUR) and the Triple A planned to place an explosive device in the drains underneath the podium mounted for the event. One of the conspirators was the engineer in charge of Havana's aqueducts and sewerage system. Explosives supplied by the CIA were seized and Federico Hernández González, Pierre Quan Diez de Ure, Francisco Blanco de los Cuetos, Jesús Rodríguez Mosquera, Orlando de la Cruz and Luis Arencibia Pérez were detained.

October–November: Desmond FitzGerald met in Paris with Rolando Cubela to coordinate a planned coup d'état in Cuba and the assassination of Fidel Castro. On the same date that President Kennedy was assassinated, November 22, 1963, a CIA case officer gave Cubela a hypodermic syringe filled with a powerful poison with which to kill the Cuban leader during an event planned for December of that year.

December: A CIA network made up of Bernardo Lucas Milanés, Roberto Caíñas Milanés, Adela Nagle, Loreto Llanes García and others planned an assassination attempt on Fidel Castro during his visit to the Potín café on Línea and Paseo in Vedado. The plan was to intercept the leader's fleet of cars when they stopped and to open fire on them with automatic weapons. After several weeks of surveillance, the operation was abandoned when Fidel Castro failed to show up.

The ELN planned an attack on Fidel Castro during a public event at the University of Havana. The plan was to concentrate a group close to the podium, and when the Cuban leader arrived, to throw hand grenades at him. Roberto Ortega, Ciro Rey and José Águila were arrested.

1964

January: A group from the ELN plotted to assassinate Fidel Castro during an event marking the fifth anniversary of the triumph of the Revolution in the plaza. The plan was to take by force one of the apartments in the blocks at numbers 1423, 1425 and 1427 on Zapata Avenue, from where the presidential podium could be seen. Once there, they would fire on him with three rifles with telescopic sights. The plan was discovered and its participants arrested, including Rafael Mir Peña and Manuel Santos Martínez.

Bernardo Milanés López returned from Madrid after discussing and agreeing on a plan of action that included the assassination of Fidel Castro with his case officer, CIA agent Joaquín Sanjenís. The plan consisted of organizing an ambush on Fifth Avenue in Miramar with a telephone company truck that would carry a .30-caliber submachine gun in the back. When Fidel Castro's cars approached the truck in their regular transit via this avenue, its rear doors would be opened and the occupants would fire on the Cuban leader. The plot was uncovered and Mario Salabarría, Roberto Sabater, Bernardo Milanés and other conspirators were arrested.

March: Individuals belonging to the National Alliance of Anticommunist Coordinators, made up of the Anticommunist Civic Action, the Agramonte Resistance and the Internal Government of Anticommunist Liberation, plotted to activate a huge subversive plan throughout the country that included an attempt on the lives of Fidel Castro and Blas Roca. The conspirators organized their actions in the vicinity of Revolution Plaza as the leaders were heading for their offices. Luis A. Casanovas Morales, Arturo Flores Zamora, Roberto Torres Alfonso and others were detained.

May: A group of counterrevolutionary elements belonging to the 1422 Military Unit conspired to take its installations by assault, seize its weapons and subsequently organize an uprising. The plot included the assassination of Fidel Castro, who they would draw to the unit by making certain economic demands. The plot was uncovered and its participants arrested, including José M. González Castellanos, José G. González Carmenate, Cándido Ruiz Palencia and Narciso P. Baró Serrano.

Members of the Internal Anticommunist Front, a subsidiary of the FRD, planned to ambush Fidel Castro in Puente Cabrera in Marianao. The plot consisted of firing automatic weapons from previously selected locations. The operation was discovered and the plotters arrested, including Manuel Fordán Diéguez, Ricardo Solana Zayas de la Paz, Armando Prieto Puig, Jorge García Rodríguez, Pedro Lemagre Zárate and José A. Villamil Arias.

August: A group from the ELN plotted to assassinate Fidel Castro in an ambush with automatic weapons at the intersection of Presidentes and Zapata Avenues, Vedado. In order to acquire the weapons they planned to assault a Revolutionary National Militia garrison. Gregorio Mena Perera, Miguel Tomey Peláez and Pedro Aguilos Montoy were arrested.

September: Members of the Internal Liberation Front plotted an attempt on the life of Fidel Castro in the home of Celia Sánchez, after previously attempting it at the intersection of Zapata and Carlos Manuel de Céspedes Avenues in Vedado. They were equipped with a Czech 7.62-caliber submachine gun and a number of hand grenades. Francisco Muñoz Antunes, Nemesio Cubillas Pérez, Juan M. Vailac Valdés, Ángel M. Arencibia Bidau, José R. Montano Meneses and Manuel A. Torquemada Tendero were detained.

A plot to assassinate Fidel Castro when he was in the presidential box at the World Youth Baseball Series by launching hand grenades at him was uncovered. Alberto Grau Sierra, Reinaldo Figueroa Gálvez, Valentín Figueroa Gálvez and Felipe Ramos Rodríguez were arrested and three submachine guns and grenades were taken from them.

1965

January: From the United States and with CIA approval, the MRR, headed by Manuel Artime and Nacín Elias Tuma, plotted the assassination of Fidel Castro during the commemorative event for the triumph of the revolution. They recruited one of the leaders of the MRR in Cuba, whom they exfiltrated and took to Florida for training. When everything was in place they infiltrated him back into the country on December 23, 1964. The plot failed because the supposed leader was Abel Haidar Elías, an agent of Cuban State Security who had penetrated the counterrevolutionary organization. Rifles with telescopic sights and the rest of the weaponry to commit the crime were seized.

March: Members of the ELN conspired to assassinate the Cuban prime minister at the home of Celia Sánchez, or in that of *Comandante* René Vallejo, Fidel's aide. Orlando Travieso Peña, Tomás Gilberto Guerrero Matos, Justo González García, Iluminado García Pérez and Modesto García García were detained and their weapons seized.

June: A group of counterrevolutionary elements from the Democratic National Front plotted to assassinate Fidel Castro at the event for the anniversary of July 26 in the city of Santa Clara. To that end, they stole a FAL rifle and various pistols from a military unit. Ramón Medina Machado, Alejo R. Álvarez Santana and Santiago Apóstol Gómez Gutiérrez were detained.

July: Elements from the Revolutionary National Unity plotted to assassinate Fidel on the corner of 21 and L Streets in Vedado when the revolutionary leader passed by. For that action they had a .45-caliber Thompson submachine gun. Enrique Abreu Vilahu, Julio Ruiz Pitaluga and Carlos Sánchez Hernández were arrested.

CIA agents planned an attempt on the life of Fidel Castro during his visit to an agricultural project in Los Arabos, Matanzas province. The same network also devoted itself to acts of espionage and sabotage. Roberto Ramos Rodiles, Antonio Alonso Soca, Rolando Quevedo Negrín, José Pellayá Jústiz and Mirta Beatriz Pérez López were detained and two M3 submachine guns of US manufacture were taken from them.

August: A CIA network acting in Cuba under the command of agents Benjamín Acosta Valdés and Antonio Ramírez Méndez plotted the assassination of Fidel Castro. The conspiracy consisted of a planned commando operation of 30 armed men on the residence of Celia Sánchez. León R. Martínez Gómez, Felipe Hernández García, Raúl Hermida Lafita, Juan A. Morera Suárez, Enrique Fernández and others were arrested. The CIA agents managed to escape from the country. A sizeable arms cache was seized.

September: Rescate planned an attempt on the life of the prime minister at the commemoration of the anniversary of the CDRs, for which they had various bars of C-4 explosive. Roberto del Castillo Fernández, Salvador del Castillo Atkinson and Lorenzo Medina were detained.

December: Members of the ELN plotted to fire an 81-millimeter mortar at the home of Celia Sánchez when Fidel was there. Elio Diáz García and Sergio Romero were arrested.

1966

January: An attempt on the life of Fidel Castro was plotted for a conference bringing together representatives from the international revolutionary movement in Havana. Various automatic rifles were to be used in the attack. The plot consisted of an assault on the Havana Libre Hotel where the Cuban leader was to make an appearance. Guillermo Valdés Sosa, Amado Santana Correa and Carlos M. Vidal Fernández were arrested.

The Democratic National Front plotted an attempt on the life of Fidel Castro during an event in Revolution Plaza. They had in their possession 10 pistols as well as fragmentation grenades. Luis Fernández

Rodríguez, Raúl Martínez Lima, Ricardo Padrón Acosta, Aurelio Gascón Díaz, Luis Mitjans González, Mario Valdés Cárdenas, Francisco Palomino Castillo, Felicio Valdés González, Sabino Villar Suárez and Jesús González Ramos were arrested.

Counterrevolutionaries Víctor Rodríguez Landerer and Giraldo Suárez Martín, who had organized an ambush of the prime minister in the vicinity of the Presidential Palace, were captured. The place selected was the Fausto movie theater building on Prado and Colón, where Suárez Martín worked as an administrator.

February: Rolando Cubela Secades — CIA agent AM/LASH — and a group of his collaborators were arrested while plotting an attack on *Comandante* Fidel Castro during an event at the University of Havana planned for March 13. Subsequent investigations revealed that Cubela and his associates, in conjunction with the CIA, had previously planned to ambush his vehicles when he visited Varadero. On the cited occasions sharpshooters were positioned in the selected locations, but Fidel Castro did not appear. The dates concerned were March–April 1964 and June–July 1965.

March: Members of the counterrevolutionary groups MRP and the Revolutionary National Union plotted an attempt on the life of Fidel Castro at the baseball stadium located in El Cerro district. The plan was to throw a number of fragmentation grenades at him as he entered the stadium. The weapons were seized and counterrevolutionaries Juan Pereira León, Juan Valdés López and Oscar D. Sáenz Rodríguez were arrested.

April: Members of the counterrevolutionary organizations MRP and the United Western Front planned to assassinate Fidel Castro during a visit he was to make to the Emergency Hospital on Carlos III Avenue in the Cuban capital. The conspirators hid in a corridor of the hospital armed with a submachine gun and a pistol awaiting the leader, who, on that occasion, did not go to the institution. Roger F. Reyes Hernández and Jorge E. de la Torre were arrested.

Gustavo Gil Hernández was arrested for planning an attempt on the life of Fidel Castro with fragmentation grenades. The place selected was the highway leading to the Liberación sugar refinery in Cuatro Caminos, Havana province.

May: Rodobaldo Hilarión Fariñas Lumpuy was detained while preparing an attack on Fidel Castro in El Cerro baseball stadium. His plan was to throw two fragmentation grenades, which were seized from him.

A CIA special missions group was captured infiltrating the coast near Havana with the objective of assassinating Fidel Castro. The members were surprised by the Cuban militia and fighting broke out. Terrorists Herminio Díaz García and Armando Romero were killed and Antonio Cuesta Valle and Eugenio Zaldívar detained.

June: A counterrevolutionary group plotted to assassinate Fidel Castro when he was crossing a bridge in the Biltmore district, Marianao. The plan was to fire on him from the cover of nearby shrubs. The main organizer, Francisco A. Díaz Valdagil, was captured and a M3 submachine gun seized. The other conspirators managed to escape to the United States.

July: Elements from Alpha 66 and the MDC planned to assassinate Fidel Castro by throwing fragmentation grenades at him while he was receiving the Cuban delegation that had attended the Central American Games in Puerto Rico. The event and the attack were organized for El Cerro stadium. Francisco Bernal González, Pedro Gervasio Pérez Jorrín and others were arrested.

September: An attempt to assassinate Fidel Castro en route to his residence in Cojímar on the outskirts of the capital was foiled. The plan was to ambush his vehicle and toss fragmentation grenades at him from motorcycles. An additional plan was to assault various police units and subsequently to stage an uprising in the mountains in Havana province. Guido Farmiñán Fernández, Rodolfo Sierra Cabrera, Vicente Rodríguez Molina and José L. Alfonso Calderon were detained.

October: Members of the Brigade Battalion organized a plot on the life of Fidel Castro via an ambush on Paseo Avenue in Vedado. This route was frequently used by the Cuban leader in his movements. The conspirators possessed various guns and pistols and also had an apartment in one of the buildings in the area. Ramón Luis Arias Cuña, Narciso Oseguera Rodríguez and Pantaleón Rivera Rodríguez were detained.

1967

July: An ex-sergeant from the army of the Batista dictatorship planned a solo attempt on the life of the Cuban prime minister. He plotted to shoot him with a Czech machine gun in the vicinity of Revolution Plaza. Pascual Peña García was arrested and the weapon taken from him.

September: Several individuals from the Anticommunist National Group plotted to eliminate Fidel Castro. The plan was to shoot him with various automatic weapons during his visit to a farm in the Aguacate neighborhood of Havana province. José Paradela Ruiz, Rodolfo Suárez Sardiñas, Roberto Milián Sánchez and Alfonso López were detained and their weapons seized.

November: An attempt on the life of Fidel Castro was planned during the inauguration of the National Baseball Series in El Cerro stadium. The plot consisted of positioning a man next to the main electricity cable to interrupt the electricity supply, and at the same time, to throw fragmentation grenades at the leader's box. José A. Acosta Corona, Marcelo Ramos González, Segundo Rodríguez Pérez, Isidro Benavides Segura and Reinaldo Barrios Romero were detained.

1968

March: Oscar Rafael Planas Madruga and Juan Sánchez Gómez plotted to assassinate Fidel Castro during his visit to a genetics institute in Havana province. They were in possession of weapons and hand grenades for the attack. Both conspirators were detained and their arms taken.

A group of counterrevolutionaries planned to assassinate Fidel Castro and then flee from Cuba to the United States. To that end the conspirators were watching the access roads to the home of Celia Sánchez. Julio Pedrosa Gómez, Norberto Vega Salas, Felipe Israel Cruz Saavedra and José Buenaventura Ruiz Hidalgo were detained and their weapons seized.

April: A plot was hatched to assassinate Fidel Castro during one his visit to the Nazareno genetics institute in Santiago de las Vegas, Havana province. The counterrevolutionaries made a careful study to ascertain the number of cars in the leader's bodyguard, as well as access routes and suitable locations for an ambush. Digno Pereira, Valentín B. Fernández and Pedro E. Chang were arrested and two M3 submachine guns seized.

May: Another plot to assassinate Fidel Castro in an ambush on a street that he used to go to the Palace of the Revolution failed due to action by the Cuban security agencies. The conspirators possessed various weapons and were studying the selected location. Santiago Oliva Ramos and Berto Gutiérrez were arrested.

A counterrevolutionary plotted to assassinate Fidel Castro during his visit to the Chullima shipyard in the bay of Havana. To that end he made contact with criminals who agreed to supply the weapons for a sum of money, and who, without warning, fled the country before the date of the planned crime. Nemesio Rafael Rodríguez Amaro was arrested in relation to this case.

Criminal elements resident in Florida contracted Bartolomé Hernández Quintana and Antonio Muñoz González in Havana to assassinate Fidel Castro during one of his trips through the capital. They were arrested and their weapons seized.

Pedro Luis Sabina plotted to assassinate Fidel Castro during a visit to his aide, *Comandante* René Vallejo. He staked out the house on various occasions and obtained a .45-caliber pistol. The plot failed when he was discovered and arrested.

June: Members of the Democratic National Front conspired to assassinate Fidel Castro via an ambush in a Havana avenue that he regularly used. They had four .22-caliber pistols with silencers and rockets poisoned with cyanide. Desiderio Barreto Martínez was detained for this action, while the others involved escaped to the United States.

Onelio León Zayas and Luis E. Monzón Painé planned an attempt on the life of Fidel Castro during one of his regular trips through the capital. Monzón Painé was a demobilized officer of the Ministry of the Interior and possessed information on the leader's itinerary, as well as various automatic weapons. Both individuals were detained.

July: Desiderio Conrado Pérez and Ramón E. Salazar Román conspired to assassinate Fidel Castro during one of his visits to Villa Clara province. They were detained and their weapons taken.

A group from the Montecristi Group plotted to assassinate the Cuban leader during one of his visits to Quivicán municipality in Havana province. The plan was to intercept his vehicles and fire on him with various automatic weapons. Justo Páez Santos and Mario Llorens Hernández were detained and their weapons seized.

Rafael Domingo Morejón Recaña was arrested for plotting to assassinate Fidel Castro during the event celebrating the July 26 anniversary in the city of Santa Clara. Morejón Recaña had decided to shoot him from the public audience, a suicidal act for which he was equipped with a .45-caliber pistol.

Marcos Ortiz González also planned to assassinate Fidel Castro during the commemoration of July 26 in Santa Clara. He selected one of the access routes to the plaza where the event was to take place. He was arrested and his pistol seized.

August: Members of the 30 November Revolutionary Movement plotted an attempt on the life of Fidel Castro. To that end they selected snipers from the ranks of Batista's army. The attempt failed, and Pedro Pablo Montes de Oca Martínez, Bernardo Montero González and Eladio Ruíz Sánchez were detained and their weapons seized.

Marcial Mirabal, Flor Damaris Garlobo Pérez and Daysi Valdés Sánchez were arrested on the discovery of a conspiracy mounted by them to assassinate Fidel Castro during the commemoration of the July 26 anniversary in Santa Clara. The operation consisted of firing on the leader from the public area with .32-caliber pistols. The conspiracy was frustrated as they were unable to reach the selected location in time and did not have the required view of the podium.

September: Carlos Alberto Mata Escobar, Rigoberto Castro Gutiérrez, Juan Antonio Loureiro Padilla and Roberto Osvaldo Catá Gómez plotted to assassinate Fidel Castro on a main avenue in the capital and then flee to the United States. They also planned various acts of terrorism to coincide with the attempt. The location selected was the Alcoy Bridge in San Miguel del Padrón. All those involved were arrested.

October: CIA officer David Phillips organized a plot to assassinate Fidel Castro from the US naval base in Guantánamo. The plot consisted of infiltrating a heavily armed commando unit that would organize an ambush in the vicinity of Manzanillo, Oriente province, the location of an event to celebrate the centenary of the struggle for Cuban independence at which the revolutionary leader would speak. The operation failed as the men could not be infiltrated.

November: Argeo Hernández Durán, Emilio Montes de Oca, Antonio Torres Torres, Pedro Matute and Juan F. Moreno were arrested in the vicinity of the residence of Fidel Castro when they were checking the movements of the Cuban leader. Under interrogation they confessed that they were plotting to assassinate him. They had a rifle with a telescopic sight, which was seized.

1969

February: Hugo E. Rojas del Río, David Hernández Tiant and Miguel Finlay Villalvilla, members of the Internal Government of Anticommunist Liberation counterrevolutionary group, were detained conspiring to assassinate Fidel Castro with a fragmentation grenade.

March: Félix Olivera Castillo, a member of the National Internal Front, was directed by his organization in the United States to prepare an assassination attempt on the prime minister. To that end he devoted himself to studying the routes taken by Fidel Castro, during which time he was detained. At the moment of his arrest he was found awaiting a vessel from Florida bringing him a gun with a telescopic sight and various pistols to execute the action.

Counterrevolutionary Agustín Rivero Rodríguez, a member of the MRR, decided to make an attempt on the life of Fidel Castro with a pistol that he owned during a speech by the leader in El Cangre, Havana province. He was arrested.

Salvador J. de la Torriente and Rayné M. Hernández, individuals belonging to the Agramonte Resistance, plotted the elimination of Fidel Castro at a public event in Havana province. To achieve their objective they planned to approach the stage and then throw themselves on him with knives. Both were detained.

April: Mario Ramón Echevarría Camejo, Juan Hermida Salinas and Eugenio Ledón Aguilar from Havana province were arrested for plotting an attempt on the life of Fidel Castro. The action was to be carried out when the leader was touring agricultural projects in the area. Various small arms prepared for the aggression were seized.

Luis M. Acosta González and Francisco Hernández were arrested for plotting the assassination of Fidel Castro during his visit to an agricultural project in the town of Quivicán, Havana province. Various fragmentation grenades were taken from them.

June: Fulfilling instructions from terrorist Armando Fleites, leader of the Alpha 66 organization located in the United States, Guillermo del Carmen Álvarez Teijeros planned to assassinate Fidel Castro during one of his public movements in the capital. He had been promised a safe exit from Cuba with all his family as soon as the crime was committed. He was detained and a .45-caliber pistol taken from him.

July: Damián U. Cruz González, Félix Alfonso Santiago and José García Gutiérrez plotted an attempt on the life of Fidel Castro during the events celebrating the anniversary of July 26. To that end they acquired a truck in which they installed a .30-caliber machine gun. They planned to intercept the leader's cars with the vehicle and fire on him and his bodyguards. They were arrested.

August: A counterrevolutionary group drew up a plot to assassinate Fidel Castro during an anniversary celebration of the CDRs. The plan was to cause a power cut in Revolution Plaza once the event had started and to then throw a number of fragmentation grenades at the platform. Julio Sánchez Almeida, Manuel Pérez Medina, Rubén Arango González, José Antonio González Delgado, Luis Gervasio Márquez Gómez, Eduardo Rivas Pizarro, Delio Germán Sánchez Rius and Orlando de la Caridad Concepción Maura were arrested.

October: A counterrevolutionary group made up of Gregorio Nieves Rojas, Justiniano Lorenzo Espinosa García, Luis Orlando Román López, Hipólito Espinosa García and Ramiro Castillo Garcés was captured planning an assault on the Civil Defense headquarters in the town of Santiago de las Vegas, Havana province, with the intention of stealing weapons to be used to assassinate Fidel Castro.

November: Members of the Democratic National Front, prompted by their leaders in the United States, planned to assassinate Fidel Castro during one of his visits to the towns of Güines and San Nicolás de Bari, Havana province. The action was to be executed via an ambush on one of the access route to a genetics institute in the area. They planned to use various .12-caliber shotguns and two .45-caliber pistols. Gerardo Figueredo Durán, Gertrudis Cabrera Acosta, Jorge Sarmiento Lazo, Israel Ramos González, Cristóbal González Pérez and Pedro Mourdoch Benítez were detained.

December: Daniel Alberto Pérez Cruz and Samuel Nisembaun Waiider, members of the Rescate organization headed by Manuel Antonio de Varona in the United States, plotted the assassination of Fidel Castro during one of his tours of the city of Santa Clara, as instructed by their chief. During the preparations they made contact with people they knew in that city who helped them with details for the operation they were planning. They were arrested when their plot was uncovered.

1970

January: Jorge Luis Faroy Abreu and José A. Camejo were detained while organizing an attempt on the life of Fidel Castro on the occasion of his visit to the Cuban Institute of Friendship with the Peoples, on 17th and I Streets, Vedado. To commit the assassination they had three AKM guns and three fragmentation grenades.

February: Counterrevolutionaries Edgardo M. Barrera Abreu and Bernardo Ramírez Batista plotted to assassinate Fidel Castro during one of his visits to the house of Celia Sánchez. They thus made a detailed study of the area, during which they were surprised and detained, and their weapons taken.

October: Common criminal Julio Guerra Guedes, influenced by radio stations broadcasting from the United States, planned to assassinate Fidel Castro with a P38 pistol. He selected the Antillana steelworks on the outskirts of the Cuban capital for the action. He was arrested.

December: A group composed of Emérito Cardoso Vázquez, Pedro Pablo Pérez Páez, Antonio Martínez Chávez and Santiago Felipe Martínez Chávez plotted to assassinate Fidel Castro during one of his regular visits to La Bijirita genetics institute in the vicinity of Santiago de las Vegas, Havana province. For this action they drew up a plan of the selected location and obtained khaki uniforms and two AKM rifles from a military unit. They were detained.

1971

February: Nelsón Pomares Fortes and José Ulpiano Torres Hernández, members of the United Army in Arms counterrevolutionary organization, conspired to assassinate Fidel Castro via an ambush on 146th Street and Fifth Avenue in Miramar district, Havana. The idea was to take up positions on the flat roof of the pharmacy at this intersection — where Pomares Fortes worked — and to open fire with a rifle as soon as the leader's cars passed by. They were arrested.

October: Elio Hernández Alfonso, a counterrevolutionary who worked in a steel mill, tried to recruit a number of workers from his plant to assassinate Fidel Castro during a visit. The plot was to make the leader fall into a large vat full of melted iron when he passed by. The plot was uncovered and its author arrested.

November: Fidel visited the Republic of Chile at the invitation of President Salvador Allende. On that occasion the CIA planned three attempts on his life. One of them was to be executed when the Cuban leader came out onto the balcony of La Moneda Palace. The plan was to fire on him from the Hilton Hotel, situated beside the presidential palace. Another attempt was planned during a press conference to be given by the Cuban prime minister. Two terrorists of Cuban origin armed with a revolver placed inside a TV camera were to shoot Fidel. The operation failed due to the perpetrators' fear of losing their lives in the act. Finally, during Fidel's return flight to Cuba, two more attempts were planned. One was during a stopover in Lima, Peru, where two CIA agents were to throw explosives from the airport terrace, and the other during his transit through Quito, Ecuador, where it was planned to fire on him from an aircraft close to where the Cuban plane would come to a stop. Both plots failed due to the assassins' fear of the response of the Cuban bodyguards. The conspirators involved were David Phillips, Antonio Veciana Blanch, Luis Posada Carriles and various terrorists in the service of the CIA.

1973

September: Lázaro O. Hernández Valdés was detained while attempting to fire on Fidel Castro during the welcome tour of Chilean President Salvador Allende. The plan was to ambush him in Ermita de los Catalanes, near Rancho Boyeros Avenue, where both leaders were to pass by in an open car. To commit the crime Valdés had a .22-caliber rifle with cyanide-laced bullets. He confessed to being an avid listener of the counterrevolutionary radio stations funded by the CIA that were transmitting from Florida during that period.

October: Juan Ortiz Ribeaux, a worker at the Antillana steel plant in Havana, planned to assassinate Fidel Castro and Raúl Castro, minister of the armed forces, taking advantage of a military maneuver in which a brigade from his workplace was taking part. The idea was to fire on them with a mortar when both leaders were located on the stage. In his statement to the court Ortiz Ribeaux confessed to being a regular listener to the counterrevolutionary radio stations.

December: Counterrevolutionary Pablo Alfredo Álvarez Alvarado, influenced by letters from friends in the United States who urged him to assassinate Fidel Castro, planned to ambush the leader on Third and Paseo in Vedado, a road he used periodically. On being arrested, a sketch of the area was taken from him along with a pistol.

1975

February: Aureliano García Calderón planned to assassinate Fidel Castro after listening to radio stations calling for that objective from the United States. He got hold of a .38-caliber revolver and a .22-caliber pistol and began checking the routes used by the Cuban leader. He was arrested.

March: Jorge Crespo Brunet, a worker at the Cuban Film Institute, was detained for plotting to place an explosive device in that institution during a visit by Fidel Castro. He had drawn up a plan of where to place the device and had stolen various cartridges of dynamite to carry out his objective.

1976

September: Through one of its officers calling himself Harold Benson, CIA headquarters directed one of its agents in Cuba to compile information on the imminent voyage of Fidel Castro to attend the first anniversary of the Angolan revolution. The task was related to an attempt on Fidel and various terrorist attacks to be carried out by a commando unit headed by Orlando Bosch Ávila and Luis Posada Carriles. The plot on Fidel was uncovered by Cuban State Security agents; however, regrettably, other acts of terrorism, including the sabotage of a Cuban passenger plane off the island of Barbados in which 73 passengers lost their lives, were not uncovered in time.

1979

October: Antonio Veciana Blanch and Andrés Nazario Sargent, two Alpha 66 leaders in the United States, plotted to assassinate Fidel Castro during the Cuban leader's attendance at the 34th session of the United Nations. The plot consisted of throwing a contact bomb disguised as a baseball at his car during one of the Cuban leader's transits through New York. The operation failed, being neutralized by the FBI.

1982

April: Intelligence sources reported that counterrevolutionary Luis

Llánes Águila was planning an infiltration of Cuba from Florida with the objective of assassinating President Fidel Castro and *Comandante* Ramiro Valdés. He was captured in May attempting to enter national territory in order to execute the action with Rogelio Abreu Azcuy. The weapons for realizing the operation were also seized.

1985

January: Intelligence sources learned that elements linked to the Saturnino Beltrán Commandos, made up of anti-Sandinista Nicaraguans and Cuban émigrés in Florida, were plotting to bring down the airplane taking Fidel Castro to the inauguration of Daniel Ortega in Managua, Nicaragua. This was to be effected by firing a ground-to-air missile when the aircraft was flying over the Nicaraguan capital. Orlando Valdés, Adolfo Calero Portocarrero, Manuel Reyes and Roberto Milián Martínez were involved in the operation. The plot was frustrated.

1987

April: Intelligence sources discovered that the veteran CIA agent Mario Salabarría, who went to Miami after his release from a Cuban prison, was plotting to assassinate Fidel Castro during a tour of Spain that he was making. The operation was planned to take place when the Cuban leader traveled to his ancestors' native village. Salabarría, Marco Tulio Beruff, Cándido de la Torre and an unidentified Spanish citizen were to execute the action. The conspiracy was neutralized by the heavy security measures taken in the selected location.

July: Intelligence sources discovered that terrorist Eduardo Tamargo Martín was devising a plot to assassinate Fidel Castro during a visit to Brazil. To that end there were various meetings in the offices of the Independent and Democratic Cuba group in Caracas, Venezuela, attended by Ramón Méndez, Ariel Clavijo and Eduardo Tamargo himself. This group linked up with the Venezuelan police, who assumed the task of training the group selected to fire on the Cuban president. The plot failed due to the heavy security measures taken.

1988

November: Intelligence sources revealed that Cuban terrorist Gaspar Eugenio Jiménez Escobedo was organizing a plot to assassinate Fidel Castro when he made another visit to Brazil. Jiménez Escobedo was linked to the Orlando Mendoza and Luis Posada Carriles project and had everything he needed to carry out the act, but failed due to the heavy security measures adopted.

December: Intelligence sources reported that, from a Venezuelan jail, terrorist Orlando Bosch Ávila was plotting an assassination attempt on President Fidel Castro on the occasion of the inauguration of President Carlos Andrés Pérez. He designated an explosives expert called Eusebio for the operation, who was to prepare various devices manipulated by remote control. Pedro Corzo Eves, Pedro Martín Corzo, Gaspar Jiménez Escobedo and Eusebio himself were to take part in the action, which once again failed due to the measures taken.

1990

October: A counterrevolutionary commando unit from the United States was infiltrated into Cuba on the 14th of the month to undertake diversionary actions and to assassinate Fidel Castro, for which they brought weapons which were seized by Cuban security forces. Gustavo Rodríguez, Tomás Ramos, Sergio González Rosquete, Richard Heredia and Higinio Díaz Duarte were detained.

1994

November: On the occasion of the 4th Summit of Ibero-American Heads of State and Government in Cartagena, Colombia, intelligence sources discovered that the Cuban American National Foundation (CANF) was plotting to assassinate Fidel Castro. The plan was to fire on him with a .50-caliber Barrett rifle brought from Miami. The plot failed due to the fact that the conditions anticipated by the conspirators did not materialize. Cuban terrorists Alberto Hernández, Roberto Martín Pérez, Luis Posada Carriles, Ramón Orozco Crespo, Gaspar Jiménez Escobedo, Félix Rodríguez Mendigutía and Raúl Valverde were involved in the operation.

1995

November: On the occasion of the Fifth Summit of Ibero-American Heads of State and Government in the San Carlos de Bariloche resort, Argentina, intelligence sources reported that terrorists of Cuban origin Roberto Martín Pérez, Gaspar Jiménez Escobedo and Eugenio Llameras were plotting to ambush and assassinate Fidel Castro with the support and funding of the CANF. The plot failed due to the strong security measures taken.

1997

November: Luis Posada Carriles, in complicity with Arnaldo Monzón Plasencia and the leaders of the CANF, organized a conspiracy to assassinate Fidel Castro on Margarita Island, Venezuela, during the Seventh Ibero-American Summit of Heads of State and Government, taking advantage of his attendance at the meeting. The attempt failed due to the capture in waters close to Puerto Rico of the team of assassins: Ángel Alfonso Alemán, Francisco Córdova Torna, Juan Bautista Márquez and Ángel Hernández Rojo. When they were detained the terrorists were on the boat *La Esperanza*. Two .50-caliber Barrett rifles were seized, one of them owned by Francisco Hernández, an executive of the CANF.

1998

November: Intelligence sources uncovered a plot by the CANF to assassinate Fidel Castro during a visit to the Dominican Republic, for which it contacted terrorists Luis Posada Carriles, Ramón Font, Ramón Orozco Crespo, Francisco Eulalio Castro Paz and Enrique Bassas. The conspiracy failed once again due to strict security measures adopted given prior notice of the homicidal plot.

2000

November: Intelligence sources learned that terrorist elements were plotting to assassinate Fidel Castro during the 10th Ibero-American Summit of Heads of State and Government in Panama City. Those individuals included Luis Posada Carriles, Guillermo Novo Sampol, Pedro Crispín Remón and Gaspar Jiménez Escobedo, who, under instructions from the CANF, were planning to plant an explosive device in a university auditorium, the venue for a Cuban solidarity event at which Fidel was to speak. After being exposed by the Cuban authorities, the terrorists were caught and detained by the Panamanian authorities. Three years later, after they had been sentenced in a public court for their criminal acts, President Mireya Moscoso took advantage of the conclusion of her mandate and, following the instructions of the US ambassador, granted them a pardon.

THE SECRET WAR SERIES
by Fabián Escalante

A four volume account of the Secret War of the United States against Cuba by the internationally recognized authority on Washington's covert operations in Cuba and Latin America.

The Cuba Project
CIA Covert Operations Against Cuba 1959–62

An intriguing tale of a "regime change" project that failed, this is the secret war the CIA lost. The "Cuba Project," initiated to remove Fidel Castro after the 1959 revolution, included assassination plots, sabotage and terrorist activities, paramilitary invasion plans and psychological warfare operations.
ISBN 1-876175-99-0

JFK: The Cuba Files
The Untold Story of the Plot to Kill Kennedy

Cuba's investigation into the Kennedy assassination uncovered a conspiracy that brought together three groups that violently opposed the Cuban revolution — the Cuban exiles, the Mafia, and the CIA — who felt betrayed by the Bay of Pigs debacle and Kennedy's apparent moves toward a rapprochement with Fidel Castro.
ISBN 1-920888-14-4 (Also available in Spanish ISBN 1-920888-07-1)

Executive Action
634 Ways to Kill Fidel Castro

A review of four decades of CIA plots to assassinate Fidel Castro, a project code-named "Executive Action." Although melodramatic and at times almost comical, these CIA plans were deadly serious — and unconstitutional — as US government enquiries concluded.
ISBN 1-920888-72-1 (Also available in Spanish ISBN 1-920888-55-1)

oceanpress
e-mail info@oceanbooks.com.au
www.oceanbooks.com.au